Enjoy these
of our NBA Champions!

Jay Marcuk

mo. HOF '06

FULL COURT

THE UNTOLD STORIES OF THE ST. LOUIS HAWKS

BY GREG MARECEK

Reedy Press, LLC
PO Box 5131, St. Louis, MO 63139, USA

MathisJones Communications, LLC
PO Box 569, Chesterfield, MO 63006-0569, USA

This book is printed on acid-free paper.

Library of Congress Cataloging-in-Publication Data: on file
ISBN: 1-933370-03-3

For all information on all Reedy Press publications visit our website at www.reedypress.com.

Printed in the United States of America
06 07 08 09 10 5 4 3 2 1

Cover Design By William Mathis, MathisJones Communications, LLC

Design by Ellie Jones and William Mathis, MathisJones Communications

Contents

To my wife Helen,
son John, and daughters Leslie and Jennifer
for their support and understanding
of my passion for the Hawks.
While our lives have been permeated by sports for these many years,
know always that nothing has been more important
than all of you.
Of all the things I've done in my life,
nothing compares with the pride I take in each of you
and the happiness we have been blessed to share.

Preface
Dedicated to John Marecek, Jr.
My Father

I am proud to be the author of a book that needed to be written. It brings back to life a professional sports team that was as colorful and successful on the court over a relatively short period of time as any sports franchise in St. Louis history.

I dedicate this story to my father, John Marecek, Jr., who provided me with lifelong guidance and a love of sports. He passed away succumbing to disease on March 2, 2005, but not before seeing and experiencing almost every exciting event I've been privileged to attend and cover in my sportswriting and broadcasting career.

It was my father who took me to the very first St. Louis Hawks home basketball game on November 5, 1955. I didn't know anything about the National Basketball Association and couldn't imagine a sport where teams could score 100 points in a game!

As we walked into Kiel Auditorium, which seemed huge to a grade school kid who'd never been in a big arena before, my dad was trying to describe what I was about to watch.

After he finished, I said, "Dad, nobody scores 100 points in one game doing anything. I don't believe it."

He didn't reply. He just waited until we watched the pre-game practice and the opening tip was thrown into the air. As the 13-year era of Hawks basketball began, dad looked over at his mesmerized almost 7-year-old son and said, "I'll bet you an ice cream sundae that one team scores over 100 points!" I took the bet.

The powerful Minneapolis Lakers and our Hawks pounded up and down the Kiel floor under the glowing lights that focused only on the hardwood court. I watched the great second-year star Bob Pettit, the gentle giant Charlie Share and the rest of the Hawks battle the five-time champion Lakers. Our Hawks had finished last the year before in Milwaukee.

But that first day proved to be a sign of things to come. It was the beginning of exciting Cinderella seasons. At game's end, the St. Louis Hawks had won their first-ever game at home, and of course, dad won the bet. The final score was Hawks 101, Minneapolis 89. I lost a sundae but the Hawks had a new, young fan.

Dad knew how much I loved that night, and over the next 13 years he proceeded to bring home the company tickets night after night for hundreds of games. I still own and cherish the Hawks' game programs with many of the box scores filled out from the games we attended. We almost always had courtside seats so I could see and hear it all. Yes, I was there the day Bob Pettit poured in those 50 points to win Game 6 and the 1957–1958 World Championship.

My No. 1 fan, supporter and greatest friend was my Dad, whose never-ending, never-compromised love and support has been the true inspiration for the writing of this book. It is the first and only narrative exclusively telling the stories of the team, the players and the events that made up the history of the St. Louis Hawks.

And I still think about that great day with my Dad, the very first day of the Hawks. I hope in heaven he's reading the book.

I love you, Dad.

Introduction

If I would ever write an autobiography, the title should be *Privileged* because that's what I was as a child. I was given so many opportunities to experience things in life by my loving parents, and one of those was Hawks' basketball. From the first game in St. Louis to the last, I attended hundreds of games, saved every game program, every ticket stub and tried to imitate Bob Pettit and Cliff Hagan as would every other kid on the block.

The baseball Cardinals and basketball Hawks were all we had in St. Louis through the second half of the 1950s, and what earned my loyalty as a fan was winning the 1957–1958 National Basketball Association championship against the dreaded Boston Celtics. The Hawks were much more than a cult following, they truly had the interest of the masses. The Cardinals didn't win a championship in my youth until 1964, and there too, I was given the chance to be at the final six games during that remarkable end of the Redbirds' regular-season comeback to win the pennant. Then I attended two of the four World Series games against the New York Yankees, including Game 7.

I was privileged to be sitting in west floor seats behind the Celtic bench at Kiel Auditorium with my dad and a business associate of his for that magical Game 6 performance by Bob Pettit. I was nine years old and could fully appreciate every thrilling minute of this intense game. We were screaming for Pettit to keep shooting and scoring, never knowing how many points he really had until it was announced during the pandemonium at the end of the game. Imagine, 50 points by Pettit to win a world championship by one point—it was a once-in-a-lifetime performance, and I was there.

Those memories are my reasons for writing this book, and the rest of this forward are the reasons my principal adviser and supporter, Ed Macauley, believes the book needed to be done. It is amazing that there is no other work about the Hawks despite their incredible contribution to the sports history of St. Louis. That's why these are "The Untold Stories of the St. Louis Hawks."

The story of the Hawks begins and ends with a self-made businessman who, without vast financial resources and little knowledge of the game, found ways to develop a professional basketball team that became a perennial championship contender in the National Basketball Association. His name was Ben Kerner, originally a promotional specialties salesman in Buffalo, N.Y., who worked his way to St. Louis where his team became the No. 1 challenger to the Cardinals for the top spot in city's sports fans' hearts.

Once upon a time in the NBA, there were no $10 million player contracts and teams weren't bought and sold for $200–$300 million dollars. The times were much different in the 1950s and 1960s, the setting of this book. Teams didn't fly in chartered planes, players didn't receive hundreds a day for meals, and they didn't stay in luxury hotels. Most players made less than $10,000 per year and a superstar like Minneapolis' George Mikan made a whopping $25,000.

There were many more "have-nots" in the early NBA. Players didn't have lucrative endorsement contracts and there was no player pension plan. When playing in New York or Boston, for example, players traveled by railroad for between 24 and 30 hours from say Minneapolis. Our meal money was $5 per day.

Players were playing for the love of the game and owners weren't getting rich. Teams were more likely to fold in bankruptcy than announce any profits at the end of the season.

All of those facts make this story of the St. Louis Hawks all the more enriching to sports fans. Kerner's team achieved a goal that many wealthy owners in the league never sniffed—winning an NBA championship. Most dismissed the blue-collar squad in St. Louis as incapable of competing at a high level. How could they succeed in yet another home city after failing so miserably in Tri-Cities and Milwaukee?

A lot of things had to come together just right or the Hawks would have become vagabonds headed to another city as fast as they got to St. Louis. All the elements did come together and the team was embraced by a hungry city looking for something to revive its sagging sports image.

This is the story of that time and that team that brought St. Louis into the national picture for a sport other than baseball and set the table for other teams in other sports to make St. Louis their home. We hope you enjoy reading this story, which likely is all or mostly new to you. It was the catalyst for the city's future reputation as America's Best Sports Town.

—Greg Marecek and Ed Macauley

Chapter One

Tri-Cities, Milwaukee, St. Louis

The St. Louis sports landscape was barren in 1954 with only the St. Louis Cardinals available on the professional level for the fans to quench their thirst. Add to that, the Redbirds hadn't won anything since 1946 and were headed to two dismal seasons in 1955 and 1956 finishing sixth and seventh, respectively.

Meanwhile in Milwaukee, a new baseball team, the Braves, had arrived from Boston. They quickly took over the town, garnering the interest of the media and fans. When Braves' centerfielder Billy Bruton's fishing exploits earned front page headlines in the Milwaukee newspaper over an actual game story of the Milwaukee Hawks of the National Basketball Association in the middle of January, it was a signal that would change the futures of the two cities, Milwaukee and St. Louis.

Before getting to Milwaukee and then St. Louis, the trail for professional basketball's seventh oldest franchise had five other stops. It all began in 1946 in Buffalo, N.Y., where a pair of advertising men, Ben Kerner and Leo Ferris, got the idea of starting a team, thinking the post-war era would spur new forms of entertainment in America. The two had plenty of experience producing and selling advertising in sports event programs, including auto racing, wrestling, and yes, basketball.

These new sports entrepreneurs settled on Bisons for their team's nickname in the National Basketball League. The price to play in the league was an entry fee of $1,500 with another $5,000 to the league as a performance bond. But few victories and fewer fans had the enterprising duo scurrying to look elsewhere by mid-season. Kerner and Ferris eventually moved the team to the tri-cities area of Moline and Rock Island, Ill., and Davenport, Iowa, creating the Tri-Cities Blackhawks.

However, while Kerner and Ferris were struggling to win games and draw people in small markets like Oshkosh, Wis., Waterloo, Iowa, and Sheboygan, Wis., a group of executives from major cities met in New York in June 1946 to form a new competing league. These men were largely arena owners or hockey general managers looking for alternate-night sources of revenue for their buildings.

They formed a new league—the Basketball Association of America—with members in New York, Chicago, Boston, Philadelphia, Toronto, Detroit, Washington, Providence, Cleveland, Pittsburgh and St. Louis. The St. Louis Bombers were born and would survive four seasons with such players as John Logan, D.C. Wilcutt, Red Rocha and a budding star, Ed Macauley, who was an All-America performer fresh out of St. Louis University.

The competition of college and the two pro groups led to the merger of the National Basketball League and the Basketball Association of America, which became the National Basketball Association. However, little did two men in that new league realize their paths would cross later in St. Louis. Macauley became the leading scorer for the Bombers, while Kerner joined the NBA with his Tri-Cities team in the 1949–50 season.

The newly christened NBA found a 17-team league, broken up in three divisions, to be unwieldy and cumbersome. After just one season, restructuring began. Six teams were failing, including the last place and financially ailing St. Louis Bombers. The players were dispersed around the league with Macauley landing in Boston with the Celtics. Kerner's Tri-Cities team was also an underachiever at the gate and on the court, finishing 29–35 and in third place in 1949–50 and a sorry 25–43 and in last place in the 1950–51 campaign. Kerner's head coach in the final season in the old National Basketball League in the 1948–49 season was a fiery young guy who challenged the decisions of his domineering owner, a trait that would make it easier for Kerner to dismiss the coach after just one season.

Why bring up a coach from Tri-Cities who had a poor 28–29 season? His name was Arnold "Red" Auerbach, who would never have another losing record in his career. Instead of staying in Tri-Cities, which would eventually lead to St. Louis, he was booted by Ben at the behest of the NBA office to Boston to coach the struggling Celtics. The Kerner-Auerbach relationship would be just one of many ironies over the years between the franchises representing Boston and St. Louis.

The "new" NBA wanted their teams in big cities, not the Tri-Cities of the world. Kerner picked out a new destination for his team. He chose Milwaukee and shortened the nickname to the "Hawks," but neither change improved his club's win-loss record. The Hawks had five straight last-place finishes in their first five seasons in the NBA from 1950 through the 1954–1955 season.

Hall-of-Fame *St. Louis Post-Dispatch* sports editor Bob Broeg quoted Kerner in his May, 10, 1959, column about Ben's first decade of owning a pro basketball team (1946–1956). "I'd been in pro basketball 10 years," he said sadly. "I'd lost $108,000 and hadn't taken a cent in salary. As much as I loved the game, I'd lost my shirt. I wanted out."

A Milwaukee Hawk who would become a town favorite in St. Louis was Charlie Share, a 6-foot-11, 245-pound center, who was a first-round pick of the Boston Celtics out of Bowling Green in the 1951 draft. Share was sent by Boston to Fort Wayne for the rights to future star guard Bill Sharman and then was moved to Milwaukee 2 1/2 years later. Share remembers those bleak days in Milwaukee.

"Ben Kerner tried a lot of promotions such as a $1.25 ticket admission where the fan would receive an 89-cent pound of coffee. Still almost nobody came to the game," said Share. "Then since we were the doormat of the league and not drawing any fans, the NBA decided to use us as guinea pigs for an experimental game that would count in the standings using 12-foot baskets.

"We played the league champion Minneapolis Lakers at their place for the game. They widened the lane and used 12-foot hoops in an attempt to take the game away from the big men in the NBA. The great 6-11 George Mikan was the center for the Lakers and he was averaging between 25 and 29 points per game every season.

"It did affect his shot as Mikan had to put the ball up over the light fixtures with enough arch for the ball to come down. It did help one of our players. Usually noted for his defensive play, Bill Calhoun, for some reason, was the game's leading scorer. However, it wasn't interesting enough to ever try again."

Share recalled another depressing evening in Milwaukee against the champion Lakers when the Hawks were humiliated, losing by a 58-point margin, 133–75. Kerner had tried every promotional ploy he could think of in Milwaukee to bring the fans back after the persistent losing was in its third nightmarish season. Even giving away products and drafting Louisiana State University All-American Bob Pettit, who would become the NBA rookie of the year, didn't work. Kerner's flamboyance and energy were being sucked away in a sea of red ink. He even borrowed money from relatives. So before he lost more he decided to sell his franchise for $90,000. Thank goodness nobody bit on the offer.

Pettit, the player around whom the franchise would be built, remembers that one year in Milwaukee. He had been a spectacular college player at

Louisiana State, averaging 27.4 points and 14.6 rebounds per game during his varsity career, leading LSU to the co-championship of the rugged Southeastern Conference, along with coach Adolph Rupp's storied Kentucky Wildcats.

"I liked the city of Milwaukee very much," Pettit recalls. "The problem was the baseball Braves were everything in Milwaukee, and it was very difficult getting space in the newspaper. We didn't draw very well, and the arena never filled up unless the Globetrotters came to town."

The Hawks were clearly in a scramble mode. Kerner and Ferris had three choices: sell the team to one of several suitors who'd made low-ball offers, fold the franchise and write off the losses or gamble again in a new city. Two unacceptable offers were made, one by a Washington, D.C., businessman who pitched $65,000, and the other by an Indianapolis group that wanted a steal at $50,000. Kerner publicly called them "stinking offers," but the NBA wanted a decision so they could complete the 1955–1956 league schedule.

This proud man was not about to stay in Milwaukee where the atmosphere for basketball had grown maudlin and the town's sports interest had changed to a small white ball with stitches. But he had to decide where to go on very short notice as the Wisconsin snow was melting and the cry of "play ball" was in the air. Baltimore had wanted him to move there, but there was one city that Ben had played a game in that had drawn 8,000 fans just a couple of months earlier on Ash Wednesday.

The city, of course, was St. Louis. But when Kerner said that's where he wanted to move, there were dissenters in the written press all around the league. Eastern writers were quoted as saying, "What? St. Louis? Why they've lost pro basketball before and their hockey team … St. Louis University gave up football and the American League Browns had just left for Baltimore. What a lousy sports town!"

St. Louis did have to pass one test before the Hawks could pack their balls and sneakers to come south. Before the NBA would approve a transfer, the owners wanted some evidence St. Louisans would be excited about the return of basketball and buy tickets. Kerner put the City Fathers to the test, giving them less than a month to sell 1,000 season tickets. Three weeks later 633 season tickets had been sold and sales were increasing daily.

Now it was up to the NBA Board of Governors. The group met on May 11, 1955, in New York City to discuss and vote on the move of the Hawks from Milwaukee to St. Louis. Hawks' owner Ben Kerner reported his satisfaction with the rushed ticket campaign and other promises of support from business leaders and the media. The late, great Bob Burnes, sports editor of the old morning newspaper, the *St. Louis Globe-Democrat* has always been tabbed as the most influential media member who pursued Kerner and his Hawks.

Based on the ticket-selling campaign and the availability of Kiel

BOB PETTIT, ROOKIE OF THE YEAR AND ALL-PRO IN HIS FIRST PLAY-FOR-PAY SEASON WITH THE HAWKS... SCORED *1,466* POINTS FOR **20.4** AVERAGE... 6-FOOT-10 LSU GRADUATE PICKED BY WRITERS TO FIGHT IT OUT WITH NEIL JOHNSTON FOR SCORING HONORS AGAIN THIS YEAR

Auditorium with its almost 10,000 seats, the league members voted unanimously to immediately transfer the Hawks franchise to St. Louis. On May 12, 1955, the headline in the *Globe-Democrat* read: "Milwaukee Hawks Shifted to St. Louis by NBA." By the way, owner Ben did offer to consider a new nickname if local promoters wanted to use a selection process to help rally the fans behind the new team. Fortunately, no one popped up with any great campaign and "Hawks" stayed.

Besides the recent history of sports team failures, there was also the temperament, the politics, the economics and the overall climate of the city that Kerner had chosen for his franchise. Memories of the 1950s belong to the generation of baby boomers who today wait at the cusp of social security. The Cold War was beginning, segregation was in full force and St. Louis was a solid business community.

The political climate had St. Louisans solving the global and national topics of the time. Communism, Cold War evacuations or sheltering, the Soviet's atomic bomb, the arms race leading to the space race, the United States coming to the aid of the South Koreans, segregation, desegregation, radioactive fallout, and Eisenhower's Interstate Highway System dominated the headlines of the two St. Louis newspapers. Interestingly, commentators of the decade noted the 1950s as being sober, contented, and conventional. And in comparison to the turmoil of WWII, they probably were.

In 1916, a vote for segregation passed in St. Louis at a count of 52,220 to 17,877. Approximately one-half of all registered voters cast their ballots on February 30. The special election was held to create segregation ordinances within the city of St. Louis. Ten days following the vote, the law was writ. The Republican-pushed agenda really had no chance of failing. Only 9,846 blacks were registered to vote.

Fast forward to the 1950s, the progress of "Negroes" in St. Louis was severely stunted by the ordinances. Richard G. Baumhoff of the *Post-Dispatch* wrote at the time, "Negroes of St. Louis get the short end of several things. The short end of education. The lower rungs on the job ladder. The smallest figures on the pay scale. The meanest housing, the most overcrowding. The poorest, most limited recreational facilities. The worst conditions for health." The racial climate of the nation needed to be changed. Using St. Louis as a microcosm of society, it is easy to understand the need for Thurgood Marshall to win the Supreme Court case of *Brown v. Board of Education of Topeka*. It is easy to see that the civil rights years of 1954 to 1965, brought a long overdue change to the nation.

Segregation of schools, restaurants, all forms of transportation, theaters, drinking fountains, and virtually all public and private facilities was not only a St. Louis issue, it was a national crisis. When Rosa Parks joined the Montgomery Bus Boycotts in 1955 and when 14-year-old Emmitt Till was slain in Mississippi for "flirting" with a white woman, the nation and St. Louis watched and gradually began the change.

Similar to the changing racial overtones in the city, St. Louis also underwent numerous changes in the business sector during the decade. With its prime location hugging the Mississippi River and the onslaught of a computer revolution being years away, St. Louis business prospered. In 1950, St. Louis reached its peak in population. For the working population, it was a great place to be.

St. Louis was the second largest trucking center in the United States. There were approximately 50,000 trucks in the city, 303 carrier lines with connections to 25,000 U.S. cities and towns operating out of the city. A total of 28 common carrier lines had their home offices in the area. Partially causing the industry's great expansion since WWII was the fact that St. Louis was a hub of the grain markets. Nearly $200 million in business was generated in the St. Louis grain market in each year of the early 1950s. Nearly 40 million bushels of grain were exported from St. Louis through the gulf ports.

Who used so much grain? Well, St. Louis operated 14 mixed feed plants, three corn grinding plants, three flour mills, three soybean processing plants, two stockyards, and six breweries. Schlitz, not Anheuser-Busch, was the largest national brewery. To cut into the Schlitz lead, A-B made three significant marketing decisions, one of which stabilized the sports market.

The brewery added horses, a farm and a team to its St. Louis operation in an effort to catch up. The advertising campaign that began a great tradition and has come to symbolize Anheuser-Busch was born with the acquisition and development of the "Clydesdales" program. In 1954, the late president, August Busch Jr. opened Grant's Farm to the public in south St. Louis County. A year later Busch Beer was unveiled and the St. Louis Cardinals Baseball Club was purchased by the brewery.

In 1954, Edward D. Jones, chairman of the board for Griesedieck Western Brewery Co., brewers of Stag and Hyde Park beers, announced Carling Brewing Co. of Cleveland bought Griesedieck out for $10 million cash. Mergers and diversity were the key words of St. Louis business in the 1950s. Rawlings Manufacturing Co. purchased A.G. Spaulding and Brothers, Inc. of Chicopee, Mass., for $5,635,000. Monsanto bought out Lion Oil of Arkansas. Magic Chef acquired Dortch Stove Works of Tennessee, and lastly, Illinois Terminal Railroad was purchased by a group of 11 railroads. The face of business in town was being altered.

Coinciding with the business shifts in the city was dramatic growth at McDonnell Aircraft Corporation. In 1939, the company had two employees, but in 1954, the firm employed 12,000 people, used 2 million square feet of space, and had a payroll of more than $1 million. Its sales had skyrocketed from zero to $431,289,410 in only 15 years. The company's recent firsts included: the Army-Air Force XV-1, the Air Force F-101 long range twin-jet fighter, the building of John Glenn's Friendship 7 spacecraft and other Mercury and Gemini spacecrafts for the first Americans in space.

St. Louis, while becoming a giant in the aeronautics field, was also a huge cog of the automobile industry. The city was second in the nation in auto production. General Motors moved its production of the Corvette from Flint, Michigan, to St. Louis in 1953 and built the flashy sports car there for the next 28 years.

Finally, in response to the growing use of nuclear power and research, uranium plants in St. Louis County began construction. The area supported Mallinckrodt expansions through $39 million in funds from the Atomic Energy Commission. An additional $6.5 million were used in support of the company's expansion to the county and addition of uranium processing downtown.

With all those good things happening in the business world, it was time for the sports entertainment segment to pick up the pace. The addition of a professional basketball team in St. Louis was the needed tonic in a sickly sports scene.

There was little fanfare for the arrival of the Hawks as they went through pre-season drills in 1955 while preparing for their first season in St. Louis. The timing seemed good to attract the curious sports fans who just had endured the worst Cardinals baseball season since 1918, finishing in seventh place in the National League with a 68–86 record.

The Cards' new owners, Anheuser-Busch, fired manager Eddie Stanky and at the end of the season fired interim manager Harry Walker as well. Not everything was bad for the Redbirds, however. Stan Musial batted .330 with 33 home runs, and rookie centerfielder Bill Virdon hit .281 and won Rookie-of-the-Year honors. Another youngster named Ken Boyer took over third base and showed great promise with the glove and at the plate, where he hit .264 in 1955.

Charlie Share vividly recalls his first reaction to coming to St. Louis: "My wife and I were coming back from a Colorado vacation when we came through the city to meet with Ben Kerner before training camp," Share said. "What we saw was a lot of rustic old buildings and the temperature must have been 100 degrees. It was miserably hot.

"Our first impression improved dramatically when we saw the enthusiasm and interest from the fans who we began to meet. It was obvious Ben had put together a very coordinated effort with local businessmen in a very short time to pull off the move."

Jack Levitt, a former minor league baseball player and lifetime St. Louisan, quickly became an untitled "Jack of all trades" in the hard-working Kerner front office. Levitt, who had risen all the way to Triple A in the Cleveland Indians organization before returning to St. Louis, didn't want it mentioned it was an unpaid position without which the Hawks couldn't have gotten along.

"I didn't really have a title. I worked with the Hawks for about 11 years," recalls Levitt. "I'd met Marty Blake [general manager] when I played in the minor league system for Cleveland. He was a public relations guy for the Indians I met at spring training previously. When the Hawks moved here in 1955, Blake called and asked if I would come down and help, which I was happy to do.

"I had just retired from baseball and had a big sports void in my life. One thing led to another and I had a fairly responsible position with the Hawks," Levitt added with pride. "I think there were a lot of guys with different teams working on a "comp" basis because NBA clubs didn't have any money."

It was true. Kerner had come to the Missouri river town with no money and wondering if he wasn't just beating his head against the wall. That desperation nearly spelled disaster before the first ball was tossed into the air in St. Louis.

Kerner was so hard up for cash that summer he nearly traded his two young stars—Pettit, the NBA Rookie of the Year in 1954–55, and collegiate scoring sensation Frank Selvy. The New York Knicks quietly offered Kerner $100,000 cash for each player, which he seriously considered. Pettit was a hot commodity. He finished fourth in the league in scoring (20.4 points per game) and third in rebounds as a first team all-NBA performer. Selvy had averaged an impressive 19 points per game in his freshman season, giving the Hawks the best one-two scoring punch in all of the NBA.

Fortunately for St. Louis and basketball history, Kerner never pulled the trigger on any deals with his two budding stars. Selvy, however, never became a star with the Hawks, being crippled by a stint in the U.S. Army. Pettit, of course, would become one of the greatest NBA players of all-time.

Getting ready for that first season meant finalizing a lot of details like where the Hawks would play their games, who would be the radio announcer and on what station, plus who would be responsible for promoting the team and creating publicity besides Kerner.

Two buildings could accommodate the NBA, The Arena and Kiel Auditorium. The Arena was capable of seating 20,000 and the smaller downtown facility with 9,300 actual seats. The Ash Wednesday game against the Boston Celtics that had drawn the 9,000 fans in the spring that convinced Kerner to move to St. Louis was played at the cavernous Arena. Ben determined that the Hawks would never be a "tough ticket"

9

Kiel Auditorium

in such a spacious building. In addition, The Arena wanted too much rent money.

In the end, the intimate Kiel, built for $5 million in the mid-1920s, became home to the greatest basketball games played in St. Louis history for 13 seasons. While no one ever saw construction done or seats added, the actual capacity for a Hawks game seemed to be the deep, dark secret of owner Ben. For instance, the game program of the 1957–58 season had a picture of Kiel with a cutline saying capacity was 9,432. But the 1959–60 game program had the same picture and a cutline that proclaimed the capacity was 9,816.

The guys who really knew how many people were cramming into Hawks' games during the best years were the fire marshals for whom Kerner would find a seat to keep them happy.

"I would get the turnstile count and then I'd go to Ben's seat, show it to him and ask him what the attendance announcement should be," smiled Levitt. "I can tell you every time we played Boston, the attendance we'd show was 10,100, but for the life of me, I don't know where the other 800 people were! Kiel was a great place to watch a ball game."

The next piece of the puzzle in the development of the Hawks franchise was the hiring of the radio announcer who, in the days of minimal media access, was critical to the image and exposure of the team. On Grand Avenue at Busch Stadium, the Cards had assembled one of the greatest radio broadcast teams of all-time in any sport with Harry Caray, Joe Garagiola and new kid, Jack Buck. That famous trio was making ground outs exciting and telling colorful tales that made radio listeners crave every moment of a Cards' broadcast.

The Cardinals already had 50 years of tradition, the Gas House Gang era and a handful of World Championship teams to build their fan base. Kerner had the daunting task of finding someone to build interest in the NBA and make heroes out of these new athletes in town that were playing in a league less than 10 years old!

The call went out to a native St. Louisan, a graduate of Beaumont High School who had played major league baseball briefly and was currently making a national name for himself as baseball's Game of the Week announcer alongside colorful former Cardinals' great Dizzy Dean. His name was Robert Garnett "Buddy" Blattner, who would become the "Voice of the Hawks" for the most exciting eight seasons in the city's basketball history.

Buddy Blattner

"I had no connection at all with the NBA, and I don't remember ever having done a basketball game on either radio or television," said Blattner, who also broadcast Major League games for the St. Louis Browns, Anaheim Angels and Kansas City Royals. "I was representing Falstaff Beer doing the Major League Baseball Game-of-the-Week with Dizzy Dean and making appearances for the brewery. We were making an appearance for a distributor in Houston, Texas, when I got a phone call from the president, Joe Griesedick.

"He told me he had a job for me as the new announcer for the St. Louis Hawks. I didn't know if the Hawks were a water polo team or what, but they had already committed me. They told me that a man named Ben Kerner and his NBA team was coming from Milwaukee and had asked for my services."

It was a no-brainer decision for Falstaff, the other nationally recognized beer with headquarters in St. Louis. Providing Blattner, an announcer with a national reputation yet a native of St. Louis, was icing on the cake for Falstaff to win the exclusive beer sponsorship rights for the Hawks' radio and television broadcasts.

Bud doesn't remember what he was paid as the Hawks' play-by-play voice, but he knew baseball and little, if anything, about the inner workings of the NBA. He was next introduced to Kerner, with whom he would enjoy a very close relationship for years to come.

The first radio station to broadcast Hawks basketball would not be KMOX, the 50,000 clear channel red hot watts of what would become in the 1960s the Voice of St. Louis. Instead, the games were carried on KXOK 630 AM. It didn't matter to Kerner who carried the games, but who was willing to pay for that right. In those days, sponsors paid for programs and in this case Falstaff Beer offered $10,000, arranged the station and brought Blattner on board from the successful Baseball Game of the Week crew.

"I went to their version of 'spring training' in of all places Minneapolis where it was already pretty cold, and I would sit at the top of building with my little recorder and practice doing the play-by-play," remembers Blattner. "Later, I'd go back to my room, listen to the tapes and want to throw up. Thank goodness we didn't broadcast practice games then."

But Blattner would become a very important piece of the Hawks' history as he described the action in his colorful, exciting style emanating from one of the smoothest radio voices in sports. His player nicknames became legendary and his basketball jargon was spoken every day in backyard imitations by admiring young Hawks fans.

There was one more man who came with Kerner from Milwaukee, without whom the Hawks' success may never have reached its incredible run or won a championship. In 1954, Marty Blake was introduced to Kerner after the 23-year-old promoter had delivered a crowd of 12,000 to a ball park that seated 6,000 for the Wilkes-Barre Barons baseball club, a Cleveland Indians Class A team. The spectators came because the enterprising Blake convinced a team of NBA all-stars to come and play the Harlem Globetrotters as part of a doubleheader.

Blake took the job for $70 a week as the Hawks' public relations director, promotion director and as he would quickly find out, team general manager. When he went to Milwaukee to meet the staff, it was head coach Red Holzman who took Marty aside and said, "Look in the mirror and you'll be looking at the staff!"

Blake would be instrumental in almost everything the Hawks would do, but always with the final blessing of boss Ben who would have to sign off on every detail. It was no corporate empire that marched into St. Louis with this NBA franchise, but just Ben, Red and Marty. The trio would soon to be joined by Blattner and 10 players that made up the St. Louis Hawks.

Chapter Two
The First Season, a Playoff

n opening night, November 5, 1955, amidst little civic fanfare, the Hawks' era began in the Gateway City. That first jump ball was thrown in the air as the Hawks' Charlie Share challenged for the tip with the Minneapolis Lakers' Vern Mikkelsen, both well-known NBA players, but whose names had those fans in attendance scrambling to their game program to find out something about each of them.

The game program, a 25-cent investment, featured Share on the cover above an ad for Cresyl 110 gasoline from your neighborhood Mars Service Station. The inside cover was a full-page ad from the Wabash Railroad with the headline: "When the Hawks are on the go." Pictured with their suitcases in hand, something today's athlete would never be seen doing, were players Alex Hannum, Tiger Bob Harrison, Bob Pettit and Med Park. The Hawks and other teams frequently traveled by train.

The regular season was 72 games long, 36 at home. The Hawks played at two sites for their home games, Kiel Auditorium and the Washington University Fieldhouse, which the press guide said had 6,000 seats. The Fieldhouse was used when a conflict arose at the Kiel, but Kerner didn't mind using the university site because his teams over the years posted a hefty winning percentage on campus. He often scheduled important games and playoff games at Washington University, sacrificing attendance for the cozy confines and home-court advantage.

Charlie Share

As the Hawks and Lakers thundered up and down the court for the first time, this was the St. Louis roster on opening night:

Head Coach Red Holzman	
Charles Cooper 6-6	Duquesne
Al Ferrari 6-3	Michigan State
Alex Hannum 6-7	Southern California
Chris Harris 6-3	Dayton
Bob Harrison 6-2	Michigan
Med Park 6-2	Missouri
Bob Pettit 6-9	LSU
Dick Ricketts 6-7	Duquesne
Frank Selvy 6-3	Furman
Charles Share 7-0	Bowling Green
Jack Stephens 6-2	Notre Dame
Charles Whiteman 6-8	NYU

Buddy Blattner began his colorful career as the radio voice of the Hawks without a color commentator, perched midway in the second deck of Kiel where he preferred to look down on St. Louis' first NBA action. *Post-Dispatch* basketball beat writer John Archibald described the game in his Sunday, November 6, 1955, story: "A crowd of 7,452 persons, passive at first but gradually rising to college-like enthusiasm as the Lakers threatened in the second half, welcomed the Hawks to their new home."

In the first quarter, virtually the only Hawk to take off was Selvy, the second-year starter with the high-scoring reputation from college, who sparked the Hawks to a 32–23 lead by pouring in 18 points. The year before in Milwaukee, Selvy, nicknamed "the Fordham Flash," had averaged 19 points per game including three nights with 40 points or more. He had finished fifth in league scoring average and had made the East-West All-Star game lineup.

The second quarter was a low scoring affair as the Hawks outscored the perennial contending Lakers, 22–19, for a 54–42 halftime lead. Pettit couldn't find the basket in the first half, reflecting the nervous energy that was all over Kiel on opening night in a new city. It would change in the second half, and the greatness of No. 9 from Baton Rouge, La., would begin to show.

The Lakers, led by future Hawk Clyde Lovellette and husky Ed Kalafat, rallied in the third quarter, outscoring St. Louis 26–22. The home team was nursing a 76–68 advantage into the final period.

During the first four minutes of the final quarter, St. Louis couldn't make a shot and Minneapolis closed to within one point on a hook shot by Kalafat. The crowd began to exhort the home team to pull together with the score 78–77.

Then things began to turn around when Chuck Cooper hit a pair of free throws and Jack Stephens got the first Hawk field goal of the period to push the lead to three. Despite the 6-9 Lovellette's nine field goals and 27 points, the Hawks pulled away.

Pettit final got rolling with three of his five field goals in the final two minutes. He added 11 free throws for the night to equal Selvy's point total of 21, while Share contributed 16 points and was a dominant rebounder. Opening night was clearly a successful debut for these transplants from Wisconsin.

St. Louisans didn't know much about the National Basketball Association in 1955. The quality of basketball was so good in large part because there were only eight teams in the league. The Eastern Division consisted of the Boston Celtics, New York Knickerbockers, Philadelphia Warriors and Syracuse Nationals. In the West, it was the Minneapolis Lakers, Ft. Wayne Pistons, Rochester Royals and St. Louis Hawks.

The defending division winners and league champions weren't exactly big marquis cities. The West had been won by the Ft. Wayne Pistons in 1954–55 and the East by the Syracuse Nationals, who also won the NBA title. The top stars in the league were represented on the All-NBA first and second teams:

First Team All-Stars
Bob Pettit—St. Louis Hawks (Milwaukee at the time)
Dolph Schayes—Syracuse Nationals
Neil Johnston—Philadelphia Warriors
Larry Foust—Ft. Wayne Pistons
Bob Cousy—Boston Celtics

Second Team All-Stars
Vern Mikkelsen—Minneapolis Lakers
Bill Sharman—Boston Celtics
Harry Gallatin—New York Knickerbockers
Paul Seymour—Syracuse Nationals
Paul Arizin—Philadelphia Warriors

The Hawks were a novelty to a lot of local sports fans that first season. The team was on a roller-coaster ride of ups and downs regarding wins and losses. They climbed to 7–4 on November 30 after edging the Lakers again, 99–97, but after losing to defending division champ Ft. Wayne, 83–67, the day after Christmas, their record stood at 10 wins and 11 losses.

December's chill turned into a frosty January as wins were hard to come by. A seven-game losing streak between December 29 and January 8 was followed by losing streaks of three and five games. The club hit a season low on January 22, starting the day 13 games under .500 at 13–26.

However, a mid-season trade for two veterans triggered a run by the muddling Hawks. The deal sent first-round draft choice Dick Ricketts, who had not fulfilled his early promise, and rookie Chris Harris to the Rochester Royals for 6-7, 32-year-old forward Jack Coleman, and scrappy guard Jack McMahon. The two were clutch performers and deadly outside shooters. Coleman would be the third leading scorer, rebounder and leader in assists for the Hawks, while McMahon would be a playmaker and strong defender.

The timely trade would be a tip off of things to come. St. Louis would become a team always ready to trade to fill a need and seldom did the combination of Blake and Kerner make a mistake in deals. Meanwhile, after a great start, Selvy was drafted into the armed forces in November.

On January 22 at Syracuse, the Hawks began picking themselves off the floor. With their new, productive front line of Pettit, Coleman and Share, with McMahon anchoring the backcourt, they battled the defending NBA champion Nationals to the wire. At the buzzer, St. Louis had captured a 109–105 victory.

The Hawks would split their next two games, winning at Rochester and losing a return visit to Syracuse, but then they reeled off six victories in a row. Included were impressive back-to-back wins over division favorite and eventual winner, Ft. Wayne on the road, boosting their record to 22–26. But prosparity wouldn't last.

A six-game losing streak, three at home and three on the road against good clubs dropped the Hawks back to 10 games under .500 at 22–32. The loss of Selvy had really put a crimp in the Hawks' backcourt and team depth in the heart of the grueling season.

Then, over the final month, the club really battled. St. Louis beat the Pistons again at a neutral site in Kansas City, 84–82, and the Boston Celtics, 101–97, at Kiel the next evening. The Hawks went 20–13 in their final 33 contests to grab a second-place tie with the Minneapolis Lakers at 33–39 to earn both a tiebreaker game and a semifinal round spot. The winner would play division champion Ft. Wayne.

This match up was about as even as there could have been. The two teams had played 12 times in the regular season with the Hawks winning seven and losing five. In St. Louis, the Lakers had lost all four games at Kiel with other games having been played at neutral sites as often happened for cash opportunities in the NBA. The Hawks also had an extra day of rest while Minneapolis was traveling.

But the veteran, playoff savvy Lakers were ready to compete in this newest of NBA cities for the right to claim second place outright and home-court advantage in the first round of the playoffs. Minneapolis was led by two giants under the basket, soon to be Hall-of-Famers George Mikan and Lovellette.

Clutch Man in Drive to Playoffs

The Hawks could only hope their big man, Share, could outduel the awesome twosome. Pettit, meanwhile, had pounded the Lakers in the last two regular season games with 44 and 34 points, respectively.

The first game was a battle all night long as the Hawks and Lakers played like it was the seventh game of the NBA Finals. Remember the Hawks had finished dead last the year before so this pressure was a new experience. However, in retrospect, it gave them a chance to get adjusted to the tension before the real playoffs began. The Lakers won the tiebreaker game, 103–97, giving them the home-court advantage in the best-of-three round that would begin the following night in St. Louis.

In this first season, St. Louisans had been privileged to witness one of the great individual performances in league history. Pettit scored 1,849 points and pulled down a league record-breaking 1,164 rebounds to lead the NBA in both categories. He averaged 25.7 points per game to earn the league's Most Valuable Player honor after winning the All-Star Game's MVP Award as well. Nobody felt the Hawks could compete in postseason unless Pettit dominated every night, but it didn't happen that way.

Pettit was his usual tireless working self in the playoffs and had some big games, but with the big bulls eye on his back from each opponent, he was less effective. What did happen, however, was that a team came together with help coming from other sources. One of those players was their first-round draft choice, Al Ferrari, who blossomed in the postseason. Ferrari had hung in there playing in 68 games but not much as a starter.

"I was drafted third by the Hawks as the 17th overall pick in the draft," recalls Ferrari. "Jack Stephens, their second pick from Notre Dame, was starting ahead of me, and their No. 1 pick had been Dick Ricketts.

"In 1955, my first with the Hawks, I wasn't playing at all and people weren't coming to the games. (Ben) Kerner calls me into his office and says 'I've got to cut your salary, you're not scoring.' I said, 'Wait a second, I'm averaging a minute per game, it makes it pretty tough to score.'"

Kerner shook his head and replied, "I don't care. I look at results. I've got to cut so you're going to $400 a month (down from $5,000 per season)."

"I was furious," Ferrari said. "How could he cut a contract? I thought that was wrong so I went to Coach Holzman and told him I'd been cut in half by Ben and I needed to start a game right now.

"We were playing Ft. Wayne and their great guards, Frankie Bryan and Andy Phillip, for two straight games. So he starts me. I told myself I'm going to shoot every time I get my hands on the ball. It's the only chance I have to save my money. So I scored 18 points the first night and 17 points the next night and we won the two games."

Back home in St. Louis after taking the train, Ferrari went from the station, unshaven and unchanged directly to Kerner's offices where he

Al Ferrari

demanded his original contract be restored.

Kerner retorted, "Holy cow, you have two good games and you think you're a superstar."

I said, "I don't think I'm a superstar, but it was wrong to cut my signed contract and if you don't want to give it to me, go ahead and release me and I'm sure Ft. Wayne would pick me up fast.

"I really wasn't that sure they'd want me, but it was enough to get Kerner thinking and he decided to give me back my contract. It certainly gave me great incentive the rest of the season."

Ferrari became the Hawks secret weapon in the playoffs. He averaged 33 minutes of playing time, was the team's second leading scorer, averaging almost 15 points per game with 24 assists. Whenever Pettit was throttled, Ferrari would come up big, often when the game was in the balance. The Lakers would be the first to find out Ferrari's worth in the division semifinals.

Still, the Hawks were an unproven new product with many St. Louis sports fans and only 5,148 came out to watch Game 1. After the Hawks' Share rattled in five quick points to give the hometown team a 5–0 lead, the Lakers went on an 8–0 run to grab an 8–5 lead. The Hawks would tie the game at 8, 14, and 16, even led 20–16 on the strength of another Share bucket and two jump shots by Pettit. But it didn't last as the Lakers pushed to a 31–25 first quarter edge.

The second quarter was all Lakers, who built their lead to 44–27 before the Hawks could manage a field goal. The Hawks battled back, but veteran star guards Dick Garmaker and Chuck Mencel got hot and carried their club to a comfortable 60–45 halftime lead.

Early in the second half the Lakers moved out to a commanding 19-point bulge when St. Louis showed signs it was building a basketball team to be reckoned with for years to come. A 19-point lead had been chipped down to eight by the end of the third quarter as Ferrari, the Michigan State flash, poured in 16 points in the quarter, including eight of eight from the free throw line.

In the thrilling fourth quarter, the Hawks didn't take the lead until 5:13 remained. Coleman nailed two free throws for 101–100 edge. The Lakers stayed close and trailed 109–105 when Ferrari and Pettit took charge.

In the final two minutes, Ferrari hit a driving layup and Pettit bagged two free tosses to sew up a 116–115 victory in St. Louis' first-ever playoff game. Pettit led all scorers with 25 points, Ferrari added 22. Feisty guard Slater Martin, soon to be a Hawk, had 19 points for the losing Lakers. The Hawks now had to find a way to win one game on the road while Minneapolis would have to sweep at home in the best-of-three series.

Game 2 in Minneapolis was an entirely different and forgettable affair for the River City boys. In the first quarter, the Lakers jumped out to a 6–1 lead, an advantage St. Louis cut to 6–4. But by the end of the first period, the Lakers

21

led 25–15. The second quarter was worse and the rout was on. Minneapolis outscored St. Louis by a whopping 36–15 margin to take a 61–30 halftime bulge.

The lucky number for the night was "36," which the Lakers scored in both the third and fourth quarters for a new Laker single-game scoring mark. Down 97–54 after three quarters, the Hawks limped to the finish getting rolled, 133–75. The Lakers hit on 44 of 101 field goal attempts, while St. Louis managed just 22 of 91 shots. The rebounding battle was another slaughter, 71–44, for Minneapolis.

Obviously, all the stats went heavily for the Lakers. The 58-point margin of victory and 72-point half were new club records, and the final spread was also an NBA playoff record. Leading the winners was Martin with 19 points, while Dick Schnittker added 18. Pettit led the Hawks with a measly 14 points, but losing coach Holzman was philosophical after the series-tying loss.

"Fortunately this game only counts as one win and one loss, and we'll regroup by the tip off of Game 3," he said. "After all, the Lakers beat us in the second-place playoff game and we came back and won the very next night. Why can't we do it again tomorrow even up here in Minneapolis?"

With the series now tied 1–1, Minneapolis was a solid favorite to wrap up the best-of-three series and move on to the semifinal round in the Western Division. After all, the experienced Lakers had won three out of the last four NBA championships whereas the Hawks were used to finishing in last place, never competing before in play-offs.

If the Hawks were to have any chance of winning their first-ever playoff series, particularly on the road, they would need somebody to rise to the occasion. Following the Lakers 133–75 debacle, *Post-Dispatch* writer Harold Flachsbart wrote, "The Hawks are still looking for a really good scoring output by their league champion (led NBA in scoring) Bob Pettit, everybody's hero in the NBA. Pettit two-time guarded much of the way, scored only 14 points. One of these

Bob Pettit and Connie Hawkins

nights, if the Hawks last that long in the playoffs, he's likely to tally 46 and then it won't matter if Minneapolis is a hot shooting team."

The next night, March 21, 1956, Flachsbart's words looked like a prophecy, and with a better ending. The Hawks withstood an early furious charge by the home team Lakers and trailed by just four at the half. Then the determined Pettit took charge. He scored 13 points in the third quarter as St. Louis took a surprising 85–84 lead.

The Lakers had never missed winning the first round of the playoffs in their nine-year history, but the crowd of just over 5,000 recognized that mark was tottering. Pettit had been rested for much of the first quarter so he had a full tank almost every minute the rest of the way.

The fourth quarter saw the two teams trading baskets until the Hawks eased out to a 95–89 lead with nine minutes to play. But with 2:33 remaining, the Lakers knotted the score 110–110 and their fans were in a frenzy. Then Minneapolis rocked the arena when Lovellette hit a hook shot for a 112–110 lead. But the newfound confidence of the St. Louis contingent became more evident. Ferrari hit a basket and two free throws to put the Hawks back on top, 114–112, with two minutes remaining.

Now the question was whether or not the young Hawks could show some poise. With 1:54 left Lovellette connecting on a three-point play giving the Lakers a one-point lead. However, the hard-charging Ferrari was fouled and sent to the line for a pair of free throws. In front of a jeering crowd, he calmly sank them both for a 116–115 edge, ironically, the same score by which the Hawks had won Game 1.

With under a minute to play Minneapolis still had time. With 42 seconds left, Kalafat was fouled and with two free throws had the opportunity to tie or take the lead. He'd averaged just six points per game all season against the Hawks, but had 13 on this night. He took a deep breath, as did the packed crowd, then missed the first shot . . . and then the second. Pettit grabbed the rebound and the Hawks clung to its one-point lead. The seconds ran down and the buzzer sounded with no more scoring. The Hawks had shocked the Lakers in Minneapolis to win the series, two games to one and advance to the division finals.

The heroes for St. Louis were many, but the two who stood out were the 41 points by Pettit and the 16 points by Ferrari. Al was a perfect eight-for-eight from the free throw line and as Blattner had christened him on the airwaves, the Bombardier from Baton Rouge, Mr. Pettit, had hit 13–19 from the charity line. Coleman and Share each added 13 points with 11 from the steady McMahon.

Elsewhere in the league, the defending NBA champion Syracuse Nationals had beaten the Boston Celtics in three games and were set to meet the Philadelphia Warriors for the Eastern Division title. Despite having won the

NBA trophy the year before, the Nats had fallen to last place in the East, so their win over second-place Boston was truly an upset. Meanwhile, the Warriors had done the opposite, rising from a last-place finish in 1954–55 to a 45–27 record and first place in the 1955–56 campaign.

The city of St. Louis wasn't prepared for victory and tickets for the division finals had to quickly be put on sale March 22. St. Louis fans still new to the league and the game were saying, "That's great, now who are we playing?" The answer was the high-powered Ft. Wayne Pistons, winners by four games over the Lakers and Hawks in the regular season standings.

This would be a best-of-five series with Game 1 in Ft. Wayne, and then a rotation of the two cities for each of the remaining four games, if necessary. The first St. Louis contest would be Saturday, March 24, a nationally televised game to be played at the Washington University Fieldhouse instead of Kiel. It was announced that all seats would be $1.50 for adults and 80 cents for children. Just 6,000 could be jammed into Wash U., but the Hawks liked the closeness of the fans, always looking for that hometown edge.

Going into the series, it looked like the Hawks could give the Pistons a battle. St. Louis had the momentum of their spectacular win over the Lakers while Ft. Wayne sat around and could have gotten rusty waiting to play. In the regular season, the series was close with the Indiana team winning seven and losing five including two defeats at the hands of the Hawks in Ft. Wayne. The teams had played five games on neutral sites at Rochester, N.Y., Lansing, Mich., New Orleans, Elkhart, Ind., and Kansas City. Talk about travel!

While the Hawks were all about Pettit, Share and Coleman offensively, the Pistons had their own scoring machine. Veteran All-Star George Yardley averaged 17 points per game and 15 against the Hawks. He was followed by the league's 11th leading scorer, center Larry Foust who averaged 16 points per game. They also had a steady scoring guard in Chuck Noble with 11 points per game and a solid performer. (Ironically, both Foust and Noble would become Hawks.) The best-of-five for the Western Division title and the right to play in the NBA championship round was at stake and the city of St. Louis was getting excited.

Ft. Wayne had been one of those teams in the old National Basketball League of small midwestern cities that had wisely jumped to the Basketball Association of America in 1947. So when the NBL folded before the 1949–50 season, this town was already in the loop. They had won the West and advanced to the NBA Finals in 1954–55 losing Game 7 by just one point to the champion Syracuse Nationals. They were 43–29 that year during the regular season, but only 37–35 in winning the weak Western Division in 1955–56.

The Pistons, coached by a former referee Charley Eckman, featured a loosely run offense. Set plays were not part of the plan for Yardley, Foust, Mel Hutchins and assist leader, Andy Phillip. They were owned by Fred Zollner, whose company made "pistons" for engines, and he named them the "Zollner Pistons" from their inception in the early 1940s. He was instrumental in the merger of the BAA and NBL, which became the NBA. His contributions to the merger were so significant that in 1975 he was named "Mr. Pro Basketball" at the Silver Anniversary NBA All-Star Game for his status as a founder.

What would help doom Ft. Wayne as an NBA city was its size and facilities. Even today at about 170,000 citizens it would be too small for the league. The Pistons of those early days had played in high school gyms, armories and ballrooms. But at this point, they were housed in the 9,300 seats of Memorial Coliseum. Still, opening night of the conference finals drew just 3,491 fans.

Despite no day off between their dramatic win in Game 3 at Minneapolis and this semifinal series, St. Louis gamely took it to the veteran but aging Pistons in the opening quarter. The first half saw a lot of offense before the defense took over. At the end of the first quarter, the Hawks surprisingly led, 27–25, although superstar Pettit was called for three personal fouls.

Pettit's absence changed the Hawks' strategy, putting pressure to score on Coleman, Share and Ferrari, who was off to a great start in the playoffs. The second quarter resembled the first and St. Louis still held a five-point lead, 50–45 at half. Pettit would play just 18 minutes all night as the officials tabbed him for fouls number 4 and 5 early in the second half.

The play was ragged, and free throws would play a big role in the final outcome. Each team was whistled for 29 fouls in the game, and each shot 44 times from the charity stripe. The difference in the score would be reflected in the made attempts.

The third quarter belonged to the Pistons. The Yardley, Hutchins and Foust connection helped Ft. Wayne outscore the Hawks 23–19 to cut St. Louis lead to one point entering the final quarter. But these Hawks were getting used to the pressure cooker and were becoming great road warriors.

"It's too bad St. Louis basketball fans can't see the great road shows of the Hawks," declared the *Post's* Flachsbart in his game story in the March 23 edition.

The fourth quarter was tense and the veteran Pistons weren't going easy. At the five-minute mark, the Hawks were down six, 81–75. Ferrari, who was winning many admirers around the league for his smooth but aggressive style, made a clutch field goal and former Mizzou star Med Park hit a free throw. The 6-10 Share then swept in a classic hook shot to cut the deficit to one, 81–80.

The defense put up an iron curtain around the Piston stars, frustrating their scoring machine. Meanwhile, the Hawks kept rolling as the clock clicked inside three minutes. Park, Share and former Notre Dame star, Jack Stephens, each popped in a bucket before Share connected on another hook shot to give St. Louis 86 points. Those were their last points of the game, but they were enough.

Two field goals, one by Foust, moved the Pistons to 85, but that's when this gutsy St. Louis team stepped up its defensive intensity. Time outs and possession changes passed with no points being scored with 1:19 now on the clock. Pettit, who finished with just seven points, finally returned to the lineup for rebounding strength.

The play ran down to 23 seconds and the Pistons would get one more shot. Newspaper reporters called it some sort of fate when Ft. Wayne's Frank Brian, Pettit's cousin from Louisiana, swept down the lane and missed a left-handed layup with three seconds left and cousin Bob wrestled away the rebound to preserve victory for the Hawks.

The victorious Hawks raced into the locker room shouting "go-go-go," their new "mantra" symbolizing their scrappy play. They had come from behind for the second straight night on the road, and the victory was especially pleasing because they didn't have to rely on Pettit to get it done.

Ferrari had another great game banging in 17 points, Share and Coleman each added 12 points, while Harrison and Park both had 11 points. Ft. Wayne was led as usual by future Hall-of-Famer Yardley with 23 points. Foust had 15 and Hutchins 14 points.

The series moved to St. Louis, but not to Kiel. Since the downtown auditorium was previously booked not knowing if the Hawks would get to the second round of the playoffs, an alternate site had to be found. One thing was for sure, Kerner didn't mind that his Hawks had to play Game 2 in the tight quarters at Washington University.

Despite the Hawks sudden success, playoff tickets still weren't tough to obtain in town. Although the old Wash U. Fieldhouse could seat 6,000, just 3,622 were on hand to witness Game 2, which was televised nationally, including locally on KSD-TV, Channel 5. Still the atmosphere was great and the crowd sitting so close to the floor was loud and intimidating for Ft. Wayne.

The St. Louisans were loaded with confidence after their last two road wins. And even though Park had to miss Game 2 because his father had suddenly died the day before in Lexington, Mo., St. Louis was able to explode in the first quarter. The big guns, Pettit, Ferrari and Coleman each ripped the cords for three field goals and the Hawks soared to a commanding 30–12 lead after one period.

The barrage continued in period two as the cheering crowd saw the lead stretch to 37–15 before the Pistons could slow the Hawks' attack. Ft. Wayne fought back to within 12 at the half, 47–35, but it still didn't look like a run was coming.

The low scoring second half saw a lot of basket trading. After three quarters the Hawks led 66–53 and cruised to a final of 84–74 to take a shocking and commanding two games to none lead in this best-of-five series. They had hit on 13 of their first 25 field goal attempts to put the Pistons away early. The substitutes got plenty of playing time in this one.

Again the scoring was well distributed. Ferrari stayed hot, leading all scorers with 21 points, Pettit added 19 and Share 14 points. For the losers, Foust had 16 points, Yardley 14 and Hutchins 12. St. Louis hit 35 of 88 shots, with their second team unit hitting just 6 of 23. On the other end Ft. Wayne connected on only 28 of 84 shots. Rebounding was key. Pettit controlled the boards with 17 rebounds, while Share and Coleman split 30 more for a team edge of 66–51.

It was starting to look easy after that second game, with the Hawks dominating on both ends of the court. However, the Ft. Wayne veterans were neither scared nor intimidated. Yardley had been held down dramatically by Ferrari's tough defensive play, but the series wasn't over—not by a long shot.

The upstart Hawks were due for a letdown as they headed back to Indiana for Game 3, and the hometown fans were waiting to rally their Pistons. The red-shirted Hawks were razzed and taunted by the 4,800 Piston fans who as reporters later said, "Came to give St. Louis the business."

It worked, although at the start it appeared a repeat of Game 2 could occur as the visitors from Missouri bolted to a 6–0 lead. But they would make only two more field goals the rest of the quarter and Ft. Wayne took a 29–19 advantage after one period. The second quarter was more evenly played, as the Pistons moved ahead 55–43 at halftime. Again it was Ferrari who kept the Hawks in the game scoring all 12 of his points in the first half with several great drives to the hoop.

Maybe inspired by a couple of lineup changes which created a new backcourt, the Pistons got 40 points from a three man rotation of 6-5 Corky Devlin, 30-year-old veteran Odie Spears and the sharp-shooting Noble. Noble connected on five long field goals and added five free throws for 15 points and Devlin threw in 16. Yardley got his usual 19 points to lead the Pistons to their 107–84 triumph, cutting the St. Louis series lead to 2–1.

Holzman saw the writing on the wall early in the game and used the second half as a time to rest some of his regulars. Hannum came off the bench to score a season-high 18 and Stephens added 11 in a reserve role. Pettit had 16 for the losers and was nursing an injured hand at the end.

"We were entitled to an off night after three tremendous efforts weren't we?" asked a still-confident Holzman. "I just hope our rooters will be there at Kiel at the next game in large numbers and with large voices. I would like to see what a really geared up big St. Louis crowd is like."

Game 4 would be back home and, indeed, at Kiel. Winning would mean a lot to the small salaried players who could earn $3,500 more by winning than losing the NBA semis. The winner would take home $7,500 per man. A loss would send the series back to Ft. Wayne for what would be a perilous Game 5 for the Hawks.

While Kiel still was not full, support got better as more than 6,300 screaming fans came to Kiel in an effort to get their high-spirited Hawks into the division finals. Maybe the Hawks were too juiced. They missed shot after shot and found themselves down 24–21 in the first quarter. Yardley came to play right out of the gate, popping in 12 of his 30 points in the opening stanza.

Pettit hit the first bucket of the second trimming the deficit to a point, but before one could blink, the Pistons got a Yardley three-point play and a Bob Houbregs' hook shot gave Ft. Wayne a 44–35 lead. The half ended 52–48 bad guys at Kiel.

For a time in the third quarter the fans got excited about the possibility of an NBA Championship Series in town. A Tiger Harrison set shot, Ferrari fast-break bucket and a Coleman free throw gave the Hawks a short lived 53–52 lead that swayed back and forth throughout the quarter.

Going back to Ft. Wayne tied with the Pistons on a two game roll was not what the doctor ordered for the Hawks, but the vets from Indiana showed their poise in the fourth stanza. The Hawks never gave up but Ft. Wayne managed to even the series with a 93–84 verdict. Momentum and the favorite's role had swung to the division champs for the fifth and final game.

Adding to the Hawks' woes was a wave of injuries heading into the decisive game. Stephens, a double-digit scorer and playmaker, injured his ankle so severely he didn't even make the trip. The 6-7 Hannum couldn't walk without limping and now the hustling, high-scoring Ferrari had aggravated an ankle tendon making him questionable. Cinderella was losing her good looks heading into Game 5.

The pressure fell heavily on Pettit, who had been shackled by Hutchins' tough defense up to now. Bob had scored just 7, 16, 19 and 15 points in the four games after scoring a league-leading 1,871 points during the season, the second highest total by anyone in NBA history.

"We promise to have some interesting surprises offensively and maybe something on defense as well for this game," promised Holzman, the red-haired leader of the Hawks. "We naturally want to try to increase the scoring output of Pettit in order to win. He is our main weapon and with our backs to the wall, we have to go to our bread-and-butter guy."

Holzman was good to his word about having a surprise ready. In fact, it was shocking. Right after the opening tip, he pulled his two scoring stars, Pettit and Ferrari, replacing them with Park and McMahon hoping both to confuse the Pistons and jolt Pettit out of his slump by coming into the game later. Ferrari's break didn't last long because Bob Harrison was nailed for three fouls in the first quarter.

Coleman and Share kept the period close. The Hawks were down by five before Pettit re-entered the game. However, his slump didn't end and Yardley and Foust would play a duet all night on St. Louis. The Pistons' lead grew to nine, 46–37, at half. The Hawks let it all hang out in the third period, rallying to tie the game and even taking a one-point lead, 68–67, after three quarters. Year No. 1 and the franchise's first playoff appearance would either be extended to the NBA Finals or end in Ft. Wayne based on the final 12 minutes.

St. Louis, which actually built a five-point lead briefly in the third period, put up a gallant finish, but fell just short. In the game to the final minute, the Hawks couldn't hold on down the stretch. At the buzzer the score read Ft. Wayne 102, the Hawks 97, ending a thrilling first campaign, but igniting the fire that was NBA basketball in St. Louis for years to come. Coleman had 20, Ferrari 17, Pettit and Share 16 each and Harrison 13. Yardley had 26 and Foust 20 to carry the day for the champions. Ft. Wayne would take on the Philadelphia Warriors in the NBA Championship, but go home the losers in a rout, four games to one.

St. Louis, though disappointed at losing the last three games in the division finals, was satisfied at how far they had come, especially after losing Frank Selvy and Dick Ricketts, two players the team had counted on, at the beginning of the season. They had improved the club through trades, acquiring Coleman and McMahon, and their late-season heroics had won over a new and fast-growing fan base itching to start the 1956–57 season.

Chapter Three
Trades—How the Hawks Were Made

S t. Louis entered the off-season knowing changes would have to be made if they were to take the next step and win a conference final and play in a league championship series. They'd made two great draft selections in back-to-back years, drafting Pettit No. 1 in the spring of 1954 and Ferrari as their third pick in 1955. But with only veteran Coleman supporting Pettit as a scoring forward and Ferrari going to the military leaving a gaping hole at guard, the Kerner-Blake combo needed to find starting lineup help.

The 1956 draft was about to unfold with the Hawks having the second pick behind the last-place Rochester Royals. The Hawks had finished with the second poorest regular-season record in the NBA after losing the tiebreaker play-off game to the Lakers. The stage was set for what is still today one of the most important trades in NBA history because it resulted in two franchises assembling championship teams.

Everyone's No. 1 pick, or so it was thought, was the center for the University of San Francisco, 6-foot-11 Bill Russell. In those days of limited media coverage and minimal television, plus playing in the West Coast time zone, Russell had only modest exposure to even NBA recruiters. However, it was widely known the Boston Celtics, who owned the third pick in the draft, were coveting Russell's services.

Boston was determined to make a deal for his rights with either Rochester

Bob Pettit, Bill Russell, Cliff Hagan at the Boston Garden

or St. Louis, whoever was standing with Russell available. The Celtics thought Rochester would take Russell and worked out a trade with St. Louis for the No. 2 pick so they could offer it to the Royals. The Hawks, meanwhile, were looking for some veteran scoring power and a local attendance draw so they asked for former St. Louisan and all-pro forward "Easy" Ed Macauley.

A two-time All-American at St. Louis University, Macauley was named the Most Valuable Player in the 1948 National Invitation Tournament, widely considered to be the country's true national championship tourney at that time. He was also selected Associated Press National Player of the Year in 1949. He had led his SLU Billikens to the NIT title in 1948 beating New York University, while Kentucky won the NCAA Tournament.

Macauley had been the first draft pick of the St. Louis Bombers in the ill-fated Basketball Association of America, in an attempt by the local team to save the franchise. He averaged 16 points per game as a rookie, but nothing could save the Bombers. With that team's demise, Macauley was available and the Celtics took him in the league's dispersal draft. He became a scoring machine and one of the league's premier stars over the next several seasons in Boston.

Peter Bjarkman, the author of the "Boston Celtics Encyclopedia" wrote, "With Macauley and Risen (Arnie) in the forecourt and Cousy (Bob) doing the playmaking the Celtics were already an offensive whirlwind team that could score quicker and more continuously than any team in the league."

Easy Ed was chosen the MVP of the first NBA All-Star Game in 1951, was All-NBA First Team his first three seasons and second team in 1953–54. Over his six seasons in Boston, No. 22 averaged 20, 19, 20, 18, 17 and 17 points per game, respectively. He was the perfect trade bait for the Celtics to throw out to the Hawks.

What the Celtics harried owner Walter Brown needed to know as he tottered on the verge of bankruptcy that could end the franchise in Boston, was whether Macauley would accept a trade to St. Louis. Auerbach was ready to make a deal if the pieces of the draft fell into place, but Brown wanted Macauley's blessing. At first, Ed wasn't very interested in going to a new franchise in St. Louis after he had spent six years building a career and name for himself in Boston. Then a serious personal crisis occurred that changed Macauley's mind and the NBA history books.

"It was right at the end of the season and I was in Boston with my wife, Jackie, our daughter Mary Ann and one-year-old son, Patrick," began Macauley. "With about 10 games to go our son Patrick got sick. I was playing at the Garden in the afternoon, came home, and Patrick began running a high fever. We took him to Boston Children's Hospital, one of the best in the country.

"We handed Patrick over to the doctors while they ran some tests. We sat there for about three hours before the doctors came out and they didn't look very happy. They had bad news. Patrick had spinal meningitis."

The Macauleys were told that the disease that they had never heard of was very serious and the outcome would be largely determined by how high the fever would go and how long it would last. In the end, their worst fears were realized. The fever was very high and lasted a long time before medication could get it under control.

"Patrick's brain had been destroyed by the fever, and from that point on he couldn't talk, walk, think, do anything but lay in a crib," remembers Ed. "He had to be cared for full time, and Jackie had to feed him every meal. We flew home to St. Louis after the playoffs and got a call from Walter Brown.

"Walter said he didn't want to make the deal because he couldn't imagine the Celtics without me, but I told him now the circumstances had changed and I didn't know if I could even consider going back to Boston with my son's prognosis so poor."

On the other end in St. Louis, Kerner had his own reasons for wanting Macauley and giving up the great potential of Russell, if he were available when the Hawks turn to draft came up. Ben's problems were financial and he needed a player to immediately impact his team that was ready to compete. Russell had potential baggage because he was scheduled to play for the United

Ed Macauley jump shot against the Syracuse Nationals with Bob Pettit (#9) guarded by Dolph Schayes (#21) and guard Jack McMahon watching

States Olympic Team in Australia and would not be eligible to sign before the following December. In addition, Russell wanted $50,000 in salary, a salary that would be more than Pettit was making. That wasn't going to happen in St. Louis.

If all went according to form, however, Rochester would take Russell. The Hawks would then draft Sihugo Green, the All-American out of Duquesne, and trade him to Boston for Macauley. Boston would then be on its own in an attempt to get Russell. The morning of the draft, Rochester's ownership decided against drafting Russell, a decision that would reshape the future of the NBA.

The Royals selected Green as the first pick in the draft, leaving Russell available to the Hawks. Now Kerner balked at his trade with Boston, telling the Celtics he couldn't close the deal with only Macauley for Russell. He needed more from Boston. Kerner had given up Auerbach to Boston to be their coach after the 1949 season at the request of the league, so as far as Ben was concerned, it was payback time.

Auerbach understood and was on a mission. He didn't hesitate to add Cliff Hagan, his prize draft choice from the previous season, who was now serving in the military for one year. At 6-4, Hagan was a two-time All-American from the University of Kentucky who had averaged 19.2 points per game for the Wildcats. He possessed a smooth hook shot and had great rebounding instincts.

Coach Rupp said of the polished Hagan, "If Cliff took a hook shot I didn't even have to look, it was going in. He was an outstanding center."

Ed Macauley's 1957–58 NBA championship ring

"We were not going to get Russell and were very happy to get the all-pro Macauley and a star waiting to happen in Hagan," said G.M. Marty Blake. "The way it worked Boston was going to actually tell us who to take. We would draft for them because of NBA rules, but everybody knew we would make our pick (Russell) and pass him on to Boston. Eddie was a hero in St. Louis and could obviously help us, and Hagan was a great addition.

"Don't kid yourself, the Celts weren't crazy about giving up Hagan, too, and they weren't positive Russell was their next superstar. By the way, about the race issue that's mentioned all the time regarding the Hawks and Russell, that's a lot of baloney. We already had a black player, Chuck Cooper, it was just the fact that Russell was going to miss half the season and we couldn't meet his financial demands.

"In retrospect the trade made two great franchises that would battle each other for championships for years to come. If Rochester had drafted Russell, it is my contention that the NBA would not be as popular as it is today and the Celtics most likely would have folded."

There is really another piece of the puzzle that links directly to the Macauley-Hagan trade for the rights to Russell. Since the Hawks didn't keep their first choice in the NBA draft of 1956, their second-round pick became their top selection. He was UCLA forward Willie Naulls who, had it not been for Russell, would have been the best ballplayer on the Pacific Coast. This is what the St. Louis press guide had to say about this 6-6, 225-pound forward from Los Angeles:

"Willie Naulls was one of the most underrated players in the country last season. Many thought Naulls was actually the better of the two players when matched up to Bill Russell. A fine rebounder, great shooter from every post on the court, Naulls was in fact a much better shooter than Russell. He made every All-America team and decided not to play on the Olympic team after being selected as an alternate. He became the first UCLA player to score 600 points in a single season, averaged 23 points per game and set conference scoring marks. He is fast for a big man and could develop into one of the stars of the game."

However, with Coleman, Macauley and Hagan sure to get the bulk of playing time, Naulls would see little action the first part of the 1956–57 season. Instead, he would become the perfect trade bait for the Kerner–Blake braintrust to get their much needed backcourt leader. What made the Celtics great with Russell was the presence of two fantastic guards who could take his outlet passes off the rebound and fast break down the floor. That pair were the incomparable future Hall-of-Famers Cousy and Sharman. The Hawks needed a match for Cousy to compete for any titles, and it was Naulls who would be sacrificed.

Getting ahead of the timeline a bit, the trade that elevated the Hawks into the league's upper echelon in just their second season in St. Louis, occurred in December 1956. Struggling to get the basketball up the floor against any competition because it turned out the experiment to make Hagan a guard was a mistake, the wily Kerner set out to solve the problem himself.

William "Red" Holzman was beginning his third season as the Hawks' head coach having replaced Andrew "Fuzzy" Levane in Milwaukee. Under Holzman the club had drastically improved and now had a chance to break into the upper half of the league. Despite losing two-thirds of the backcourt to the army and retirement, namely Ferrari and Stephens, Holzman thought his team could win the Western Division if Naulls could live up to his potential and Hagan could adapt to the backcourt.

"Cliff Hagan, Player of the Year in the college ranks during 1954 as a member of Kentucky's national champions, must be considered highly. He performed at center during his college career, but I plan to use him in the backcourt," said Holzman in his press guide summary of the upcoming season.

Hagan came to training camp attempting to play a new position, one that posed a drastic change from his college days as the center. He could not recall ever bringing the ball up the floor and now he was being asked to do it against the best guards in basketball. As a guard, Hagan was an invitation to disaster and wasn't going to be the answer for the Hawks.

Acquiring Hagan was good judgment, but thinking he could be converted to guard was a bad decision. How many hook shots are ever made much less attempted by a guard playing 15–20 feet away from the basket? Cliff would prove early in training camp and throughout the pre-season schedule that he was as out of place as a dolphin in the desert bringing the ball up the court and setting up the plays. Then besides making a bad first impression on the court, Hagan got injured and was relegated to the bench.

He played sparingly as the season began, uncomfortable in his new position and getting little opportunity to do what he did best, put the ball in the hole. Kerner knew a guard who could be the floor leader had to be found fast. He knew which NBA player he wanted, but also knew he would have to connive and bend the rules a little to catch his prize.

How do you get or steal the point guard from your biggest rival in your own division who'd won the NBA championship four times in the last five years? You boldly approach the player yourself, hope the league doesn't find out and convince a friendly fellow owner to participate in the plot. That was Kerner at his best.

Slater "Dugie" Martin, the feisty, fiery 5-10, 170-pound guard of the Minneapolis Lakers was the target. What was known in the small circles of the league was that Martin wanted to be paid what he was worth after winning four championships with the Lakers. Further if they didn't want to give him the cash he was looking for, Slater was ready to make good on his retirement threat.

"The Lakers didn't want to trade me, but I was going to retire because they wouldn't give me a raise," explained Dugie. "The first year they also hadn't told me they made playoff money. They gave me a straight salary. At the end of the season when the playoffs came, there was $1,500 that I was supposed to get, but they said it was part of my salary. I held out every year after that first one

(1948–1949) and over time I got it back. I mean $1,500 was a lot when your annual salary was $5,000.

"So I was holding out as usual in 1956, running the sporting goods store I'd opened in Houston, Texas, and told the Lakers the hell with you I'm staying here. They gave up trying to sign me and traded me out of the division to the New York Knicks so I couldn't beat them in the regular season, or so they thought.

"They traded me for a big boy named Walter Dukes (a 7-0 center who played one season in Minneapolis and seven more in Detroit), and at the same time I'd gotten a sly call from Mr. Kerner in St. Louis, through his messenger, a St. Louis sportswriter who asked me if I would play in St. Louis if a deal could be made.

Slater "Dugie" Martin

"I said the answer is simple, how much money will Mr. Kerner pay me? Mr. Kerner and I made a deal and he said to wait, I would go to New York for a couple of weeks and then the Knicks would announce a trade with the Hawks. It turned out it was a three-way deal but only two teams knew about it, " laughed Martin. "The Knicks owner Ned Irish was a good friend of Kerner and nobody had told the Lakers. They were hot."

Imagine today a sportswriter working hand in hand with the local professional sports team and another owner to engineer a player trade to help the home team! However, the sportswriter kept the lid on the deal and didn't even break the story in his own publication. Even 50 years later nobody can remember the sportswriter's name—or won't spill the secret.

"Again, this wasn't coincidence or accidental. The Lakers thought I was retiring and they had no idea I had been talking with Mr. Kerner and he had been talking to the Knicks," said Martin. "Mr. Kerner asked me if I thought I could come up to St. Louis and win a championship. I said to him, you've got the best player in the league, Bob Pettit, and I don't see any reason why we can't win it in a year or two. Pretty prophetic don't you think?"

Kerner got excited and uncharacteristically offered a secret bonus to Martin if the Hawks won the championship. Slater's arrival would solve the

Hawks' serious problem of bringing the ball over center court against the competition, most of whom had gotten used to pressing the inept Hawks. What his arrival didn't settle was what to do with Hagan, their touted prospect from the Celtics.

"When they talked to me about the trade, they (Hawks front office) said they'd expected to turn Hagan into that point guard, but found out he really couldn't dribble the ball down the court," explained Martin. "They had had hopes he was going to be that guy, and then they had turned to Willie Naulls wanting to make him the guard. But Naulls didn't get it done either.

"Every team was pressing St. Louis, so when I got there in December I told them just give me the ball and get the hell out of the way, and pretty soon the presses stopped.

"I had played against the Hawks in Minneapolis, of course, but I really didn't know much about them," Martin continued. "But they sure had a pretty good team and had beat us in the playoffs the year before. They were big and could score with Pettit, Macauley, the big boy in the corner Jack Coleman and Share in the middle. They needed me to compliment Jack McMahon at the other guard."

Still missing from the lineup was Hagan. Something needed to happen or trade-happy Ben might dream up a deal to move the All-American along and hope lightning would strike again for another great player. Fortunately fate, not Kerner, took over and the Hawks would become solidified in their starting five.

Hagan tells the story of how he became a Hawk beginning with being drafted by the Celtics. In fact, he and two Kentucky teammates were selected in the same draft by Boston and were looking forward to playing pro ball together.

"After we won the NCAA championship at Kentucky, there was a scandal in the program and we were put on probation," he said sadly. "While we had to sit out a year, we were drafted by the Celtics. . . . Frank Ramsey was first, I was second and Lou Tsioropoulos was third, all done by Red Auerbach. We all had taken ROTC in college and had two-year military service commitments to fulfill so Lou and I went in. But for some reason, Ramsey got a hardship dispensation and went immediately to Boston.

"I'm at Andrews Air Force Base for a year-and-a-half, and I receive this phone call from Red Holzman. I didn't know who he was, but he said he was the St. Louis Hawks' coach. He said he had Bob Pettit as his star and he had just acquired my rights from the Celtics along with Ed Macauley," added Hagan. "Well I was depressed. I was looking forward to playing for the Celtics. St. Louis hadn't been winning anything and my buddies were in Boston.

"Then Holzman tells me I'm going to play guard even though I spent my whole college career at center with my back to the basket rarely dribbling the ball. He stopped me and said again, I would be a guard and that was it."

Hagan didn't have a choice, and soon he was negotiating with Kerner. So besides trying to overcome this news that he was going to play guard instead of center, he was hit with a minimum salary offer from Kerner, something other players warned him would happen in negotiations.

"I got the very, very, very minimum dollar offer, too embarrassing to talk about," Cliff said. "I was really upset, and on the way to the airport, Ben threw out that he would give me a $500 bonus for making the team. So getting on the plane, I broke down and signed the contract, and I actually returned to my military duty at the time in Louisville, Ky. My wife was pregnant at the time, and my first child, Lisa, was born on August 31, 1956. A week later I had to report to St. Louis."

After being housed in the George Washington Hotel in downtown St. Louis, the team reported to Knox College in Galesburg, Ill., for training camp. There Holzman worked the team, running them constantly. Cliff developed terrible foot blisters in camp, but tried to play through it as the season began. In those 10 games Holzman would find out Hagan was no guard.

Hagan's struggled to bring the ball up the floor. That was compounded when he went up for a rebound and his knee collapsed, chipping a bone and putting him on the disabled list for seven weeks. Frankly, it was a blessing. If Hagan had been well and on the roster, he most likely would have been cut during camp. He was in the middle at 6-foot-4, too small for center and he couldn't play guard, an awkward situation at best.

"Kerner didn't know what to do with me," said Hagan. "We got down to 10 players and I was still around because they couldn't cut you while you were injured. I didn't have a no-cut contract, I don't think anybody did, so I would play only if we were 20 ahead or 20 behind once the season started. That's the only time I would play."

Then fate, not good coaching instincts, caused a decision that would change and cement the Hawks into a long-term contender. On February 15 against the Boston Celtics, Pettit broke his left arm and his nearly 30 points per game were out of the lineup for a few weeks. Now Hagan had his chance to play forward alongside the steady all-pro Macauley. He would play there the rest of the season and the rest of his NBA career. How well he played will be detailed later in the chapter of the 1956–57 season.

What again was a lucky turn of events occurred just before Pettit's injury and Hagan was forced into the lineup on a daily basis. Martin had arrived, but Kerner was considering yet another trade.

"Ben told me there was a deal on and he was contemplating making it official," said Jack Levitt. "He said he could trade Hagan to the Minneapolis Lakers for their outstanding guard Dick Garmaker. But in the end, something stopped Ben from making the deal and shortly after Hagan became invaluable in Pettit's stead."

Garmaker was a University of Minnesota graduate, a playmaker and scorer along the lines of Martin without the experience and savvy that Dugie had. He would play just six seasons in the NBA, the last season and a half with the Knicks. He averaged 16, 16, 13, 12 and 15 points plus three assists per game over the period starting in 1955. But with Martin and McMahon in place as starters, Garmaker wasn't needed and, as it turned out, was the best "no deal" the Hawks ever made.

From 1954 to 1959 the Hawks didn't trade often but each move seemed to make a significant impact on the team. The draft also brought some success in early rounds including unprecedented successes in the selection of Pettit in 1954, Ferrari in 1955, and Russell, who was then traded to Boston, in 1956. Of a lesser degree were forward Dave Gambee in 1958, Hub Reed in 1958 and in 1959, St. Louis U. star Bob Ferry, who went on to play for St. Louis and several other NBA teams.

Some called the Kerner-Blake front office team one that had a penchant for making astute trades. The first four seasons saw St. Louis go from the basement to championship contention annually through deals that would fill important needs. Here's how the Hawks were put together:

1954: Bob Pettit drafted No. 1 in the entire NBA draft.

1955: Jack McMahon and Jack Coleman were acquired from the Rochester Royals in exchange for Dick Ricketts and Chris Harris.

1956: Cliff Hagan and Ed Macauley were acquired from the Boston Celtics in exchange for the Hawks' first-round draft choice Bill Russell.

1956: Slater Martin was acquired from the New York Knickerbockers for Willie Naulls, the Hawks second-round draft pick.

1958: Clyde Lovellette was acquired from the Cincinnati Royals in exchange for Jim Palmer (Dayton), Ken Sidle (Ohio State), Darrell Floyd (Furman), Wayne Embry (Miami of Ohio), and Gerry Calvert (Kentucky).

1958: Dave Gambee was the first-round draft choice from Oregon State.

1958: Hub Reed was the second-round draft choice from Oklahoma City U.

1959: Sihugo Green was acquired from the Cincinnati Royals for Med Park, Jack Stephens and an undisclosed amount of cash.

1959: John McCarthy was acquired from the Cincinnati Royals for Win Wilfong (Missouri, former No. 1 pick), William Bell (North Carolina State), Tom Hemans (Niagara), and cash.

1959: Cal Ramsey (New York University) was the second draft choice.

1959: Alan Seiden (St. John's University) was also a second rounder (the Hawks had two second round selections in exchange for Frank Selvy who was traded to the New York Knickerbockers.

1959: Bob Ferry was the first-round draft choice from St. Louis U.

Walt Davis, Charlie Share, Bob Pettit, Ed Macauley, Clyde Lovellette

Two other additions came in back-to-back years, 1955 and 1956 from the University of Missouri. One would be a key piece to the depth of the ball club that would battle for titles. The other made his mark not in the NBA, but ultimately in the college coaching ranks as the greatest coach in the history of the University of Missouri.

Med Park was a 6-2, 205-pound bulldog guard, who blossomed quickly with the Hawks after a good college career at the University of Missouri where he averaged 15 points per game his senior season. His hustling and spirited play was his trademark, and he could play men four and five inches taller because of his physical strength. In the first season he proved his worth over 40 games, logging valuable minutes so that Ferrari, McMahon, Hagan and others could be rested.

The other more famous name, whose NBA career would last only five games, was one of the top scorers in the country and drafted fifth by the

Hawks in 1956. Later to become "Stormin'" Norman Stewart, he had averaged 17 points per game in the rugged Big Seven Conference over a three-year career at Mizzou. He was selected by the Helms Foundation as an All-American and was considered one of the best Tigers ever to that point. Stewart once scored 36 points against Colorado and set three Mizzou scoring records: most single season points, 506; highest point per game average, 24.1; and highest three-year scoring total, 1,112 points.

While Stewart's NBA career didn't pan out in St. Louis, he did record 731 victories against 375 losses in 38 coaching seasons of which 32 were at Missouri. In addition, Norm won eight Big Eight titles, was two-time National Coach of the Year and five-time Big Eight Coach of the Year, retiring in 1999.

His other claim to fame? Besides a tremendous college baseball career, he married Missouri's Homecoming Queen of 1955, Virginia Zimmerley, who has been by his side as his best friend for more than 50 years.

In his book, *Stormin' Back,* by John Dewey, Norm relates the experience of being cut by the Hawks. "There were just eight teams and 10 players per team so you didn't have many chances to make an impression," said Stewart. "The team acquired guard Slater Martin in a trade, giving them a backcourt of Martin and Jack McMahon. Unfortunately, the acquisition of Martin cost a rookie guard from Missouri a spot on the team. Getting released really bothered me, I wasn't used to losing a job. But in retrospect, it was probably the best thing that happened to me. What followed (for the Hawks) became a part of basketball lore."

Chapter Four
A Season of Greatness and Disappointment, 1956–1957

The second season dawned with a new radio station carrying the broadcasts, 1120 A.M., KMOX, and a trio of new players expected to bring St. Louis into a position to compete for the division and conference titles. Now wearing Hawks' colors were "Easy Ed" Macauley, Cliff Hagan and rookie Willie Naulls.

Lost to military service was practically a full squad. Five rookies and three one-year players were wearing the armed services uniforms for the season. They were Julius McCoy, rookie Michigan State; Jack Stephens, second year from Notre Dame; Darrell Floyd, a rookie from Furman; John Barber, a rookie from Los Angeles State; John Gunderman, a rookie from Sienna; Dick White, a rookie from West Virginia; and one-year veterans Selvy and Ferrari.

The starting front line of Share at center, Pettit at one forward and Macauley at the other, with Coleman subbing at either forward spot, ranked second to none in the division. The book on Naulls was a great rebounder and outside shooter who was sure to be a Rookie-of-the-Year candidate. He was very impressive in the preseason.

Again the hope was that Hagan could convert to guard, teaming up with McMahon, while Park, the impressive hustler from Mizzou, and Irv Bemoras, a military service returnee who had played well in his rookie season back in Milwaukee, would be a solid backcourt group.

Instead it was two in-season acquisitions that were the key to cementing

Kiel Auditorium, Saturday, March 14, 1964 against the Cincinnati Royals with a crowd of 10,650 in a regular season game won by the Hawks 114–110

the Hawks present and future. Both were veterans who were instrumental in guiding the team through the next two years, one as a star player and the other as a player-coach.

The season began on October 27 when the Hawks stepped on the floor against the Minneapolis Lakers, who they had vanquished in the first round of the playoffs just months before. As the teams took the court and the big crowd settled in, the atmosphere that would make Kiel Auditorium such a home-court advantage started to assert itself.

Anyone who witnessed either the Hawks or St. Louis U. basketball games at Kiel can remember the almost reverent setting. On entering Kiel, one came into what was usually a very crowded, small lobby area and proceeded through the narrow doors and turnstiles on a concrete ramp that wound its way either up or down depending on what level of the building your tickets were on.

The young were usually in awe walking from the concourse while staring at the extraordinarily high ceilings and out into the seating area, which was magnified by the beauty of the cathedral-like architecture of the rounded ceiling. The subtle, softly lit topping was in the design of large, rectangular areas separated by wide beams under which came the recessed lighting. It was the setting for an opera or concert, not a basketball game.

The court required it's own set of lights, about a dozen single bulb candles hanging on long wires and hovering about 50 feet above the court. It made for a dramatic effect setting off the court for the event while the upper areas of the lower deck and all of the second deck sat nearly in the dark throughout the game. It truly made the game the show and made for a distinct home court advantage.

"It was a great atmosphere in Kiel," Pettit said fondly. "We had great fans. The lights shined out on the court and then it was dark in the bowl. We had a great group of fans that sat right under the basket. We had to run up a ramp and through the crowd to get to the locker room and so did our opponents. Our fans were pretty intimidating to them."

The brilliant white uniforms of the Hawks set off in bright, red beaded trim, glistened every night and contrasted beautifully with the dark colors of the opponent, whether it was the silky green pants and jersey of the Boston Celtics or the candy striped shorts of the colorful Rochester Royals. The show was clearly the players and the game at the magnificent Kiel, which was showing her age but also her grandeur as distinctive as the Boston Garden or Madison Square Garden.

The Hall-of-Fame star of the Celtics, No. 14 Bob Cousy said, " I remember we dressed in those Mickey Mouse actors' rooms there and then had to come through a vocal crowd past all those seats on the way to the floor. I don't remember any other building that put you next to the fans like that. It certainly got your attention."

If revenge was on the minds of the Minneapolis club this opening night after the shocking playoff series loss to the Hawks a few months earlier, it wasn't readily discernible to the fans. St. Louis came out rolling and never stopped, dominating the once powerful Lakers, 97–75, winning their home and season opener for the second consecutive season.

The first month was encouraging. The Hawks won four of their first five games, including a two-point road victory over the world champion Syracuse Nationals and a home win against the defending Western Division champion Ft. Wayne Pistons. By November 26 St. Louis had an 8–5 mark fresh off another victory over Minneapolis, this time at the Minnesota site, 95–94.

But after getting beat by the Boston Celtics, 102–90, on November 27, the season took a decided downturn into December. The local boys went 1–8 for the next three weeks and sat on a 9–15 record on December 16. Kerner and the hometown fans were expecting more growth at this point, and the restless owner wouldn't tolerate the losing streak. Holzman's tenure was clearly in trouble.

As it would turn out later, the month of December 1956 and the first half of January would be the most pivotal time in club history. A series of off-court moves would set the stage for the next two seasons and beyond. The coaching merry-go-round would begin and the next two coaches would come from the player ranks, even though neither of them were on the Hawks' squad at the start of December.

The first move was made to beef up the front line with an experienced per-former. The rugged Alex Hannum was reacquired after being released by Ft. Wayne. Hannum had played for the Hawks for a year-and-a-half after being picked up from Rochester in December 1954. St. Louis had released him at the end of the 1955–1956 campaign. Getting him back just six months later, Hawks' management jumped at the chance to grab those 10 to 15 minutes a game Hannum was good for along with his inspiring defensive work. He worked over the league's big men like Clyde Lovellette and Vern Mikkelson of the Lakers and Larry Foust in Ft. Wayne.

Still missing with Ferrari and Stephens in military uniform was that leadership and aggressive play at what today is point guard. It's at this moment in time that the sneak attack on the Lakers took place, and Slater "Dugie" Martin came to the Hawks from the New York Knicks for Naulls and a draft choice. The Lakers had given up trying to sign Dugie and traded him reluc-tantly to New York figuring their former star wouldn't be competing in their division—wrong!

With a disappointing 14–19 record and under great pressure from man-agement and fans, Holzman was fired on Monday, January 8, 1957. With no master plan in mind, Kerner turned to his new favorite player, Dugie Martin, and asked him if he would take over the coaching position as well as lead the team on the court.

"Yeah, they fired Red (Holzman) and made me coach, about the last thing I wanted to do," explained Martin. "I told Mr. Kerner you know me and know we can win this championship here, but if I coach you ain't gonna win nothing. I can't play and coach too. I don't mind doing it for a few games, but I'd rather just play."

Finally Martin caved in and agreed to coach for awhile as Kerner searched for a permanent replacement. But after just five games, Martin was suffering in the position and wanted out. He told Kerner the team was going to lose more ground with him coaching and it was affecting his play.

"I told Kerner I didn't want to go on coaching and besides, he had a guy on the team who couldn't contribute much anymore as a player, but whose discipline would make him a great coach. The player was

Red Holtzman, first St. Louis Hawks head coach

Alex Hannum, but it was a known fact that Kerner didn't like Hannum at all.

"Hannum was a tough guy and he drank a lot, and of course, you couldn't fool Mr. Kerner," said Martin. "Finally Ben conceded and agreed to name Hannum the coach, but only if I agreed to help him. I said sure I'll help him, that's no problem and that's how I got out of the job."

Marty Blake recalled this key moment in Hawks' history. He does call Martin's acquisition pivotal to the team's elevation to the next level and Hannum's roller-coaster career in St. Louis worthy of a movie script.

"Alex was picked up in the 1954–55 season when he wanted $500 more from Rochester and they wouldn't do it. So we signed him for $6,800," remembered Blake. "We got him for $500 to be paid whenever Kerner had the money to pay it. Then we moved to St. Louis where he played for a year. Then we gave him his unconditional release to find a deal for himself and he went to Ft. Wayne.

"Six months later we got him back, make him coach in January after Martin says he can't do the job and that he was consulting Hannum on strategy and player substitutions anyway. The team had won four of five games in that short period with Martin and Hannum co-coaching."

Macauley has a vivid recollection of Hannum's effect on the club and smiles when he talks about how the coaching move affected his playing time. Macauley had already had an All-Pro career when he got to St. Louis, and he had continued to be a scoring machine as a Hawk. Hannum knew Macauley's great value, but with the team spiraling down under .500 he knew some adjustments were needed immediately.

"Alex was a very good coach," said Macauley. "He didn't have a whole lot of plays or anything like that, but he was a hard-nosed guy who expected everyone to play hard all the time. He expected his teachings to be followed, which was to pass the ball, move the ball, play defense, hit the open man, and of course, get the ball to the superstar Bob Pettit.

"One of the first things Hannum did as coach was to demote me and put Cliff Hagan in the starting lineup. I went to the bench and it worked out great. It was Hagan's time and he needed to play forward, not guard where Holzman tried to use him. That was ridiculous. Hagan took off and never looked back.

"Alex was a very good coach. Some of the guys might not have liked him, that's not unheard of as far as coaches are concerned, but one of Alex's biggest problems that led to his eventual undoing was that Kerner never trusted him."

There was no psychology applied to Hannum's style of coaching. He was a bulldog on the court and on the bench as a coach. Blattner, the Hawks' broadcaster, had his own view of the proceedings between the highly controlling owner and the player-coach. Blattner early on nicknamed Hannum "Sergeant York" after the famous American soldier of World War I who killed more than 20 Germans and forced 132 more to surrender on October 18, 1918, earning him the Congressional Medal of Honor. It was a tough guy reference that Blattner felt fit the Hannum's makeup.

"After Ben had appointed Slater Martin head coach he couldn't have been happier and thought after a few games Dugie would get used to it," Blattner said. "Kerner was at the top of his game, he's got three or four all-stars on the team and things are starting to turn around. But I knew Martin wasn't going to accept the coaching job for long.

"We're on the road at the time and I get a call to go to Ben's room in the hotel, which Ben was prone to do with me when he wanted to bounce his ideas off someone. He started by saying 'you know we've found our coach now and . . .' I stopped Ben right there.

"Ben, wait a minute. Let me say this to you. Dugie has made up his mind vehemently that he will not coach this team. If that's the only way that he can be with the team, he's going to leave.

"Well Kerner went from the penthouse to the basement. He went 'Whoa, whoa, whoa. Who does he think is going to coach the Hawks?' I said, 'Well, the players were expressing they would like Alex Hannum.'

"I'm telling you that Ben jumped on the bed and said, 'What! He can't control himself. Oh no, he can't coach my team.'

"So Ben went and talked to Dugie and got the same story, and Kerner reluctantly said 'Let's just get on to the All-Star game and we'll settle it then.'

"If I remember correctly, a few days after the All-Star game we were on the train from Boston to Ithaca, N.Y., where we were going to play the Syracuse Nationals. Ben called Alex over and told him the plan to make him the head coach."

The chronology of events clearly demonstrated Kerner's dominating, manipulative character. The *St. Louis Globe-Democrat* reported on January 7 the "mutually agreed" resignation of Holzman. It also reported that veteran Boston guard Andy Phillips was the No. 1 candidate to fill the coaching void, followed by Jim Pollard and both Martin and Hannum.

Then on Wednesday, January 9, the *Globe* headline read, "Martin to Coach Hawks for Rest of Season." At that moment, Slater was quoted as saying he "was more than happy to have the chance to coach," thinking it would help him as a player and in business. Then he asked to be relieved of his coaching duties after just eight games saying he couldn't do justice to simultaneously being a player and coach.

His January 21 quote revealed Martin had already called Kerner about quitting after just one week. "I can't do justice to both jobs, and I thought Hannum did a fine job handling the club," stated Martin. "We've got a good chance of winning the world championship, and I have to have my mind clear to concentrate on playing without the worry (of a coach)."

In typical Kerner fashion there was more intrigue in his coaching selection when he announced Hannum would be the coach the rest of the season and, in fact, coach his first game that night in Ft. Wayne. Meanwhile, a front page headline on the sports page read: "McKinney Says He Has Offer to Coach Hawks." Horace "Bones" McKinney was the assistant basketball coach at Wake Forest University and was claiming he had been offered a two-year "no-ifs" contract starting with the 1957–58 season.

Privately Kerner told Hannum on day one, "This isn't a permanent thing yet, you'll coach a few games and we'll see how it goes."

That threat rang hollow as Hannum was clearly the players' choice and they needed some immediate leadership and stability. Hannum would provide both as Macauley said:

"Though Ben was his own biggest enemy when it came to juggling coaches, having doubts up front about Alex wasn't totally unjustified. I don't know why anybody would have wanted Alex. He hadn't any experience. But Mr.

Kerner wanted to get rid of Red Holzman and put in Dugie Martin, who knew nothing about coaching. That was exaggerated by the fact that Dugie didn't want to be the coach, and then Ben rebelled against Hannum being the coach. That didn't make sense, either."

Now that the dust was settled on the coaching situation, the Hawks could get back to trying to challenge for the division title with Hannum at the helm. The old Sarge would take charge and at least for the rest of the season they could just play basketball. The 31-year-old coach was ready for the job.

"I owe a lot to basketball, and I would love to coach full-time after my playing days are over because I

Alex Hannum, player-coach of 1958 World Champs

love the sport," beamed Hannum. "This gives me a real opportunity to show what I can do and I have confidence that we'll go all right."

Despite what Kerner told Hannum privately, he publicly gave the job to Alex for the rest of the season adding he may want him to become a bench coach pending future roster changes. Hagan said having the coaching situation settled would allow things to really come together with the team and would be good for the team's prospects of winning the rest of the year.

The new coach's debut wasn't memorable (a 97–87 loss at Ft. Wayne), as it dropped the club into the Western Division cellar at 19–23. On the bright side, however, they were only two games out of first place in this very balanced division.

It was a month before Pettit would break his wrist and Hagan hadn't yet cracked the starting five. In the loss to the Pistons, Pettit drilled in 30 points and Macauley continued to be a solid scorer with 16 points. Still it seemed the Missouri squad was making progress.

The Hawks won five of their next seven games moving to within one game of .500 at 24–25. Included in that stretch was a satisfying 106–97 victory at Minneapolis, sending the reeling Lakers into the division basement. A record Laker crowd of 7,123 and a national television audience of millions caught a good look at this rising team of Hawks and of Pettit, their fabulous MVP leader. Pettit's 37 point and 17 rebounds got the nation's attention and his feats were becoming a nightly occurrence.

A couple of other noteworthy incidents in the Pistons' game were an indication of where the Hawks were headed. Share had had enough of the Pistons' rough style and initiated a fist fight with Lovellette late in the third quarter. Meanwhile, Martin, the former Laker great guard, took charge of the game halfway through the fourth period, banging in 11 of his 16 points for the game, sealing the win.

But, just as the club was ready to take off, it stumbled again, suffering what could have been a devastating injury. Pettit broke his wrist in a 123–116 double overtime loss to Boston on February 15. During the next month the Hawks would go 7–11 and fall six games under .500 at 30–36.

The front line was now Share, Macauley and Hagan, who was added up front in Pettit's absence. Easy Ed could have been called "Steady Ed" as he could be counted on for 16 to 25 points a night, figures he hit throughout the entire season, but grew more meaningful without Pettit. With more opportunities to touch the ball, Macauley was cashing in with points. He netted a whopping 36 points in a 118–115 overtime victory over Minneapolis just two days after Pettit went down with his wrist injury.

Hagan relished his chance to play forward and play a lot. He captured the fancy of the fans as he started to produce with his patented hook shot and squared up jumpers, posting games of 17 points and 14 points in back-to-back efforts. He had been getting only a couple of minutes playing time, averaging only two to five points per game.

"I guess they saw some possibilities in me when Pettit got hurt," said the hard-working Hagan. " When Pettit got hurt I got my chance and I took advantage of it."

When Pettit came back, cast and all, earlier than expected, Hannum chose to keep Hagan in the starting lineup with his double-digit scoring and rebounding stats. Macauley went to the bench, giving the Hawks the best "off-the-bench" scoring punch in the NBA.

"Hagan really got it going the last 10 games of the regular season," remembers Blake. " In the final 10 games, Cliff scored 101 points and then went on to a tremendous playoff run."

Their 30–36 record was cleaned up with a four out of five spurt, though two losses at the end, 117–104, at Minneapolis and a season-ending road five-point loss at Rochester left St. Louis with a 34–38 record, tied with both Ft. Wayne and Minneapolis for first place in the weak West. Tiebreakers were nothing new for St. Louis, which had just played one such game the previous season, a loss to Minneapolis that cost the Hawks home-court advantage in the first round.

A flip of the coin forced St. Louis to play at Ft. Wayne in the first tiebreaker game. Minneapolis would wait and play the winner for the right to the Western Division's No. 1 seed and home-court advantage in the playoffs. This time the Hawks got sweet revenge for the previous year's playoff beating by whipping the Pistons, 115–103, for their ninth win in 13 games against Ft. Wayne. The Hawks stayed home for Game 2 as well, and in an overtime thriller took down the Lakers, 114–111, at Washington University's Fieldhouse, giving Kerner his first regular-season Western Division championship.

Speaking of Washington U., a feature article accompanying the victory was the reaction of the team after winning. The players dragged Blake, their colorful public relations director, off the floor and in their exuberance, threw him fully clothed into the indoor pool inside the Fieldhouse. Along with Marty went several hundred dollars in change and bills from the day's ticket receipts. Kerner was quoted as saying, "No one leaves the pool until all the money is collected!"

Pettit gave an MVP performance in the overtime, scoring 10 of his 14 points, and Hagan was spectacular in the clutch pouring in a game high 28 points. Macauley played inspired basketball with 24 points, including 14 straight free throws.

Kerner called it the toughest season of his 11 years of ownership with two coaching changes, and a serious injury to his superstar Pettit. But it also gave Hannum a chance to demonstrate his coaching ability and win in his first attempt as a coach.

The Hawks thus won the right to sit around and watch Minneapolis take on Ft. Wayne as the Nos. 2 and 3 teams in the West. That best-of-three series was brief. The Lakers twice took it to the defending West champs, winning 131–127 in the opener at home and 110–108 in a nail biter at Ft. Wayne. The Hawks had their opponent and what had become a great home-court advantage in the first two games of a best-of-five series.

The Hawks and Lakers knew each other like a book after 24 head-to-head contests over two regular seasons, and the upstart St. Louis squad had won both season series, including an 8–4 edge for the current year. With Martin guiding the Hawks instead of the Lakers, a pair of St. Louis wins were posted at Kiel, 118–109 in Game 1 and a heart-stopping 106–104 decision for a 2–0 series lead.

In Minneapolis, defense went out the window as the Hawks showed a killer instinct for the first time. Needing just one win over the next three games to win the Western Division championship, it was a loose bunch of Hawks who took the floor in the hostile environment of Minnesota. The two clubs raced up and down the floor all night pouring in the baskets, and at the final buzzer St. Louis had a scintillating road victory, 143–135. The Hawks had earned the franchise's first-ever berth in the NBA Finals against another team looking for their first championship, the green and white clad Boston Celtics.

The city so familiar with baseball's World Series was now preparing for what the newspaper called, "The World Series of professional basketball." The hated Boston Celtics had whipped St. Louis seven of nine regular-season meetings, leaving the Hawks a decided underdog going into the series. Game 1 from the Boston Garden was scheduled for 1:30 p.m. on Sunday, March 31, to be broadcast locally on KSD-TV and on KMOX Radio.

The two clubs had contrasting personalities that would lead to an interesting battle to see which approach would prevail. The Celtics would use their speed and skill in an up-tempo game, while the Hawks would use their height and inside strength. The two most important matchups were at guard with Cousy, Boston's ball handling wizard, against Martin, his St. Louis counterpart. The other confrontation would pit Bill Russell, the Celtics' sensational rookie center, against Pettit, the Hawks' scoring and rebounding machine.

Russell said of Pettit in a *Globe-Democrat* pre-game story, "Pettit just hurts my pride." All season, even in losses, Big Blue, as Pettit was nicknamed, had little trouble dissecting the gangly big man. Pettit had averaged 25.1 points per game in the regular

Cliff Hagan gets punched by unidentified player as referee watches

season. He scored 39 points against Boston during the year.

Understand the Celtics were not turning New England upside down either. While they had a hard core of loyalists, the Celtics, too, were only filling half their building. Game 1 in the 13,900-seat Boston Garden was played in front of 5,976 raucous fans. Nonetheless, the Celts were usually dominant at home.

Any thoughts that the Hawks would be easy pickings for the Celts in this series went away in the first half of Game 1 when St. Louis blew out to a 31–18 first quarter lead. Boston woke up in the second period to close to 49–47 at the intermission.

The second half was a nail biter from start to finish. The momentum Boston built in the second quarter continued in the third. A 27–22 advantage in the quarter gave the home team a 74–71 lead going into the fourth period. Martin and Hagan had kept the game from getting out of hand in the third period and Pettit rallied the club with his free throws at the close of the period to cut a five-point Celtic lead to just three. But the Hawks came back strong in the final period.

The Hawks, led by Pettit's 10 points and Martin's 9 points in the fourth, began pulling away. But just when it appeared St. Louis was ready to put Boston away, Bill Sharman, the great Celtics' great shooting guard, brought Boston. Sharman's sharpshooting put Boston ahead, 97–95, with 2:30 left to play, but 30 seconds later the Hawks had rallied to build a 102–97 lead. Then Sharman made three points, and after both teams missed on a pair of possessions, Cousy stole a pass and Tom Heinsohn tipped in a basket to tie the game as regulation ended.

In the first overtime, the Hawks again broke into the lead by four, and held a 113–111 lead with 22 seconds to play. Again the Celtics stole the ball and Cousy connected on a game-tying shot. On to the second overtime.

This time Boston took a three-point lead, 121–118, but the Hawks fought back. Pettit took charge and scored five straight points to tie the score at 123 with 27 seconds remaining. It was then that Coleman, the "Old Rancher," would connect on a running one hander to give St. Louis a 125–123 lead. St. Louis tried to give the game back with Hagan and Med Park each missing two free throws in the final 27 seconds, making it interesting. But Cousy missed a desperation shot at the buzzer, giving the Hawks a stunning first-game road victory.

The locker room scene was wild as Hannum praised his dynamic duo of Pettit and Hagan for their dazzling play and leadership. Hannum called it a tremendous defensive effort, in spite of Sharman's 36 points and Cousy's 26-point performance. Pettit scored 37 points, Macauley buried his old teammates for 23 points, Martin added 23 and Hagan 16. The great city of Boston had been jolted by the country boys in the Midwest.

The excitement of Game 1's double-overtime verdict just might have been the turning point in Boston Celtic history. The next night instead of 5,900 showing up, the Garden was packed with a standing-room-only crowd of more than 13,900 screaming fans. It was already developing into the NBA's greatest playoff series to date.

The Hawks rode in with a six-game playoff winning streak, but on this night the Celtics, who had beaten St. Louis like a drum all year, showed up. St. Louis trailed by 10 after one period and 19 at the half. It grew to 24 after three periods and Boston coasted to a 119–99 victory to square the series at one game a piece. Macauley led the anemic attack with 19 points and Pettit had a measly 11.

For Boston it was a showcase for the guards. Cousy and Ramsey each tallied 22 points, while Heinsohn added 14 and Russell 11 with 25 rebounds. The patented Celtic fast break buried the tired and beaten Hawks.

A capacity crowd at the Boston Garden in the late 1950s

Game 3 had the whole city captivated with these newly discovered stars and hard working teams. It was St. Louis' turn to shine and demonstrate its newfound love for this young franchise. The first full house, standing-room-only crowd of 10,048 jammed into the Kiel and the ensuing game would have columnists calling it "the greatest of basketball spectacles." It was a game that left fans breathless.

The Hawks appeared overanxious and tight on their home floor and the first quarter went back and forth. The keys were Pettit's incredible rebounding, hauling in 15 boards, and the fact that Russell picked up three personal fouls that sent him to a prolonged stay on the bench. But the Hawks hit only five field goals and the Celtics eight and the first quarter ended with the score tied at 19.

This was a rough tough affair all night long and every hard-earned basket seemed monumental. Two Macauley jumpers and three Share free throws gave the home team a seven-point lead in the second period, but the irrepressible Cousy and the sharp-shooting Sharman took the visitors to the halftime locker room with a 45–40 lead.

The first part of the third quarter was all Boston. Bad passes gave the Celtics two baskets, and Boston snared a 51–42 lead before Pettit and

Coleman led a comeback. The Hawks went on an 11–3 run, and when Share hit back-to-back hook shots the Hawks took a 59–58 lead, bringing the crowd roaring to its feet. Still, Boston led 72–69 after three quarters in a game that would go down to the wire.

The Hawks played the fourth period shorthanded as their important big man, Share, had fouled out. But everybody began chipping in, led by the combination of Pettit and Martin, whose determined work earned a 95–91 lead with 3:16 to play. The intensity led to several skirmishes among the fans and several Bostonians were ejected from the building for fighting by the St. Louis police.

It was the spirited Martin who finally took control for the Hawks. After two riveting comebacks from nine-point deficits in the third period, the smallest player in the NBA became a clutch-scoring machine, tallying 11 points in the final quarter.

Both two teams flashed their best defensive efforts in the final frame, with the Hawks shutting down Sharman, Cousy and Heinsohn when they had to. Then, with 44 seconds left to play, the Bombardier from Baton Rouge launched a jumper from 30 feet that swished through the basket for a 100–98 margin. Kiel went delirious as the final seconds ticked off and the desperate Celtics couldn't find the basket. Basketball history was made in St. Louis with their first-ever home playoff victory in a championship round. The Hawks now led the series, 2–1.

Probably fueling the animosity of the crowd on both sides was the now historic incident that occurred before the game. Cousy describes today what created an on-court, front-office confrontation.

"The fight between our coach Red Auerbach and the Hawks' owner Ben Kerner was really my fault," said Cousy. "We're going in to take practice layups and I think the hoop is a little off. It was innocent and I went over to Arnold (Auerbach) and said 'Arnold, I don't know if you want to change hoops but either way we're going to have to shoot at this one and there's something wrong with the height.'"

Auerbach went over to Marty Blake and Marty got the proverbial 10-foot pole. The Celtics weren't accusing anyone of anything because the Hawks would have had to shoot at the basket, too. But the Hawks' Kerner wouldn't see it that way. All he was seeing was "red," figuratively and literally.

"Benny had a history with Auerbach back in Tri-Cities remember, and all Kerner could see was Red out there measuring his hoop which was an infringement on Ben's character," Cousy went on. "Kerner came running on the floor screaming at Arnold, and just as Kerner got to him yelling obscenities, Auerbach had heard enough and punched him in the mouth sending him backward. He cold cocked him right in front of a capacity crowd in the championship round."

The *Globe-Democrat* story headline on the bottom of the front page read, "Auerbach vs. Kerner in Non-Title Bout," and in the story, sportswriter Joe Pollack (later of the *Post-Dispatch)*, described it as a one-punch, no-decision in which Kerner claimed the victory.

"Look," said Kerner as he pointed to a slightly reddened lip, "I took his best punch and nothing happened. That's real bush, with all the talent he has, and he still pulls tricks like that. It isn't the first time he's done this. In Minneapolis about eight years ago he claimed they were using illegally high baskets, and he was wrong then, too."

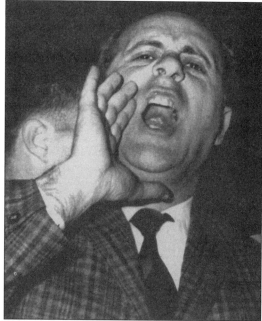

Celtic Hall-of-Fame coach Red Auerbach.

Auerbach's version was, "He called me a bunch of bad names and I just didn't want to hear him anymore."

Red was proven wrong by the Kiel janitorial service that measured the basket and found it to be exactly 10-feet high. Auerbach, according to the media at the time, was sometimes accused of being a "weeper" (complainer) but the event definitely incited the already tense crowd.

The next day, NBA Commissioner Maurice Podoloff fined Auerbach for the punch, a $300 hit that angered Boston owner Walter Brown. The owner blasted the officiating in the NBA Finals saying the officials, not the Hawks, had won those two games. Hannum lashed back ripping the Celtics owner.

"I'm disappointed that a man who has done so much for the game would stoop to such low tactics as blaming officials to explain his team's losses," said the Hawks' coach. "I would expect statements like that from Auerbach, but not from Brown."

Down by a game for the second time in the series, Boston set its sites on a split in St. Louis and regaining their balance back home in Game 5. The Celtics did find their game getting more comfortable in the loud, unfriendly confines of Kiel. This time they wouldn't give it back down the stretch and at the buzzer, Boston had won, 123–118, and the series was even 2–2.

Back in the Garden and with 13,900 hanging from the rafters again, the green and white overcame an early St. Louis outburst that had the Hawks up 12. The Pettit, Hagan and Martin combo built a 30–21 first quarter lead, but by the half, the Hawks led only 60–59. Pettit's 14 rebounds to Russell's 13 was a big reason why St. Louis was in the game, but astonishingly, Big Blue would only get one rebound the rest of the game to Russell's game high 23.

Cousy and Sharman were fabulous in this one. Cousy had an NBA play-off record 19 assists and 21 points, while Sharman posted a Celtic-high 32 points hitting 13 of 24 field goals, including had 13 points in the third quarter. After the Hawks built a 70–69 lead, Russell slammed home a dunk and his team pulled away for a 124–109 victory and a chance to clinch the championship in Game 6 in St. Louis.

There were arrangements made for the Celtics champagne victory party in St. Louis after Game 6, but a team that wasn't even supposed to make the play-offs had nothing to lose. The intensity of Game 3 at Kiel returned for this do-or-die setting. The 10,053 fans in the stands would bring the total over the last three games to more than 30,000, new heights for the young league.

The tight first half saw Boston lead by one after the first quarter and by two at the half. The Hawks picked one back up in the fiery third quarter, trailing 78–77 heading into the fourth and final period. Feeling the tension, the Celtics were all over the refs again, while Cinderella was pushing the issue to the limit wanting to be the giant killer.

All night Pettit came up with clutch baskets, and old pros Coleman, Martin and McMahon were steady influences. But in the end, it was a rookie whose driving and jumping ability was the difference between ending the season and playing a seventh game in the finals. The good-looking idol of the lady fans and demon around the bucket would put on the hero's cape.

The score was knotted at 94 with 1:29 to play. After a succession of missed Boston shots by Heinsohn, Jim Loscutoff and then Cousy with 12 seconds remaining, the Hawks called a timeout. Coleman inbounded the ball to Park who slipped it to Pettit, but Bob was well guarded and could only take an off balance shot that bounced off the rim. Hagan, who had 20 rebounds from his 6-4 frame, then jumped four feet off the floor and tipped it in for a 96–94 victory.

The post-game scene was wild. Hagan was carried from the Kiel floor, and it was a jubilant dressing room as the Hawks players knew that they had taken the Celtics to a final Game 7. Hagan sipped a cup of orange juice, while his teammates held court with the media. On the Boston side, neither the players nor the generally boastful Auerbach had any comments.

For the first time the Hawks thought about the possibility of winning it all and that, just maybe, Boston had spent their last bullet. The pressure was still squarely on the heavily favored Celts, particularly on their home floor. Hannum made a bold prediction saying, "They couldn't win this one (Game 6), which meant so much to them and I'll wager we'll get them in Boston. We can always rise to a peak for one game."

The teams flew back to Boston with the final game being hailed by the media as one of sports classic battles of all-time. The business-first Kerner was jumping on the hot streak and local enthusiasm to negotiate a new two-year television contract with Falstaff for a schedule of road games and one special anniversary home game in year four.

With a day off in before the final game, there was a lot of reflection about the series and the season for both teams. The Celtics were called "jittery" and anything but confident after being defeated three times by a team that was in last place at the All-Star break. Boston had a fantastic season, was a team full of stars and had been told by the owner, "Win it all or their will be a shakeup and it won't be the coach who goes."

The winner of Game 7 would secure the $10,000 first prize and the loser would collect $5,000. The total was for the whole team to share, not per man! The Hawks had already collected $7,500 for winning their division and conference. But neither team, despite Boston's lofty reputation, had ever won a championship ring.

In his "Bench Warmer" column in the morning *Globe-Democrat*, St. Louis sports editor Bob Burnes talked about what the Hawks' success was doing for the city.

"Maurice Podoloff, president of the National Basketball Association, a man not given to excessive praise, said after watching the games here (in St. Louis) last weekend that, 'I've never seen fans like this anywhere in my life. It's been a splendid response.'

"The enthusiasm of the fans has been a factor in the Hawks spectacular play and that is taking nothing away from the Hawks themselves. But the job is only half done. It is one thing to get a team or an event to St. Louis and it is still another to get them to stay so there will be no regrets any place later on."

Kerner said with great pride, "Win or lose they're champions in my book. They never quit in the face of seemingly impossible odds."

The fans, the media and the owner had expressed satisfaction with the season. But representing the players, captain Pettit dispelled the notion that the season was fulfilled saying, "What do you mean lose it?"

Meanwhile, the Celtics were bickering and upset about being beaten by a rookie who was actually their property before the season. Hagan was fast becoming a star and a principal worry for Boston. His tip-in of the Pettit missed shot to win Game 6 was a sore spot. His responsibility was that of Heinsohn, Boston's rookie star, who said he was trying to help cover Pettit when Loscutoff allowed Pettit to break free for the shot. The man complaining the most was Cliff's old Kentucky teammate, Frank Ramsey, who moaned, "The last thing we said was to make sure we block out everyone from rebounding, but Hagan wasn't blocked and we lost."

Cliff Hagan makes a layup over the back of Celtic forward Tom Heinsohn as Sihugo Green (#17) watches.

Officiating and timekeeping were still hot topics. Auerbach nearly came to blows while confronting game official Jim Duffy at the St. Louis airport en route to Game 7. Auerbach claimed the clock had time left on it after Hagan's tip-in and Cousy attempted to call time out, but Duffy ruled the game was over. Reportedly, Auerbach then said to Duffy's face, "You've got no guts," to which Duffy responded, "Don't say that to me you phony, you've always been a phony."

Ironically, broadcast conflicts existed back then, although today coopera-tion and sanity would rule and no one would stop the airing of a Game 7 broadcasts by its originating station. But in 1957, the radio broadcast of the final game moved from KMOX to WIL because the Cardinals' game took precedent. On television, it was lack of equipment that almost stopped the local telecast. KSD-TV, Channel 5, the NBC affiliate in St. Louis, had the Baseball Game of the Week between the Boston Red Sox and New York

Yankees on its Saturday schedule. The game was in Boston and there just wasn't enough equipment in Beantown to broadcast the basketball game as well. However, by game time, enough equipment was found and St. Louis was able to witness another classic battle on television.

Sunday, April 13, dawned in Boston and the scene was set for an epic contest. *The Boston Celtic Encyclopedia*, written by Peter Bjarkman, says of this Game 7: "Then came the game they still debate and discuss on Congress Street and on the steps of Faneuil Hall. No single NBA contest has been often more relived, its climactic moments more often retold, than the Saturday afternoon final in which the Celtics more than a half dozen times seemed to take command of the game's ebb and flow, only to have St. Louis roar back on each and every occasion."

The entire game was memorable, but game stories dispensed with a play-by-play of the game until the end of the fourth quarter, and then the first overtime, and then the second extra session.

The game was played with a fury as neither side would give in. The lead changed hands an incredible 32 times and was tied seven times. The Celtics broke out of the gate fast, but the Hawks regained their balance and led after the first quarter, 28–26. Again Boston pulled out in front, 41–32, in the second frame but a six-point Hagan run put St. Louis up at the half, 53–51. The third quarter saw 10 of those lead changes, but in the end, the Celtics ran out to an 83–77 advantage.

The fourth quarter was a thrill a minute. Boston led by eight when the fearless Hawks rattled off a 9–0 run to take the lead. With less than two minutes to play St. Louis fans were starting to believe they would be popping champagne. The Hawks went up by four, 101–97, but the roaring crowd helped bring the Celtics back again. Three Boston free throws made it 101–100. Now inside one minute, Coleman went up for a shot to add to the St. Louis lead, but Russell swooped in and blocked the shot. When Boston scored at the other end, the Celtics had a one-point lead.

St. Louis couldn't connect on its next possession and was forced to foul the great free-throw shooting Cousy. But he made just one of two for a two point Boston lead. The Hawks came down and in dramatic fashion, No. 9, Big Blue was fouled with seven seconds remaining. He coolly sank two free throws to send the game into overtime at 103 a piece.

Fouls began playing a major factor as Boston's Risen and the Hawks' fouled out. The Hawks stepped up their intensity and the visitors went up 109–105 in the overtime only to have Ramsey score two baskets to tie it at 109 and again at 111. Then, with 50 seconds left in the first overtime, Hagan took his 24 points to the bench for the night because of fouls. Each team then missed a pair of free throws, but Sharman popped in a bucket to give Boston the lead. This time, Coleman evaded Russell and made a basket with 10 seconds to play sending this heart-stopper in the second overtime period.

Short on manpower but not on heart, the red and white Hawks wouldn't quit. St. Louis went ahead twice in the second overtime, but each time "Tommy Gun" Heinsohn brought back his Celts. It would be his greatest individual performance in the playoffs scoring 37 points.

Inside the final two minutes, Martin made a three-point play and another free throw for St. Louis, while Russell and Heinsohn hit baskets and Ramsey a free throw adding up to a 122–121 Boston edge. In heroic fashion, perhaps remembering how Coleman had hit a long shot to win Game 1 at the buzzer, Russell used his great leaping ability to block a Coleman shot. Cousy grabbed the ball and fed Ramsey for a fast-break layup.

Med Park made it 124–123 when he made the first of two free throws. The Hawks, however, managed to grab the rebound and called a time out with 17 seconds on the clock. Player-coach Hannum now in the game for the foul-plagued Hawks, got the inbounds pass, but was called for traveling. The Hawks had no choice but to foul. Macauley fouled out giving Loscutoff a free throw for a 125–123 lead with one second to play.

The Hawks again called time out, and on the sidelines Hannum outlined a bizarre and seemingly impossible play to try to tie the game and send it to another overtime. The players on the floor describe the final play.

"I remember getting into the huddle expecting Alex to set up a quick play to pass Pettit the ball, but we were all in shock when he told us how," chuckled Macauley. "Alex said he was going to go in and take the ball out of bounds, throw it the length of the court against the backboard with Pettit instructed to stand there and be ready to catch it off the board and put it in.

"We looked at each other and said this is the same guy who can't hit the basket from four feet and he's going to hit it from 90 feet? By God, he did it!"

Martin had the best lines from this serious, yet comical moment, "When Alex outlined the play in the huddle I thought he's nuts. He couldn't spit in the ocean if he was on the beach.

"You stand down there and try to throw it that far. You'll throw your arm out of socket, and when he did it, Boston didn't know what the hell was happening."

Cousy gives the Boston version of the last play and why it almost worked.

"Arnold (Auerbach) didn't have us, like they've done ever since, put our big guy on the guy taking the ball out of bounds to block his view and make it a difficult pass. We let Alex just wind up and he threw a damn strike off the backboard and it rebounded to Pettit at about the free throw line just like he planned it. It was incredible. Fortunately, Pettit's touch shot rolled off the rim. If we'd have blown that, it would have been the greatest basketball play of all-time and we'd have been the fools."

Says Macauley: "My recollection is that Bobby didn't have that good of a shot and he didn't go up unmolested, he was covered. I haven't asked him, but I think Pettit was so amazed that Alex really hit the backboard, he couldn't control it."

Cousy concluded, "I don't remember what we discussed in the huddle, but why we didn't put someone on Alex was pretty basic. To let him wind up and throw that sucker without any intervention was just crazy."

But when the ball fell off the rim, the Garden exploded with cheers and Boston had it first NBA championship. A happy Auerbach said, "We both had this game four or five times, but neither of us could grab it."

Russell, the series star, kept a pre-game promise in the post-game locker room, allowing the fiery Auerbach to grab a straight razor and shave off Russell's goatee beard.

"It's worth it to win this, besides I still have my mustache," Russell smiled.

Pettit had been a hero in defeat despite the final missed shot. He poured in 39 points and grabbed 19 rebounds. And as the unselfish warrior that he was, Pettit could only mention that "they had fought all year for this chance and he had blown the big shot at the end of the game."

The Hawks had disappointed only themselves, not their owner or their fans. They played with fire, they battled through injuries, they ignored the overwhelming odds, and they nearly pulled off a major upset. It had been the greatest championship series in the league's history and would remain forever as arguably the greatest ever. The Hawks place as the "city's darlings" were set and the following season would reach even greater heights.

Chapter Five
The Championship Season

ever before had sports fans in St. Louis had their attention diverted from their beloved baseball team in the months of March and April, but it happened in 1957. The thrilling seven-game series against the Boston Celtics ended 48 hours before the Cardinals first pitch of the regular season in Cincinnati and had clearly captured the affection of the local sports aficionados.

Maybe inspired by the excitement of the near-miss NBA championship, the batsmen got it going and challenged for the National League pennant with, of all teams, Milwaukee, the city from which the basketball Hawks had moved to get away from three years earlier! The likes of the Braves' Hank Aaron, Eddie Mathews, Warren Spahn and Billy Bruton would pull away from a tight race late in the season to beat the Cards by eight games.

But it was a great season for the Redbirds. Stan Musial won his seventh batting title, hitting .351, pitchers Lindy McDaniel and Larry Jackson won 15 games, a youngster named Ken Boyer hit .307 with 23 home runs, and the city hosted the baseball All-Star game (was won by the American League, 6–5). The Cardinals won 87 games and seemed on their way.

But basketball writers couldn't stop talking about the amazing growth of the NBA and its fan base in the past three years, with a major jump in the just finished 1956–57 campaign. The last shot of adrenaline to the season, was of course, the classic championship series between the Hawks and Boston. The

Celtics' average attendance had escalated from 5,000 per game in the 1951–52 season to 7,000 per game in 1955–56 to more than 10,000 this season. St. Louis in just two seasons had seen a meteoric rise, more than doubling its average attendance to almost 10,000 per game to compete with the league-leading New York Knickerbockers and Boston.

There was an interesting observation to make as the eve of the 1957–58 season opener approached, and it would provide a comparison that could be made in future seasons. From the coach to the roster, there was no significant change in the Hawks' makeup from the team that had just taken Boston to the final game. What would prove to be an Achilles heal in future seasons was owner Ben Kerner's phobia over coaches. It resulted in some great St. Louis teams falling just short of their championship aspirations.

That phobia will be dissected later as the Kerner effect on the club is studied in more detail. But for this one great season, there was continuity on the court and chemistry in the locker room. The players could just play and not look over their shoulder waiting for someone to make personnel changes. Martin appreciated the stability and the camaraderie that carried over all season.

"I really had a good time that year (1957–1958)," he said. "That was one of my best years on the court. Everybody got along. We went every place together. We ate together. We did everything as a team. It was a real good situation," he says fondly.

"You've got to have that closeness on a pro basketball team to win over the long haul. You can't have somebody sulking over only scoring 10 points or way below his average. You just can't worry about that. Jack McMahon and I got along great and really complimented each other's style."

In the off-season, Pettit had done something that would revolutionize the game in future years, though when he did it, his only thought was, how do I get stronger to not get beat up rebounding with the big guys in the league. When Pettit left St. Louis after the seventh game of the playoffs, he headed to Louisiana and called a trainer by the name of Alvin Ray of Baton Rouge. He was a noted expert in the use of weights.

"I had led the league in rebounding, was second in scoring and was taking a pounding on the board," he recalled. "Alvin Ray had a series of health studios around the country, and when we first came to St. Louis, Med Park and I went to his studio. He was light years ahead of anybody else in things like isometrics and workouts for athletes. He said to me, 'Bob, I'll take what you have without pumping you up, put on 8-10 pounds a year and it will be all muscle. It's going to make you think you're strong and when you get under the boards you're going to feel like your stronger mentally.'

"I really did get much stronger, particularly in my hands. When I got the ball, I put a clamp on it and it was very seldom someone could get it out of my hands on a rebound. I worked with Ray for the next five years, built

ST. LOUIS HAWKS

MAJOR LEAGUE BASKETBALL

WESTERN DIVISION CHAMPS '56 - '57

WESTERN DIVISION CHAMPS '57 - '58

WESTERN DIVISION CHAMPS '58 - '59

WORLD CHAMPIONS '57 - '58

up to about 245 (pounds) and thought I was the strongest man in St. Louis.

"I really think I was the first NBA player to ever get on weights, and it gave me a real advantage."

Recalled Martin, "When Pettit first came into the league, you could just grab his hand and he'd drop the ball. When I got to St. Louis you'd hit him and he'd take you right up with him and get the ball. All the stories in those days said that you shouldn't lift weights because you'd get muscle-bound, but Bob became strong as the devil and proved weights did work."

The only changes in the Hawks' roster on opening night from the one which ended the previous season were the additions of three reserves: center Dwight Morrison, and guards Worthy Patterson and Puxico, Mo.'s Win Wilfong. The starters were the same five that played in the Boston Garden in Game 7.

No longer a stepchild in town, the Hawks opening night was the banner headline in the *Globe-Democrat* and the hot topic at the water coolers in St. Louis. The first full house to open a basketball season in St. Louis sports history was anxious to see the first rematch with the now world champion Boston Celtics. The rivalry had been borne out of those closely contested and bitterly played games in the finals. The same went for the Celtics whose lineup was identical to their championship quintet of Russell, Cousy, Sharman, Heinsohn and Loscutoff. Expectations were through the roof.

When the tip went in the air, the fans got into it like they had left it the spring, creating an exciting, tension-packed atmosphere in the first half. Pettit came out thumping with 10 first quarter points, got in his licks on the boards, but Cousy's all too familiar ball-handling flair gave Boston a 28–26 lead. In the second quarter, St. Louis played well, leading on several occasions bolstered by two Wilfong buckets that brought the crowd to life. But Russell and Cousy took charge for a 54–51 halftime lead.

In the second half, the Hawks hung tough, but ran out of gas down the stretch. In the third period, Hagan and Martin baskets brought the Hawks to within one at 56–55, and later Macauley, Pettit and Wilfong accounted for five straight to close to 81–75 at period's end. The minds were willing but the flesh didn't follow in the fourth stanza and Boston rolled out to a 115–90 blowout victory diminishing a great night by Macauley, who had 24 points to go with Pettit's 26. Russell scored 20 and Cousy 24 to earn Boston the road win.

The club started slowly the first 10 days, but looking back, the low point of the entire season was a 1–3 record after just the fourth game. A three-game losing stretch in early December, again in mid-January and another over the last three games of the season, were the only bad streaks all season long.

It was December 8, the first afternoon game of the year at Kiel against the

Knicks after the 12–8 Hawks had lost three straight. Played up in the newspaper's preview story was the appearance of the famed clown, Emmett Kelly. Kids 18 and under were able to get in for 75 cents. If the Hawks' play that day didn't give the fans something to be happy about, clown Kelly would.

The Hawks were clinging to first place with seven of their losses coming on the road. After this home encounter, the road would be their partner for three straight, against Cincinnati in New York, the Knicks at Boston and Boston at Philadelphia, three doubleheader games. The Hawks' road record to date was 2–7. But the final score this day would be another loss, 113–110 to New York, dropping St. Louis' record to 12–9.

Hannum pondered the problems and concluded the Hawks needed more balance by getting more production from their guards and relying less on their big men, Share, Pettit, Hagan and Macauley. The games in which Martin, McMahon and Wilfong scored in double figures, the ball club produced more points and usually won. In the next string of games, the chemistry clicked and this St. Louis steam engine began to pick up speed.

Five of the Hawks' next nine games were on the road, mostly neutral sites, and the club began rolling offensively. The Hawks scored more than 100 points in eight of nine games, scored over 130 points in four games and consequently, won nine in a row to boost their record to 20–9. By New Year's Eve, they were surging at 23–10.

Their eighth straight victory in the streak was an example of what propelled the club. Rookie Wilfong, who had already had a 37-point game, collected 24 on December 23 in a 123–115 victory over the Minneapolis Lakers. Wilfong had a flair. He was a younger Dugie Martin with even more shooting skill. He could wow a crowd with his shifty maneuvers, driving the lane or taking a running hook shot that was better known coming from Hagan.

In this one, the Hawks were in a tense struggle at 95–95 in the fourth, but Martin and Wilfong connected again and St. Louis pulled away. Just the night before, St. Louis had blistered Syracuse for 146 points and frankly could have just had some tired arms from all that shooting! Hagan led all scorers with 31 points and Pettit chipped in his normal 27 to carry the day.

The new era of Hawks' basketball was hitting its stride, and consistency, consistency, consistency was spewing from the rafters of Kiel Auditorium. The club would bounce back and forth very little the rest of the season. Always between 11 and 13 games over .500, the only losing streak of note was the last three games to finish at 41–31 and in first place by eight games over Detroit and Cincinnati.

The opening best-of-seven playoff series with the Pistons held some intrigue because despite the Hawks eight-game spread in the standings, Detroit had won five of the last six games against St. Louis in head-to-head competition. The games had been rough as well. Pettit had broken his left hand against them, and in another contest, one of the biggest fistfights in basketball history had broken out.

The menace for the Hawks to contend with was the wiry, 6-11 center Walter Dukes known for his shoving and holding tactics while guarding Pettit. Hannum had vocally complained to the officials privately and publicly throughout the season, and would surely be on them again in this critical series.

Globe columnist Bob Burnes expressed his concern over the threat the Pistons posed and the Hawks some-times-lackluster performances over the last month having put the division title away so early. His thoughts the day before the opener were:

"The Hawks have blown hot and cold since February 21, but tonight they will be going against a team that has been red hot for two months, and has shown a startling facility for beating the Hawks. George Yardley of the Pistons has had a tremendous season and has had a couple of his best nights against the Hawks. When they have stopped him, they've stopped him cold.

"There is also the matter

George Yardley, Piston's scoring machine

of Walter Dukes. His defensive play against the Hawks, literally sprinkled with rugged tactics, has been as important a factor in Detroit's recent success against the Hawks as Yardley's scoring. That's where a man of the stature of Bob Pettit is nice to have on your side. Nobody has stopped him over a long series."

Tempers flared in Game 1 and a fight broke out between Yardley and Wilfong. But fans and players who had rushed from their seats to the floor stopped before much harm could be done. Later the two instigators would threaten to go at it again.

Finally this tense one went into the win column for the hometown team. While Pettit played through the flu, Hagan tallied 38 points. Pettit added 14 with 16 gutsy rebounds, and Macauley chipped in 13 as the Hawks won a squeaker, 114–111. Not only was it close down the stretch, but Hawks fans had their panic moments when their club was down by 15 in the second quarter.

The Hawks won Game 2 on national television in Detroit, 99–96. Again Hagan led both teams with 27 points, edging Yardley who had 26. Pettit's 15 points practically nullified Dukes' 17. Wilfong again was an important factor with his aggressive style and 10 points. He took the role held for Park the previous season and stepped it up to another level with his bulldog defensive work, tough rebounding and flamboyant drives to the bucket.

The next two games were polar opposites. Detroit bounced back and upset the Hawks at Kiel in a shocking blowout, 109–89, to cut the series lead to two games to one. But just as surprising, St. Louis walked into Detroit against a fired up crowd, and embarrassed the Pistons by setting all-time playoff scoring marks.

Hagan's 28 points, plus the efforts of Pettit and Coleman, who had 23 and 22 points, respectively, paced the Hawks. The St. Louis squad scored 72 points in the first half and 73 after intermission, including 42 points in the fourth quarter, for a 145 total—all of which were playoff records. The final score was 145–101. Detroit got only 18 points from Dukes and 16 from Yardley, who was hampered by the flu.

Cliff Hagan

Finally the Hawks and Celtics clinched on the same night. Boston beat Philadelphia, 93–88, to win the Eastern Division playoffs 4–1. The Hawks did the same to Detroit, winning the finale, 120–96, with a steamrolling attack. Hagan continued his torrid scoring pace and was treated to a long-standing ovation after one of his greatest exhibitions that included 32 points.

"On to the Celts" was the cry in downtown St. Louis that March 26, 1958, night after a second consecutive game of over 70 points in the second half. It was truly a team effort as Hagan's heroics were backed up by superlative evenings from Pettit with 20 points, Macauley with 17 and Martin, who posted double digits in assists along with 14 points.

To date as good as the team had played, Hagan had been special. Why had he emerged as a playoff superstar.

"Money, money, money," he proclaimed. "Those first 72 games don't mean a thing, this is what counts."

He kept his promise in Game 1 of the championship series and for the second straight season, St. Louis upset the Beantowners on their own floor, winning a 104–102 thriller. "Hagan the Magnificent" poured in 33 points with Pettit breathing down his neck with 30 points. After being down six after one period, St. Louis carried the play to lead by six at half.

The second half was a seesaw affair, with the Hawks trailing by three after three periods, but then holding Boston to just 19 fourth-quarter points. This time it was Pettit down the stretch as the Celtics came in waves trying to catch the lead. Up by just one point, Big Blue sank a crucial free throw and converted another basket to nail down the victory.

After pumping in 33 points, Hagan was quoted as saying, "Just keeping up my average. That gives me 197 points in six games in the playoffs. Not bad but I'll have to try a little harder."

While Game 1 had just wrapped up, the excitement for the third and fourth games in St. Louis was cascading down Market Street. Such was the anticipation that Kerner had to arrange a quick meeting with KSD-TV officials to install a closed circuit TV area in the Kiel Opera House so another 3,500 fans would be able to get "the feel of being at the game" inside Kiel for the sold-out games.

Fans lined up for a block around the Arcade Building ticket office, then at the Kiel box office and over in Belleville at Rhein's Music House where championship series tickets were being sold. The Westroads Stix, Baer and Fuller was also jammed with ticket buyers.

However, the city of Boston didn't share that rabid response to the playoffs or the Celtics quite yet. This was a franchise ready to go under and fold only a couple of seasons before, and there were still barely over 3,500 in the stands for Game 1 in the cavernous Boston Garden. Therefore, owner Walter Brown tried to stop the local telecast feed of the home games on WBZ. However, the NBC affiliate had its own leverage and threatened to deny the network's use of their WBZ equipment scheduled to produce the game for the national television audience unless it could air the game locally. Brown relented when NBC agreed to write a check for the difference between the attendance of the first two games.

Boston gained vengeance in Game 2, swamping the Hawks, 136–112. Cousy carried his club with 25 points, a perfect 9–9 at the charity stripe, while Russell and Sharman turned in matching 22–point efforts. The Midwesterners were never in this one even though Hagan had 37 points in another big night, while Pettit and Martin each had 19 and Macauley just three.

In an aside, NBC had to pay an extra $15,000 to Boston for televising the game as the difference in attendance amounted to almost 7,000 fans.

In a great deal of vindication

★   ★   ★

DEAL ON TV PRIVILEGES

Celtics Tag NBC
For Fee of $15,000

By a Globe-Democrat Sports Writer

BOSTON, Mar. 30 -- It'll cost the National Broadcasting Company " approximately $15,000 extra for the privileges of television the Hawk-Celtic playoff game here yesterday just to New England fans.

after two games, Kerner was able to respond to the overbearing Boston sportswriters regarding the Russell trade for Macauley and Hagan. The 33 and 37 points scored by Hagan gave Kerner some bragging rights and he used them vociferously.

A reminder of the days Kerner and some of the players spent in Wisconsin when they were the league's worst occurred after Game 2. A telegram arrived in the Hawks' locker room from an unexpected source, bringing some satisfied smiles from the team's remaining Milwaukee veterans.

It read, "Go out and beat those Celtics. We're all pulling for you. From one champion to another." It was signed by Joe Taylor, Ed Mathews, Johnny Logan and Del Rice, members of the World Champion Milwaukee Braves. Of course, it was the arrival of the Braves in Milwaukee that had run the Hawks off to St. Louis just three years earlier.

There was no doubt St. Louis was ready to host the championship series in a grand way, a trait today's citizens proudly maintain. It was, and still is, a great city in which to host big events. And except for the Cardinals somewhat frequent visits to the World Series from 1926 to 1958, nine times to be exact, there'd been no major championship held in St. Louis. Kiel Auditorium was decked out with bunting along the balcony railings and signs around the city encouraged the Hawks to win it all this time.

More than 9,400 tickets were sold to sell out Games 3 and 4, prompting Kerner's ambitious decision to set up the closed circuit broadcast on the other side of the basketball arena in the Kiel Opera House. The broadcast was a magnanimous move by Kerner to accommodate a few thousand more fans, who wanted to get into the games.

It took meetings with the unions operating the building and a special agreement with KSD-TV to use its equipment to make the closed circuit arrangement possible. The stagehands and electricians unions had to agree to some role in the production before Kerner could carry out the broadcast.

Tickets to the closed-circuit telecast were just $2. There would be no profit and in fact, a small loss was anticipated, but Kerner wanted more fans to feel they were actually there. Even a large projector was flown in from Chicago and a producer hired from New York to execute the telecast.

Meanwhile on the court, Hannum was trying to come up with a counterattack to the Celtics' strategy that had won Game 2. Boston was planting Russell in the free throw lane prevent anyone driving to the basket. He wasn't guarding anyone but creating a zone defense around the basket while the other four players played outside in a man-to-man defense. It gave Boston the ability to fast break easier with four players outside because of Russell's domination of the boards. Hannum knew it would take more than one Hawk to battle for rebounds against Russell, so the coach worked on offensive changes.

With Pettit's parents in the stands having come up from their Baton Rouge

NBA commissioner Maurice Podoloff

home, Bob would lead his Hawks in a tremendous battle between two clubs playing at the top of their game. Not lost on the evening was the emotional reaction by Kerner towards the referees. At one point during the action, he stormed from his seat, went over to the seat of NBA Commissioner Maurice Podoloff and grabbed him by the arm while screaming at Mendy Rudolph and Arnie Heft, the game officials.

In this one, the Hawks grabbed the early lead, but Russell kept Boston in the game, even giving the Celtics an opening-quarter 25–23 edge. Boston stretched it to 42–37 and again to 49–44 when McMahon and Walt Davis scored for St. Louis to tie it at the half. Pettit was held in check at this point, but the Hawks were holding their own on the backboards.

The third quarter was the turning point not only in the game, but some would say it changed the entire outcome of the championship series. Depending on whether the story is being told by a St. Louisan or a Bostonian, the calamity suffered by the Celtics changed history.

Pettit came out at a blistering pace in the third quarter. The 49–49 half-time tie quickly became a 59–52 St. Louis lead with the Pettit-Hagan tandem taking charge. As the Hawks were streaking, Russell was trying to step up his defense and bring his team back again. However, when he went up to stop a Hawks' shot, he turned his ankle on the way down and would have to leave the game. To make matters worse, he was called for goaltending on the play. Without Russell in the way to block shots, Pettit would continue his barrage and tallied 18 points in the big 34–point third quarter.

When the smoke cleared, St. Louis led 83–71 after three quarters and Russell, who scored 14 points and had 13 rebounds before his injury, was in the locker room for the night and perhaps the rest of the series. The Hawks had been up by 15 at one point, and fouls were taking their toll on both clubs. Before it was over, Hagan and Share fouled out while Boston shooting stand-outs Heinsohn and Ramsey had been eliminated on fouls.

Although devastated by Russell's loss and the foul outs, the Celtics regrouped in the fourth period and battled on. Late in the game, the crowd of 10,148 roaring fans watched as the Celts took a 106–104 lead. With under two minutes to play, Pettit and Martin missed for St. Louis and Cousy for Boston. Then without Russell to contend with on the boards, Pettit grabbed a second missed Cousy attempt, sent an outlet pass to McMahon who relayed the ball to Hagan. The Hawks' forward missed the layup but, trailing the play, McMahon tipped it in.

In the closing minute, the Celtics' Frank Ramsey hit two free throws as did Martin for the Hawks, but Sam Jones' jump shot brought Boston to within two. The fans gasped when Coleman missed a long shot, giving Boston the ball with 15 seconds left down 110–108. But the Celtics never got off a shot. Macauley intercepted a pass intended for Sharman and the Hawks held the ball until Martin was fouled. He hit a foul shot and the buzzer sounded giving St. Louis a 111–108 victory and a 2–1 series lead.

Three nights later, licking their wounds and still without the ailing Russell, the defending world champions hit the Kiel floor with determination. Knowing their tower of defense and owner of the boards was missing, Boston stepped up its passing and worked for higher percentage shots. The wizard Cousy was brilliant playing 47 of 48 minutes.

The Hawks played one of their poorest games of the season, featuring bad passing, dropped balls and poor shooting. They missed an NBA Championship Series record 22 free throws while Boston made 37 of 42. Five Hawks hit double figures, but the numbers were soft. Hagan had a solid 27 points, but Pettit had just 12 (shooting only 3 of 17 from the field) and Macauley added 14 while playing only 21 minutes.

The Celtics were in command throughout. They led by nine after the first quarter, six at half, 13 after three and cruised to a 109–96 series-tying victory. Cousy was a magician with the basketball scoring 24 points assisting on 10 others and the little guard even grabbed 13 rebounds. Now Boston again had the advantage with Games 5 and 7 scheduled for the Garden, if the series went the full ride.

Heading back to Boston for Game 5, the Easterners were hopeful Russell would be back and they would have survived without him. There were four days between games, and on day two the bad news came—the 6-10 tower of strength had suffered torn tendons in the ankle.

"Bill Russell has torn tendons on both the inside and outside of the ankle, and in addition, there is a small chip fracture on the inside of the leg," Boston's sad team physician Dr. Edward Browne said at Carney Hospital. "I would say it will be three weeks before Russell can do anything on that leg."

The *Globe-Democrat* talked with Coach Red Auerbach who put a good face forward in the midst of this major setback. He vowed his team would still be a force.

"We're far from dead," he said. "That's a terrific blow to us but we did get it out there (in St. Louis) and we've got a home court edge. We are going to play the games and hope for a miracle in Russell's case. Whatever his status we're going out there and do a job."

Russell lamented but insisted he might be back before it was over.

"I'm not sure I'll be out as long as they say I will," he said. "If the series goes seven games, I'm still hoping to play. The last time my ankle was hurt it came around quickly."

Russell had been Boston's anchor in 2 1/2 games. He had scored 50 points and grabbed 69 rebounds. He'd missed three regular-season games for injury as well.

Pettit, meanwhile, knew what a blow it was to play poorly and lose at home in Game 4. Russell or not, the Celtics were usually untouchable on their home court, but on the practice day before Game 5, Pettit laid out the situation.

"I know how I feel and I think that's the way the others also feel, he said. "This may be our last chance to come close to a world title and I'd sure like to be able to say I belonged to a world champion. I think we're still going to beat the Celtics."

Game 5 in the Boston Garden would be another classic and take all the effort St. Louis could muster before 13,909 raucous New England fans. The Celtics spent the night searching for answers to make up for the absence of Russell, trying to employ a heavier dose of guard play as they did in Game 4.

The magnitude of Russell's influence on the defensive end quickly became painfully obvious to Boston fans early on. Pettit was a demon, driving the lane for baskets and pounding the boards for rebounds. He had lots of help. Macauley, Coleman and Share also were outstanding in controlling the boards, such an important factor against a team like Boston that depends on the rebound, the outlet pass and the long pass for many breakaway baskets.

Playing like there was no tomorrow, the Hawks played a stifling defense, found their lost offense and were eight points in the lead after one quarter and a whopping 15 points at the half. Defensively for the night, McMahon held the high-scoring Sharman to just 13 points and Martin met the challenge of shutting down Cousy, holding the magician to only 10 points and five assists.

What Hannum's bunch didn't expect was a career night from Ramsey. He wrinkled the twine for a shocking 30 points and almost single handedly pulled off a dramatic comeback. A 15-point deficit dwindled to three late in the fourth quarter, but a free throw by Martin sealed the series-saving win, 102–100. Pettit had 33 points without Russell there to contest his shots, and Hagan was sparkling again with 21. But it might have been the hard-nosed play and dogging of Cousy by Martin that won this one

The St. Louis Hawks were in a new position now up three games to two in the best-of-seven series with a chance at home to win basketball's highest honor. If Pettit thought before Game 5 the team might never have as good a chance to win a title again, it was much more pronounced before the sixth game. A team that just four years earlier was languishing for it's very survival as basketball's worst franchise while languishing in Milwaukee was now play-ing on the national stage for the world championship!

Saturday, April 12, 1958, will always be remembered as the greatest night in St. Louis basketball history. Leading three games to two in the champi-onship round the players knew they had to win Game 6 at home or face like-ly elimination in a Game 7 at Boston two nights later. Their fate would rest on their five starters Pettit, Hagan, Share, Martin and McMahon.

There was no pre-game word as to Russell's physical condition relative to playing, but the Hawks had already learned that with or without Russell, the Celtics would perform at a high level. At a practice held at Concordia Seminary in Clayton on Friday, Hannum had the highest praise for his Boston rivals.

"Sharman and Cousy were voted the top guard combination in the league, and you can't say Frank Ramsey is at all inferior to them," Hannum said. "Russell was voted league MVP, and Tom Heinsohn is an All-Star giving them five great starting players.

"I think it's great we've got the edge on them, but winning three out of five doesn't mean a thing if we can't get this one."

Everybody hoped it would be the players not the officials that would settle this championship series heading into the sixth game. The men in the stripes had their hands full throughout the series with the three fiercely competitive and volatile personalities on the floor, coaches Auerbach and Hannum and Hawks' owner Kerner seated in the first row. Remember, in Game 3, Kerner had actually gotten out of his seat went over and physically grabbed the NBA Commissioner and berated the officiating crew.

After that game, Kerner asked for and got a meeting with the commissioner and chief of NBA officials Jocko Collins. At the meeting, which included his coach, the irate owner accused the officials of giving preference to the Celtics coach (Auerbach) because they

Bob Pettit rebounding

77

allowed him to stomp on the floor and scream with no threat of a technical foul. Hannum, meanwhile, had gotten out of his seat and yelled at the officials only to be escorted back to his seat and told to stay there.

Kerner wanted equal rights or Auerbach shut down on the bench. His complaints were aimed at Mendy Rudolph and Arnie Heft. What ultimately happened was that Rudolph and Heft were ordered by the league to let the coaches know that any "unusual movements or loud protests" would not be tolerated and technical fouls would be assessed. On the other side, the officials were warned not to make themselves a show with demonstrative foul calls.

At 8:30 p.m. in downtown St. Louis with 10,218 sandwiched into Kiel, Blattner, the Hall-of-Fame broadcaster, was nervously waiting along with a national television audience for the opening tip. With a nod from the scorer's table they were ready, the ball was in the air and an entire city stopped to watch the championship chase.

It was like every pitch of a deciding game in the World Series for the fans. Tension gripped the crowd and the home team looked and acted uptight. In the first six minutes the Celtics led 7–4 as the Hawks passing was tentative and their shooting cold. To make matters worse, like Moses coming down from the mountain, Russell rose off the Boston bench, strode to the scorer's table and at 6:14 of the first period entered the game ready to give it his best effort, torn tendons and all.

It gave the crowd pause to think that a dominating Russell could stymie the Hawks front line. But a limping Russell wasn't the same. Pettit was able to dodge around the less-mobile Celtic center. Big Blue connected on long jumpers, reverse layups and drives to the hoops producing 12 first-quarter points.

The score was tied three times during the period. In the later stages, the durable Share, who wasn't known as a big scorer, provided two baskets and Pettit added a pair of buckets to give the Hawks a 22–18 first-quarter lead. It was already apparent the incomparable Pettit was on a mission and wasn't going to be stopped, particularly by a gimpy Russell.

The Celtics still would hang tough. Unaccustomed to and not liking their desperate position, their level of confidence was clearly lower than usual. They were feeling the pressure.

In the second quarter the pace quickened and the visitors took two early leads, at 26–25 and 31–30, when the Hawks' Big Red machine began to accelerate. The ancient one, Coleman, and Hagan stepped up, scoring eight points in the period to give Pettit some support. Bob had 21 at the half and the Kiel residents, who had led by as many as eight several times, settled for a 57–52 halftime margin.

Down to the final grueling 24 minutes, the Hawks had no letdown this night. Pettit broke free for six quick points to start the third period and with help from a pair of Hagan baskets, the St. Louis lead was up to 10. But the relentless Bostonians came back led by the irrepressible Cousy who had been held to two points in the first half. He popped in seven points, set up other scoring chances and kept his team close at 83–77 after three.

Now with one quarter to go in the game and a championship ring dangling in front of the eyes and minds of Hawks' players, would it be a Cinderella moment for St. Louis or would the big, bad Celtics elevate their game to retain their title? By now the fans were standing more than sitting and their hearts were palpitating.

A hush came over the crowd early as Boston showed their poise by scoring seven of the first eight points to gain an 84–84 tie. Then their big man Lou Tsioropoulos was fouled and made one free throw to give Boston the lead.

Baskets were hard to come by after that. McMahon and Macauley managed to come through to regain the lead and then Share hit Pettit with a perfect feed for a bucket and a three-point bulge. Boston came right back and a free throw and Sharman's set shot tied it at 91.

But before that basket with the Hawks up 89–87 a time out was called and what happened in the St. Louis and then on the court became both history and legend. With a two-point lead and about six minutes to go, Hannum huddled with his troops on the sideline. He was going over the strategy he wanted employed when the usually quiet, unassuming Pettit made his presence and opinion known. He had been making just about everything and already had 31 points.

"Pettit took over the huddle and as I recall, slapped his hand on the floor and said to all of us, just give me the damn ball," remembers Macauley, who wasn't in the lineup at the time. "We looked around at each other as if to say, 'why not?' and Hannum said let's go out there and get it. I recall walking out of the huddle with the guys and murmuring something like, if any of you other guys decide to take a shot I'm going to break your arm."

Blattner didn't need to know more than one name the rest of the game. It was "Pettit shoots, he scores," . . . "Pettit a jumper, it's good!" . . . "Pettit a drive to the basket, it's good!" . . . and it just kept coming.

Pettit snapped a 93–93 tie with a basket and a free throw, and made another after Martin nailed a shot, to make it 100–95 Hawks. With 2:20 to play, Pettit hit two free throws for a 105–100 lead, but Cousy wouldn't quit. Four points from the Couz put fans in possible cardiac arrest and the lead was a scant one point with still 1:45 to go.

After free throws were exchanged and the clock continued to run, Pettit broke free for a layup and a 108–105 St. Louis advantage. But Heinsohn was fouled and coolly sank both free throws cutting the margin to 108–107 with a minute to play. After Hagan fouled out, each team had a scoring chance but Pettit and Cousy both missed shots.

When Cousy missed what would have given Boston the lead, Wilfong snatched the rebound and with 16 seconds to play, Martin took what he hoped would be a game-clinching shot, but it clanged off the rim. But with hearts stopped all over St. Louis, No. 9 capped off his historic night with a perfectly timed tip-in, giving his team a three-point lead that sent the Kiel throng into delirium.

Remember there was no three-point shot in the NBA, and Hannum instructed his team to let the Celtics go in unmolested and score at the other end, which Sharman did making an easy layup. Martin describes the fantastic finish.

"There was about 13 seconds left when I got the ball inbounds and began dribbling around and I made a mistake and passed it to Macauley," he remembers. "I didn't know if he could catch it or not. The seconds were ticking towards zero and then out of the blue instead of just holding the ball, Macauley threw it up in the air with both hands just past center court and the buzzer sounded while the ball was coming down."

Said Macauley: "They were trying to steal the ball from me or foul me so that's why I got rid of it."

Pandemonium reigned as the fans poured out on the Kiel floor. Meanwhile, the Celtics were arguing with the referees that Martin and Macauley did not get the ball over the center court timeline in the allotted 10 seconds and Boston should have gotten the ball with three seconds left. According to columnist Bob Burnes, there was considerable doubt that the Hawks got the ball over the timeline in 10 seconds, but on the other hand he stated there were a half dozen fouls committed by the hacking Celtics in their attempt to steal it from Martin.

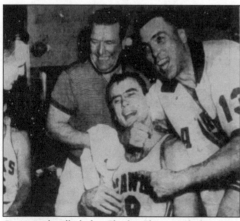

Pettit in headlock by Charlie Share in locker room moments after winning the 1958 World Title as Hawks Slater Martin and trainer Bernie Ebert look on.

Pettit had played the greatest deciding game in NBA Championship Series history, scoring a record 50 points, including 19 of the final 21 in the last six minutes. Hagan, with 15 points, was the only other Hawk in double figures. Sharman had 26, Heinsohn had 23 and Cousy 15 in vain for the vanquished Celtics. Their streak of championships was stopped at one though they would go on to win eight more in a row.

The Hawks were world champions and the city of St. Louis went crazy for their new sports heroes.

The sold out crowd didn't want to leave Kiel Auditorium. Outside, horns were honking, strangers were hugging and thousands were walking in the streets hailing their NBA champs!

St. Louis Mayor Raymond R. Tucker was like a little boy backslapping his friends along the Hawks' famous Murderer's Row, the first row on the floor. The hard-working, relentless combination of public relations director/promotion director/general manager Marty Blake ran screaming towards the locker room yelling, "Benny, Benny, Benny, we did it, we did it. . . ."

Kerner, the excitable, irascible man who wore his heart on both sleeves, got his championship wish after 13 years, three cities, bad teams and financial hardship. Over the final 17 seconds Ben just sat in his center-court first-row seat with his head in his hands just praying his team could hold on. When it was over, he celebrated.

According to newspaper descriptions, the Hawks' locker-room scene was wild. Players were all shouting testimonials and jumping around in sheer euphoria. All, except the amazing Pettit. He sat on his locker stool motionless for more than 10 minutes, his head buried in a towel. He was beat physically and exhausted mentally. His catatonic-like state briefly concerned team doctor, Stan London, who talked softly to Bob for a second and came back saying he'd be all right.

"He'll be fine, but right now he's almost in a state of shock so much has happened," said London. "What a job he did tonight."

The fans didn't leave Kiel, they waited for their heroes. First, Russell who had played just 14 minutes and had four fouls, came out and headed for his team bus. Showing the good sportsmanship that St. Louisans have become known for, the fans cheered all the Celtics who came through the crowd. Finally, the crowd cheered the champions who trickled out—Hagan, Share, Hannum, McMahon and Macauley. But they saved their biggest ovation of all for Pettit. "Oh, what a night," the song title goes. Pettit had played perhaps the best basketball game ever played to that point by an individual and he'd put his team on top of the world.

Blattner felt it was his greatest moment in broadcasting. He has glowing memories of that unforgettable night:

"My most vivid memory of the night is Pettit scoring what proved to be the winner and the ball being shoveled off to Ed (Macauley) with a few seconds left and then Ed launching the basketball towards the ceiling, but not until the clock struck zero. My thought of that game is that you seldom, if ever, get to see a person in sports that single-handily dominated the last quarter of a game that directly determined the victory."

The burning question that followed all the hoopla was: What happened to the basketball that Macauley launched into the air? Is it in a Hall of Fame or at the home of Kerner's family? Just where is the official championship basketball?

"Well, nobody knows today though I can tell you we did know where it was for awhile," says Macauley. "When I threw it up in the air and the buzzer sounded, people rushed onto the floor from every angle and I didn't wait around for the ball.

"However, sitting on the bench at the end was big Charlie Share and when the ball went up he saw that nobody on the team was going to catch it so he bolted off the bench, raced underneath the basketball, caught it, tucked it under his massive arm and elbowed mothers, fathers, grandmothers and anyone else who got in his way up the ramp through the crowd and into our locker room. Charlie stuffed it in his gym bag and took it home.

"A few days later at a team wrap-up meeting Mr. Kerner asked if anyone knew what had happened to the championship game basketball and all was quiet. Charlie had it resting on his mantle and it was going to stay there for now. Later he did give it away to one of Kerner's best friends as a thank you for helping him get a contract agreement together with Mr. Kerner. Share hasn't seen the ball since."

Share had kept the ball originally because he was angry with Kerner over his future because it didn't appear Kerner was going to offer him an acceptable contract. Share held out and didn't show up at training camp and Kerner was so mad at him that he left Share's name and biography completely out of the Hawks' 1958–1959 media guide.

As an aside, Ferrari who had played so well and been a big part of the Hawks' first two seasons had returned from military service. He was able to enjoy the championship series from the bench, this time as Hannum's assistant. But he would have given anything to be on the floor in Game 6.

In the aftermath of the championship game, Kerner began receiving calls and telegrams of congratulations from all over the country. One of them came from his bitter rival, Coach Auerbach, who expressed congratulations and his regrets for not being able to find Ben to shake his hand in the mayhem at the end of the game. He also didn't use the Russell injury as an alibi for the loss so as not to take anything away from the Hawks' tremendous showing.

Kerner received another telegram that was very important to him because it came from his one of his best friends and a man whose distinguished career in sportswriting had made him a celebrity. *St. Louis Post-Dispatch* sports editor and lead columnist Bob Broeg was in Kansas City covering the Cardinals when the Hawks victory and news of Pettit's 50 points flashed across the wire. Bob wrote to Ben:

"Hawk, congratulations on winning the championship. Why would anybody but Pettit ever shoot!"

"Hawk" was Kerner's nickname so dubbed by his buddy, August A. Busch, Jr., and Broeg's phrase stayed with Ben forever as he repeated it regularly for years after.

1957–58 Championship Team. Top Row, L to R: Max Shapiro, Slater Matin, Win Wilfong, Jack McMahon, Med Park, Frank Selvy, trainer Bernie Ebert. Front Row, L to R: Head Coach Alex Hannum, Cliff Hagan, Jack Coleman, Charlie Share, Bob Pettit, Walt Davis and Ed Macauley.

The very next day, Kerner was touting his team's success and sudden popularity. He said he was in the planning stage of creating a 55-station radio network extending through Missouri, Louisiana, Texas, Iowa, Kansas, Illinois and Arkansas. He'd had calls from cities and towns from all those states, but in the end, there is no evidence the radio network ever came to fruition.

All of this success came with a head coach Kerner intensely disliked. But for now Hannum was a St. Louis hero and nothing really mattered but savoring the championship and beating Auerbach's Celtics. Kerner put it this way:

"We didn't only beat them," he boasted, "But we beat them in six games. That I'll never forget."

Chapter Six
Owner, Promoter, Dealmaker–Ben Kerner

orld champions, toast of the town, downtown darlings, the Hawks were all of those nicknames and more. Two straight seasons of making the NBA Finals and one championship, who could ask for or expect more? Since January 21, 1957, there had been an unprecedented era of consistency and continuity within the St. Louis Hawks family and it had resulted in total success. Don't rock the boat, you say? Not in Benny's vocabulary.

Two days after winning the world championship of basketball, the Hawks' owner declared in a 36-point headline on the front page of the *Globe-Democrat* sports section, "The Job Belongs to Hannum 'If He Wants It.'" It was reported that Kerner had offered a one-year extension to Hannum's coaching contract with details to be ironed out in the next few days.

Kerner went on to say, "We have had our differences, but he did a great job with the club and I hope he decides to continue. I would have told him earlier, but I didn't want to cause any disturbance since the team was going so well."

On the other hand, insiders thought Kerner was thinking of firing Hannum if the team didn't get to the finals or even lost in the finals. Hannum was immediately impressed by the bravado in the newspaper and said, "Right now I'm not thinking about next year, but only about getting back home to Los Angeles because of pressing business matters. I've got a young construction business and it needs my attention badly."

Then after a team and owner dinner to celebrate and look ahead to the 1958–1959 season, Hannum had some prophetic words that unfortunately weren't heeded by ownership. The Hawks' steady ship was about to be flipped upside down again on a team that had just gone from a cellar dweller to world champions. In a year-and-a-half the team had posted a 56–47 record in the regular season, won two division titles, went 16–7 in the playoffs and captured one world title under Hannum's leadership.

"There have been some wonderful things said about this team, about Bob Pettit's great 50-point performance and about the final game in particular," Hannum said. "But I think the game typified the solid team spirit and the cooperation that was behind it's success for two years. They all sacrificed themselves and I'll be eternally grateful to each and every one of them."

The statement sounded more like a like a departing speech. Did Hannum know Kerner wouldn't accept his demand of a raise and a two-year contract and it would be Ben's way out with the public? Press table guru Jack Levitt summed it up best when describing Kerner's fetish for changing coaches.

"He had a thing about coaches," explained Levitt. "He didn't profess to knowing anything about coaching but he felt he knew one thing—to him they weren't very important and they weren't bigger than him on the ball club."

"It wasn't that he'd say they're not important, but in the way he handled the team and the way he handled the coach you could tell he didn't think that position was important. Ben would say, 'I've got Pettit, I've got Hagan, I've got Martin. Heck I could coach them and win.' He wouldn't ever give coaches any credit."

Ben's gracious wife, his former secretary Jean Kerner, confirmed, "With the coaching things, Ben like being in control. There's no doubt about that. In fact, even with our kids, we talked about how he always had to be in control."

And so it was, continuity and success be damned. Kerner had only one way to negotiate, his way. And while the Hawks' prospered in most of the eight seasons after the championship, it was despite his ill-timed intrusions into the chemistry of the team and its coaches. Almost to a man, the players loved Kerner over the years, but they also wished he hadn't forced them

Kerner's widow Jean with 1957–58 Western Division Title Championship trophy (L) and NBA Championship trophy (R)

Glad to Have You Aboard, Andy

to start over with new systems and coaches so often.

To everybody else, the coaching merry-go-round defied logic. But to Kerner it was all very logical. "What's the big deal? They weren't coaches until I made them coaches," he said. "What are you supposed to do, live with a guy until he breaks you?"

Public relations and promotions boss Blake tells the story about the love-hate relationship between Hannum and Kerner, including the fact that Kerner never wanted to hire Hannum in the first place but was forced into it by the players.

"So Alex becomes the coach, inspires the team, takes them to the finals the first time, so we give him a one-year contract for $10,000," began Blake. "During the championship season, he pushes Ben for a renegotiation and extension for two years and Ben says let's wait till the season's over. But Alex keeps saying, 'No, no we need to do it now.' That just made the relationship worse because nobody pushes Ben."

After the championship game, Blake called Hannum in California where the coach had gone back to see about his business. Blake told Hannum that Kerner was offering him a $2,000 raise and a one-year deal. Blake reminded him how bad his construction business was and how he should take the coaching job. However, infuriated with the lack of a two-year deal, Hannum resigned.

Jean Kerner looked back at losing Hannum as a mistake by her husband. But making impulsive decisions certainly weren't out of character for him. He wasn't always wrong. In this case, it wasn't the right call.

"If something would happen, he would just want to fix it now instead of thinking it through," said Jean. "When he let Alex go, he didn't think it through. He just got mad. Alex wanted more money right away before the season was over and was pushing for a contract, but Ben kept saying, 'No, we'll wait.'"

Losing the popular Hannum was a stunning revelation in St. Louis. Hannum told the Associated Press in Los Angeles that he was "surprised and had no comment" on the announcement out of St. Louis. But Blake said he had read the prepared statement twice to Hannum and had asked him to reconsider to no avail.

Then another bizarre development occurred. Hannum's job and business went sour and while Kerner was deciding on his replacement, Hannum called Blake back and said he wanted to come back. But the die was cast and Blake told Hannum there was no job, you quit. Kerner then announced he hired ex-Celtic Andy Phillip as his new head coach.

Hannum was in mourning in California and asked Blake what he should do for a job. Blake gave him some suggestions and Hannum got picked up by Vickers Oil Company to coach their basketball team for $17,500 and a new convertible. He would, of course, go on to a Hall-of-Fame coaching career, winning the NBA championship again with the Philadelphia 76ers in 1967 and an American Basketball Association (ABA) title with superstar Rick Barry in 1969 at Oakland.

It was an inexplicable decision to replace the highly successful Hannum with Phillip, a man the Hawks had just finished playing against, a member of the 1957–1958 Celtics. If a coaching change is being made on the world championship team, wouldn't there be a long list of highly qualified, big name coaches who would want the job? Kerner didn't wait to find out and Macauley,

Have Hawks, Will Fly'

who himself would get caught in the coaching ringer, examines the depth of this drastic decision.

"Coach Hannum wanted X number of dollars, and if it was a $5,000 or a $10,000 raise for a guy who completely turned around a bad franchise and won a championship I would have said give it to him," pronounced Macauley. "I could have reached an agreement with Alex, but Ben was funny. It was the one fault he had that he didn't understand teams, didn't understand coaching, and didn't understand that when you change coaches, you change the chemistry and style of your whole team. It always sets you back."

Phillip was known in St. Louis, being from just across the river in Granite City, Ill. He had played for the Chicago Stags, Philadelphia Warriors, Ft. Wayne Pistons and Boston Celtics, but had never coached a day for anyone. People didn't need to get to know him very well, because in another bewildering development, Phillip's reign was over before it barely began.

"His downfall began when we were playing an exhibition game in his hometown in Granite City, and he almost missed the start of the game," Macauley laughed. "He missed all of the pre-game and showed up for the tip-off saying his wife couldn't find a babysitter so he took them to the grocery store. After that debacle, Coach Phillip went 6-4 to start the season but Kerner couldn't stand it. He fired Andy and called me into his office.

"Ben tells me he wants me to be the coach and I'm thinking here we go again, changing the whole chemistry of the team. On the other hand, Andy hadn't been there long enough to instill much of anything of his own.

"But I said to Ben that I had no desire to coach and no experience. In addition, I said it's tough to bring a player off a team and make him the boss. Kerner wasn't listening and told me. I had three options—accept a trade to Philadelphia; two I could retire; or three I can be the coach. I just said where's the whistle, I'm the coach.

"Ironically, but not surprisingly, nobody had informed Phillip he wasn't the coach anymore. It hadn't made the newspaper yet, so when I went out to practice, Blake also went to practice and told Phillip after it was over. It was vintage Kerner. Three coaches in seven months on a championship team—nuts!"

On November 19, 1958, Macauley became the fifth coach of the Hawks in St. Louis in just the start of the fourth year of the franchise. In addition, the Hawks had three different coaches in their brief Milwaukee history. Kerner said of Macauley:

"In Macauley I have found a man I could trust to lead my Hawks for many years to come," Ben said publicly. The release from the Hawks said Kerner offered Macauley an unprecedented five-year, $100,000-plus contract, but added Macauley wanted only a three-year commitment.

Who really was Ben Kerner? We know the background from Buffalo to

Tri-Cities to Milwaukee to St. Louis, but what was he really like day-to-day? Personally he was a quiet, soft-spoken man who was known in business for his very practical decisions and wise policies. He was respected in the entertainment business and by noted business leaders.

Ben was born November 18, 1913, and was single for much of his adult life, choosing to take care of his mother, Helen, up to her death in 1968. His loyalty to his mother included a pledge that he wouldn't marry as long as she was alive. After his mom passed away, Ben married the love of his life, his secretary, Jean Bilbrey, on November 24, 1971, in Las Vegas, Nevada. Jean says Ben would tell his friends kiddingly, "The marriage ceremony only cost me $25, but the darn cab we held out front of the chapel cost $65, so the cab cost more than getting married did!"

They had two sons, "B.J." Ben Kerner, Jr., and Kyle Kerner. Both are married with their own families and have wonderful memories of their famous father.

The late Rich Koster, an outstanding columnist at the *Globe-Democrat* wrote a column about Kerner in 1971 a few years after the Hawks had left. He had some very apt descriptions of the man who took his chance on his own to make a living in professional basketball. Rich wrote the following:

"How do you increase the value of 10 guys in $5 sneakers 1,000 percent in 20 years? You hustle.

"You hustle, I'm the first to admit I was a hustler," said Kerner. "Basketball was my life. I spent 20 hours a day at it seven days a week, 52 weeks a year."

Starting in Buffalo and then Milwaukee, he displayed admirable enterprise and energy, but his ledgers were filled with red ink.

"Whenever I had to meet a payroll, I'd have the Globetrotters in. They'd play the first game and we'd pack the place. But then half the people would leave before our game."

Kerner did everything he could think of to attract fans. For $1 he gave away a $1.08 pound of coffee and included admission to the game. So even if the fans didn't like basketball, they would make eight cents just for showing up!

He was a fantastic promoter even if the coffee gig didn't pan out. He began at the grass-roots level initiating a summer clinic program with Hawks' players as instructors. Some 400,000 athletes attended at gyms and outdoor courts all over the metro area.

Not knowing how much it would take to get fans to come to his games early on, he did things like hiring Emmett Kelly, the famous clown to entertain at every Sunday home game in the 1956–57 campaign. He also hired the hysterical contortionist Max Patkin, the one-time, sore-armed pitcher of the Cleveland Indians minor league system, who turned himself into a baseball comedian. His pantomime act was so popular he was covered by reporters whenever he appeared.

Blake should be given credit as the man who actually did the work of booking the acts that came into Hawks' games. Blake had a Rolodex full of famous entertainer names from his days of promoting a Pennsylvania minor league baseball team. That's where Kerner found him.

The appearance of top national entertainers became expected at Hawks' games, and attending the games was THE thing to do in St. Louis after those two great seasons. Among those who appeared on the Kiel floor were Count Basie and his Orchestra, Lionel Hampton, George Shearing, Al Hirt, Guy Lombardo, Woody Herman, Harry James and Stan Kenton.

In addition, he'd have pro tennis matches by the top players in the world, golf exhibitions by touring pros and he would even set up bowling lanes after a game to hold a real professional bowlers tour exhibition. Blake remembers several humorous stories about some of the Hawks' special promotions.

"Remember there was a stage and an orchestra pit at the one end of Kiel behind the basket," Blake recalls. "I actually had the great Count Basie sitting in the pit during the game only to rise out of it just minutes after the game ended as the fans sat in amazement. We brought in a guy named Paul Hahn, Jr. the trick golfer who hit whiffle balls up in the stands.

"I'll tell you a funny one about Benny," continued Blake. "One opening night Benny heard about the St. Louis Twirling Teens who had won some kind of big contest. It was 100 little girls who twirled batons. Ben is upstairs being interviewed in the booth by Buddy Blattner for KMOX and I'm standing with Bob Burnes to whom I said, 'Watch this, it's going to be one of the funniest ever.' So right before the game the little girls march out on the court and as they throw their batons in the air, maybe 12 out of a 100 catch them and the rest are bouncing all over the Hawks' floor!

"All of a sudden Ben sees all the bouncing batons and screams down to the floor from way up in the crowd, 'Marty, Marty get the kids off the floor they're beating it up!'

"About a month later another promotional boondoggle occurs when Ben gets a call from a guy in Moberly, Mo., telling him about their state champion 'cloggers.' Without even asking, Kerner books them and even after I tried to tell him about cloggers he was insistent saying, 'They're going to be real good.' I was standing there with Ben when the kids with these huge cloggers came trudging out on the basketball floor making a terrible racket. Ben could only say, 'Oh, no, not again!'

"On another occasion, Ben found out a man and woman had met because their season tickets were adjacent to each other at Kiel. They fell in love and were going to be married, but canceled their season tickets because of the cost of the wedding. Kerner found out the circumstances, contacted them and paid for the honeymoon so they could keep the season ducats.

"Another time a fan passed away and with him was buried his season

Hawks' tickets by accident. The family realized the grievous error and actually had the grave dug up to retrieve the precious tickets."

Jack Levitt relates another funny story about an early promotion that was really a scam. Levitt remembered how tough it was to sell Hawks' tickets in the beginning. But they managed to get a watch from the incomparable "jeweler of the stars," Dorian Magwitz of Hamilton Jewelers in downtown St. Louis. The plan was to have a drawing and give the watch away, and after the first time was such a success, they wanted to do the promotion every night.

"The problem was we only asked for one watch so to keep the promotional value going with the crowd, we went out and got some students from St. Louis U. and Washington U., gave them a free ticket to the game every night, called the 'lucky number program' during the game and one of them would always win. After they came down to the floor to receive the watch, they would give it back to us after the game and come back the next game.

"It worked fine for about 20 games and now we're at mid-season. I call out the lucky number and a guy comes walking down from upstairs when we knew all the tickets of the kids were downstairs behind the basket. I was concerned and said to Marty, 'How the hell did he get up there?' Blake said 'I don't know.' So the guy comes down, his game program has the winning number we called, we shake his hand and give him the watch. All of a sudden we see the man not going to a seat, but heading out the exit behind the basket.

"'Marty, the guy is leaving, go get the watch!' I screamed, so you can picture a 250-pound Marty Blake doing the duck walk trying to catch the guy. A security guard comes back to me on the press table and says Marty caught the guy on Market Street and got the watch back so we could give it away again. Our guy we gave the ticket to had given his ticket away to this guy and he had every intention of keeping the watch."

Today that escapade would have been a news headline and a story coast-to-coast on CNN with a lawsuit to follow. But the publicity of giving a watch away every night must have been very significant to fans.

What was Kerner "the fan" like in the stands? Let's start with a complete nervous wreck. It's a good thing few cared much about blood pressure in the '50s or Ben might have been told to stay home. Kerner even called himself, "Benny the Boob" when he thought he made a mistake at anything.

He sat in the first row at center court with his feet on the basketball court and his business associates and cronies seated around him creating a section that was dubbed "Murderer's Row." He was known throughout the league as an ostentatious fan who regularly berated the officials, the opponent or whatever riled him during the games. In his pockets were cigars, cigarettes, chewing gum and toothpicks, all of which he sucked, chewed or mangled during the games. Winning

1957–58 Championship Team 30-year reunion. Back row, L to R: Medford Park, Cliff Hagan, Jack Coleman, Alex Hannum, Ben Kerner, Ed Macauley, Jack McMahon. Kneeling, L to R: Charlie Share and Bob Pettit.

or losing, during the action his face always looked in agony expecting the worst to happen.

He was a favorite target of columnists and broadcasters because he was so animated. Remember the punch he took from Red Auerbach, the night he ran across the floor and grabbed the arm of the NBA commissioner complaining about the officials, or his superstitions that caused him to do the same thing over and over again if his Hawks were having success while he was doing whatever.

One night that superstition had to do with lighting cigarettes. Jim Fox, Kerner's friend who was also a Murderer's Row member, gave Ben a pack of cigarettes right before tip-off and he took one puff and put it out as the Hawks scored a basket. Seeing what happened he continued the pattern of lighting a cigarette, taking one puff and putting it out all night long as the Hawks continued to score. Six packs and 120 cigarettes later, the game ended in a Hawks victory! Two of his favorite courtside phrases were, "Nobody's doing anything," and "We're in trouble now."

Kerner was clever, cunning, open, entertaining, lovable, passionate, caring, and a showman. Whereas in most cases and on most teams, the coach is the most colorful, prominent character, the St. Louis personality was always represented by Kerner, the out front, forthright owner.

"Ben was just great to me and I wasn't a paid employee," says Levitt fondly. "He always took me to Boston for the playoff games, and did a lot of personal things for me. When our son was born, Ben sent over a new baby carriage as an example of his generosity.

"Ben was so proud of what the Hawks had become in the city. The season his front line of Pettit, Hagan and Clyde Lovellette combined to make $100,000 combined salaries, Ben, who usually spent his time whining about not being able to afford things, wanted to blow his horn and held a press conference.

"Always looking for free publicity he staged the press conference to announce he had signed the NBA's first $100,000 front line. What's funny is the players didn't know it and in the back of the room at the Jefferson Hotel stood Hagan and Lovellette asking each other what they make to see how it could get to $100,000. They concluded, correctly or not, that Pettit must be making half the total."

His promotional efforts didn't stop at bringing attractions to games to lure

Bob Pettit signing annual contract with owner Ben Kerner in Kerner's downtown St. Louis office.

fans, but he also knew he needed to go into the St. Louis communities with his story and build supporters. Kerner started a speakers' bureau of players and team officials that went to every school, civic center and service group meetings, reportedly more than 300 per season, preaching the gospel of the NBA and Hawks' basketball. Videos and tapes weren't invented yet, so the representatives would drag around films of games and the All-Star games.

After winning the championship in 1958, the crowds had swelled to capacity on many nights in 1959, but Kiel had never been upgraded. Impatient with City Hall's delays, Ben forced the issue by loaning the city of St. Louis $35,000 to buy new seats and to improve the floor seating area. In addition, he installed a beautiful new scoreboard as a gift to hang over center court at a cost of $2,500.

Finally he broke ground nationally in the area of the baskets themselves. Again in 1959 he had baskets designed that operated on a hydraulic lift that could be moved in and out of position much quicker than the conventional way. He also advanced the city enough cash to purchase a new floor both at Kiel and The Arena for his champions.

Even in the area of broadcasting games the Hawks were trendsetters. It wasn't customary for teams to have all their games on radio much less any on television. However, Kerner allowed KMOX to carry all the preseason, regular-season and postseason games—all of them live. Kerner would also have a dozen or more regular-season and postseason games televised. Plus he took credit for triggering the interest and the concept for a national television Game of the Week on NBC.

Kerner also had a reputation for being a shrewd, if not difficult, man when it came to player contract negotiations. Players didn't have agents, so many of them were overmatched in the skill of negotiation when they walked into Kerner's office.

Unlike athletes today whose agents practically dictate their client's salaries to the teams, players were pretty much at the mercy of management in the 1950s and 1960s. Pettit was a first team All-American and known across the country as one of the coming superstars of the NBA when he signed with the Hawks. However, that didn't impress "Uncle Benny."

"When I was drafted as the second player in the draft by the Hawks, I didn't know who they were, but I found out pretty quick after meeting Mr. Kerner," said Pettit. "I went to his hotel room in Milwaukee where he took off his dress shirt and sat there in his undershirt. He told me he would pay $9,500 and I said I wanted $15,000.

"We literally sat in the room and didn't say a word to each other for three hours because I knew if I said, 'Okay, I'll take $14,000,' we were going to meet in between. But if I waited for him to say $10,000 first we would meet

Charlie Share Night, February 11, 1958. L to R: Suzanne, Cynthia, Charlie and Rose Share.

between $10,000 and $15,000. That extra $1,000 meant a lot to me.

"We finally began to talk about it and I wore down and agreed to $11,000. It wasn't what I wanted, but on top of that I got a bonus. I got to come back in a month and sell season tickets! That was my bonus."

Share was truly the original Hawk and he had many highs and lows with Kerner. He could define their love-hate relationship and back it up.

"I probably spent as much time with Ben Kerner as any other person in basketball. I was with the Hawks a year-and-a-half in Milwaukee, then five years in St. Louis and that's six-and-a-half years with the man," began Share. "I did a lot of things. I set up the Kiel Auditorium seating arrangements for games. We started out with eight-inch risers and Ben would say, 'I'm sorry, that's too high, Charlie. Bring that riser down to four inches and we'll get a lot more fans into seats.' I worked with the season ticket holders, did some of the public relations and set up the player clinics at schools and elsewhere.

"I handled the season tickets, and I arranged the seating. The problem was nobody wanted to give up their seats after the championship season. I remember we had a question whether we should play the games on Friday night or Saturday, and while Ben wanted to play on Saturday night, he wouldn't do it without a public survey. It came back Saturday, but he was always thinking of his fans.

"We had our problems, too," continued Share. "After we won the championship, I wanted a raise the following season. Kerner didn't agree so I held out and didn't come to training camp. Finally, with the season about to start, Saul Nathanson, a personal friend of Kerner's, called me up and asked if he could intercede with Ben because the team needed me to play.

"I said okay and eventually with Saul's help I came to an agreement with Kerner on the contract and joined the team. It wasn't the contract I was looking for, but I decided Saul was right and I needed to go back to the team. Later, I gave the championship game basketball I had saved that night Macauley threw it up in the air at Kiel and I gave it to Saul as a thank you. I never saw the ball again."

Ben was so angry with Share for holding out even though he knew Charlie would eventually return to the team and they would work out a deal, that he instructed Blake not to include Share's biography nor put him on the roster of the Hawks in the season press guide! Therefore, he wasn't listed as a player in the world championship season press guide for the 1958–1959 season.

Maybe Martin, with his myriad of dealings with Kerner, could best portray the various strengths and weaknesses of Ben. He too agreed that above all you had to admire and respect the owner for his accomplishments with the Hawks, The drafting of Pettit, the acquisition of Hagan and Macauley, and the trade for Martin were the three most important events in Hawks' history. But the trade for Martin was done with a bit of ingenious, legal trickery to get the star guard away from St. Louis' division rival. That really epitomized Kerner's determination to win.

"He wanted to win so bad, which is exactly what a player wants in owner-ship," recalled Martin, whose real name is Slater Nelson Martin, Jr., but who was nicknamed "Dugie" after his father, Dugan. "In that nasal tone we all knew so well, Ben would say, 'I want to win the champeenship' like the announcer would say the heavyweight champeenship of the world, not championship.

"But negotiating a contract with him was something else. It was always one year at a time and it wasn't easy. You might sit with him three days listening to him moan and groan and whine about money. You'd sit there in the room, he'd undo his tie, his hair would hang down in his eyes and you never won the discussion. When it was over, you'd just be thankful if you didn't lose anything in the negotiation that you had when you started.

"Through it all I liked Mr. Kerner and never had any problems we couldn't work out. As tough as he was on individual contract talks, the players all understood he really cared about them and he would do anything to make the team better.

Ben Kerner and 1957–58 Western Division Championship Cake

"Speaking of which Ben would ask my advice for whatever reason, before he'd make an acquisition. He asked me many times about different players and if I agreed I'd say to Ben, 'Go get him, he's a good one.' One of those guys was a great player for us—Clyde Lovellette."

Success brought Kerner a group of celebrated St. Louisans for friends. They enjoyed being a buddy with the owner of a successful and now celebrated NBA team. One of those new friends was August A. Busch, Jr., the owner of the Anheuser-Busch brewery and the Cardinals. The two used to play cards together frequently and Ben told this story about their relationship.

"One time they were sitting together along with Ben's mother on the front row at Kiel when Mr. Busch asked, 'Ben, how do you make your money?' Ben answered, 'Well, I've got this basketball team, that's my business.'

"Busch replied, 'No, no, how do you make money? How do you make your real money? Hell, I've got a damn old baseball team that doesn't make money, but I do make my money in beer! Now how the hell do you make your money?' Ben said he just shrugged as if to say I told you."

The two colorful, magnetic owners of the town's professional sports franchises had plenty of opportunities to ask questions because they would play gin rummy almost every day.

"Ben was a guy that loved to be loved," said Blattner fondly. "He wanted everything to be right all the time. He was not a social climber or very reticent in a crowd. He had his own very small circle of friends. He didn't fit in with the general society. He would always say, 'I'm not much fun.' He was obsessed with his enterprise, the Hawks. He was really pretty much a loner. He would pick up the tab, he would do anything, but he didn't want to move out of his circle."

The story of the Hawks has many pieces, but almost all of them are woven around the decisions, right and wrong, and the charismatic actions of their sometimes hated and mostly beloved owner, promoter and general manager, Ben Kerner.

Chapter Seven

Ed Macauley–Player, Coach, Symbol

Bob Pettit was the greatest Hawk—Milwaukee, St. Louis or Atlanta—period. But make no mistake that in the eyes of St. Louis fans, "Mr. St. Louis Basketball" was, is, and always will be, "Easy Ed" Macauley. Besides his all-pro career as a player, he was a championship coach, plus a national championship winner in college. And lastly, he was born, raised and still resides in St. Louis.

After the Hawks won their first NBA title and Kerner parted ways with Hannum, the owner made a second mistake in hiring an inexperienced Andy Phillip who had not been a coach. Besides the shopping incident with Phillip's wife, another habit annoyed Kerner. Phillip would schedule practice in the mornings based on the times his wife wanted him to make breakfast. Ben had enough.

"We had a ball game where we lost to Syracuse by an astronomical score (120–94 on Nov. 18, 1958) and I went up to Benny and said, 'Look, I hate to tell you this but the players are telling you something,'" recalls Blake. "You should go upstairs and fire Phillip and after he leaves make Ed Macauley your head coach."

"Fire him?" said Kerner. "I'd have to give him his $10,000 salary."

Replied Blake: "$10,000, $15,000, it don't mean a thing if your team is going to go down the drain. I don't care what the record is today, this isn't working out."

Ed Macauley

Kerner knew it was time to settle the uneasiness amongst Hawks' fans growing tired and upset with his coaching changes. Phillip's instant failure made the Hannum dumping look even worse. He needed a fan favorite fast and he found it without leaving the court at Kiel.

Macauley recalls the meeting.

"I was called into Kerner's office and he didn't mince words. After I said what do you want? Ben said in that high-pitched, whiny tone, 'I'm going to make a change. I'm going to relieve Andy as coach and I want you to be my coach.'"

As described earlier, Macauley was given three choices and accepted the one that would keep him in the Hawks' organization. Conceptually, he would be a player-coach as Hannum had been. But it wasn't long before Macauley had second thoughts about that concept.

"I think I still could have played, but as I tried it a couple of games thinking, should I substitute for myself, who should be in the game, what's the situation, there was a lot to think about as coach," said Macauley. "I found it very difficult for a big man, a front court man, to be a player-coach. I think a backcourt man could be a player-coach, and in baseball, a player could do the job. But in basketball you can't see what's going on all over the floor at the same time. So it was an easy decision to stop playing.

"It worked out fine because Hagan was already having another great season, so I could really concentrate on coaching the reigning NBA champions," Easy Ed said. "That was enough pressure, anyway."

The Macauley-led Hawks took off from his first day, a 114–109 victory over the Minneapolis Lakers at Kiel. That was confirmation enough for the fans that the Easy One would be a stabilizing force on the bench for their beloved team. The record stood at 6–4 when Ed took the reins. And from November 22 to January 4 the ball club went on an incredible run of victories, going 17–5 during the stretch.

Here's an absolutely stunning statistic about Macauley's first season as coach. In the friendly confines of Kiel Auditorium the world champions were an astounding 24–1 after November 22, losing the one game to the New York Knicks on January 4. In the string were three wins over Boston. In a strange quirk, when the club wore their home court uniforms at neutral site games, their record was a perfect 7–0! Yet when they wore their road uniforms at a neutral site, they were 0–5. Go figure.

The season didn't skip a beat as the Hawks cruised to the Western Division title, their third division championship in four St. Louis seasons. The Hawks finished the year with a team all-time best record of 49–23. Macauley had taken them to a 43–19 record under his watch, which was anchored by a second league scoring championship by Pettit, who averaged 29.2 points per game.

6–9 Clyde Lovellette in Boston uniform.

Another great trade engineered by Kerner and executed by Blake made the transition of Macauley from player to coach easier. The steady scoring of Macauley, who always averaged 14-or-more points per game, had to be replaced to keep the pressure off Pettit and Hagan. The perfect solution was the pickup of an old Hawk nemesis from the Lakers, one of the game's premier shooters, 6-foot-9 Clyde Lovellette.

On September 16, 1958, the front office pulled off the blockbuster deal that sent five players—Jim Palmer, Ken Sidle, Darrell Floyd, Wayne Embry and Gerry Calvert—to the Cincinnati Royals. Only Embry would become a significant player and star for 11 NBA seasons, eight with the Royals. Three of the four other players never played in the league.

Meanwhile Lovellette fit in beautifully in the Hawks' starting quintet. He was used to playing with marquee players in Minneapolis like Hall-of-Famers' George Mikan and Vern Mikkelsen. Thus, blending with Pettit and Hagan was a cinch. Lovellette would average of 14.4 points and almost 10 rebounds per game.

What did Lovellette think about becoming a Hawk? In Minneapolis and Cincinnati he was almost always the team's leading scorer in the 19-to-24 points per game range. He had won an NBA championship in his rookie season of 1953–1954. But going to Cincinnati on a bad ball club wasn't much fun.

"Cincinnati was floundering with the two Harrison brothers owning the team, and I asked for a little more money than they could afford," Lovellette recalls. "So it was a good move for them getting five guys and a great move for me knowing I'd play with Pettit and Hagan. Of course, I split time with Charlie Share at center, which really worked out well keeping us both fresher."

The combination of Pettit, Hagan and the soft touch of Lovellette gave St. Louis the highest scoring front-court combination in the NBA. Stamina and jumping ability were the question marks Lovellette brought with him. But he worked at both areas instituting exercise, and worked with a weighted vest to

Boston center Bill Russell hooks over Hawks center Clyde Lovellette in game at Boston Garden.

strengthen his legs and back, all to improve his game. One-time welterweight boxing champion Virgil Akins, a resident St. Louisan, and his trainer monitored Lovelette's physical programs—and it worked.

The trio of Hawks scored a league-record 4,821 points. Pettit had 2,105, Hagan added 1,707 and Lovellette chipped in his 1,009. Lovellette could step back and nail a 15-20 footer or gently drop in a hook in the lane much like Hagan.

"Our rotation in the games was beautiful," said Lovellette. "Bob (Pettit) could go in and I could go out or vice versa. Cliff (Hagan) could come in or out for either of us and nothing would be lost scoring wise. We could all shoot inside or outside, which had to be a real headache for our opponents."

Macauley remembers Lovellette's exercise workouts and wonders how he got through it.

"I saw Clyde with those ankle weights on one day and I said to a guy standing nearby, 'Take him out to the Mississippi River and throw him in. That sucker will take him right down to the bottom.' Those were brutal."

Lovellette remembers that regimen with a grimace: "In the morning we ran. They made me wear these huge shoes. They'd get me up early, pick me up at the hotel, go down to the restaurant for orange juice with four or five raw eggs in it and make me drink that sickening stuff! They said it would clear my lungs to run better."

Macauley knew Clyde was a shooter, but his defensive efforts were less than acceptable when he arrived. However, some stern conversations spelling out the team's expectations for his performance paid off in improved play on defense by the big man. Macauley remembered one specific game when Lovellette turned a likely loss into victory and spared the club Kerner's wrath.

"We were playing Syracuse and down about seven points with little time left in the game," began Ed. "I decided as the coach that we wouldn't foul them because we couldn't give up any more points. Syracuse had a little guard who could really dribble but I told our guys let him dribble and guard him close until the shot clock runs out so they can't get off a good shot.

"As I recall with about five seconds left, Lovellette hit a long shot and was fouled and we tied the game. We force overtime and ended up winning. Just minutes before Marty Blake had come over to the bench to tell me Kerner wanted to see me immediately after the game, probably to rail me and the whole team. Kerner thought we would lose. Turns out he didn't have anything left to say in the locker room, thanks to Clyde Lovellette."

The final standings showed the Lakers in second place in the West, a distant 16 games behind the domineering Hawks, followed by Detroit and last place Cincinnati. Interestingly, the Hawks had finally won a season series against the Celtics by a slim 5-4 margin sweeping four in St. Louis and winning once in Boston. Meanwhile, Macauley's boys had whipped the Minneapolis group, winning eight and losing just four.

The Pistons and Lakers played a best-of-three semifinal series while the Hawks waited. Minneapolis used the home court to their advantage winning twice at home, the series clincher by a 27-point margin. They were rolling into the division finals.

All the talk centered on a third straight championship series between the determined champion Hawks and Boston Celtics. But, of course, the St.

105

Louisans first had to get past the Lakers. The media and the fans didn't consider Minneapolis much of a threat, but nobody told the Lakers to lie down.

Initially it did look easy. St. Louis blew out the Lakers in Game 1 by 34 points, and even though Minneapolis got even at home in Game 2, the Hawks bounced up and smashed them again, this time by 30 points to lead the series 2–1. Lovellette commented about the rest of the series.

"Going in we felt we could win pretty handily against Minneapolis, and it's hard to figure out what happened after Game 3," he said. "We lost Game 4 in Minneapolis by 10 but felt okay with the fifth and seventh games scheduled at Kiel.

"Then we got caught up in a close one at home in Game 5 and get beat by one point, 98–97, to go down 3–2 and facing elimination in Minneapolis. We played tough, but the Lakers got us at the end again and we lose by two (106–104). You look at it years later and it just think it wasn't our time."

Actually, history reports the turning point came only 18 minutes into in Game 1, despite the game ending in a rout for the Hawks. Outside of losing Pettit, the most important cog in the wheel was Dugie Martin. Without their floor general, the Hawks couldn't contend with Cousy and the Celtics anyway. But early in that first game, Martin was scrambling for a ball with the Lakers' Ed Fleming and went down with a series-ending pulled leg muscle. His tenacious defense, 10 points and five assists per game plus the veteran leadership all hobbled to the bench and changed the series.

"In Game 5, we were ahead by one point with only about five seconds to play when Minneapolis took a shot and missed," said Macauley, remembering the shocker. "But we had left a player wide open underneath who grabbed the rebound and put it back to beat us. I think we were still in shock up in Minneapolis in Game 6. That's what can happen in a short series."

Incidentally, the Lakers got tattooed by Boston in the championship round. The Celtics had to be ecstatic not to be playing the defending champions. Minneapolis had used up their miracles while beating the Hawks and although some games were close against the Celtics, they added up to a four-game sweep as Boston became champs for the second time in three seasons.

Under Macauley, the Hawks had gone an amazing 43–19, a .693 winning percentage in his first season. So despite the unexpected loss in the division final, there was no doubt Macauley would coach his first full season in 1959. Ed was only 31 years old at the time, and according to the Hawks' press guide, had turned down an offer at the start of the season to become the head coach of his alma mater, St. Louis University.

In the NBA of 2005, after such an incredible run as a player and first-year coach, Macauley would be getting a three-to-five-year contract as coach preparing to lead this seasoned ball club back to the finals. Well, part of that statement turned out to be true. But Ed tells the story about what happened to him as a coach for Kerner.

The 1959–1960 Hawks made minor adjustments to the squad. Another St. Louis U. All-America player, Bob Ferry, was drafted in the first round. He was arguably the best St. Louis U. Billiken player since Macauley. He was a 6-8, 230-pound center who set a single-season scoring record at SLU and led them to a No. 12 ranking in the country in rebounding. There was hope he could bolster the center position behind Lovellette and second-year man Hub Reed.

In August 1959, after the playoff injury to Martin against Minneapolis proved to be so devastating, comrades Kerner and Blake sought to obtain some young, talented backcourt help. They found it in Cincinnati, trading for two-year veteran, John McCarthy, who had averaged 13 points per game and was a tough guy on defense. His credentials read, "great ball handler, good outside shooter and excellent driver to the basket," all elements that needed bolstering in the Hawks' attack. In return, St. Louis sent veteran guard Win Wilfong, who had produced little the year before, William Bell from North Carolina State and Tom Hemans from Niagara, plus cash, to the Royals.

The Hawks were solid favorites to win the Western Division again as prognosticators considered the Lakers playoff upset of St. Louis a hiccup. They made the Hawks their pick for a third visit to the championship series in four seasons. The Lakers had the fabulous youngster, Elgin Baylor, whose 25 points per game in the playoffs were largely responsible for upsetting the Hawks the previous spring. Baylor's play was deemed the only real threat to a regular-season repeat.

Minneapolis knocked off the Hawks at Kiel in the season opener, 94–87, but that would be the only day of the season St. Louis would be under .500. By New Years' Eve, St. Louis was 19–12 and had beaten the Lakers four straight times.

They stumbled through January at .500, and were 28–21 on January 30. But in February the club exploded, winning 12 times, and on March 9, they capped it off the regular season by beating Cincinnati, 123–116, to finish 17 games over .500 at 46–29. The Lakers dropped to third, 21 games behind the winners and the Detroit Pistons scooted into second place

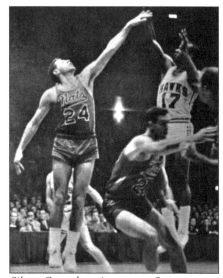

Sihugo Green shoots jumper over Syracuse Nationals player.

with only a 30–45 record. Boston ran away with Eastern Division with a 59–16 mark.

Sihugo Green, a midseason acquisition for the Hawks the year before, was an African-American and the only minority on the Hawks. He came to the Hawks from Kerner's favorite trading partner, Cincinnati. Going to the Royals were Med Park, Jack Stephenson (who shortly after retired) and cash. Green had been a heralded rookie out of Duquesne in 1956 when Rochester took him as their No. 1 pick and the first overall choice of the draft ahead of Bill Russell!

Green had suffered a brain concussion before he came to the Hawks the previous year and played just 25 games. But his importance in the 1959–1960 season becomes evident in the astonishing results of the playoffs. During the regular season, Sihugo, a 6-2, 190-pound gentle guy who played guard or forward in backup roles, averaged what would be a career-high 14 points per game. His college achievements had been considerable—a two-time All-American who led his club to the National Invitation Tournament championship his junior season.

While the Hawks sat on the couch, the Lakers upended the second-place Pistons in the semifinals, setting up a Hawks–Lakers division final again. After a good start by St. Louis, taking a 2–1 series lead, things started to look eerily like the previous year's final round. Minneapolis won Game 4 at home and then shocked the Hawks at Kiel, 117–110, in Game 5 to jump ahead three games to two while going home for the sixth game.

At this point the never predictable, always irrational Kerner did something that would cause him to lose the faith of players and fans alike. Instead of waiting to see if his team could pull off a Game 6 victory in Minneapolis, Kerner did something stupid.

"In those days, you had to change planes in Chicago to get to Minneapolis from St. Louis so we flew to Chicago and Ben Kerner went with us," said Macauley. "In Chicago Ben gets off the plane and says he has business to do and will meet the team in Minneapolis for the game.

"As the coach, I walked into the pre-game dressing room and it was very quiet. Nobody was saying very much. I kind of walked around, slapping guys on the butt saying, 'Let's go get 'em tonight,' but you don't know what that means. It could mean the guys have their bags packed already and are expecting to be eliminated, who knew.

"Everyone has heard stories about how a coach inspired a team to win the big game. As we gathered in the locker room before the game, I told them this would be one of those games we'd all remember–win or lose. I didn't make a rousing speech, I merely said we're the better team and this is the game to prove it. Play your game, get the ball to the open man and play the best defense of your life.

1958–59 team celebrates Western Division Title under coach Ed Macauley (seated) with owner Ben Kerner.

"When we hit the court the team plays their hearts out all night long and we stun them without Martin, our floor leader who had been hurt back in the All-Star game. We get to go back to St. Louis for Game 7. As usual the stars got it done, Pettit had 30 points, Hagan and Lovellette each had 29 and Green had 17, while Baylor had 38 points to lead the Lakers. But otherwise our defense was superb. We won in a rout, 117–96, and we're going back to St. Louis."

Martin struggled through injuries during the season, and a hamstring injury took him down in the All-Star classic. He pulled another muscle early in the playoffs and when he probably shouldn't have been playing. Kerner had pleaded with him to try to play in Game 6, so Dugie took a Novacaine shot to kill the pain. However, he was a non-factor in the game and was on crutches for Game 7. Martin would never play another minute for the Hawks or in the NBA, calling it quits after the playoffs.

But Game 7 provided St. Louisans with another fantastic memory in local sports history. The wounded Hawks, having just lost the last game at home, looked for leadership without Martin. Their prayers were answered when they got help from a most unlikely source—Si Green.

"In the locker room before the game, the pep talk was simple. I pointed out how the Lakers were dreading this game because they could have won it at home," said Macauley. "We didn't have our usual home-court advantage at Kiel because we played at Washington U. But the team's record there was outstanding. I told them defense was the key to winning again."

In a tense, low scoring affair, the Hawks avenged the previous season's playoff loss to Minneapolis, earning a 97–86 win to advance to the NBA Finals and again challenge the highly favored Celtics. One of the heroes of Game 7, Green, scored 16 points and added 13 assists.

"Si was not a good shooter, and if somebody would have said we needed to get 16 points from Green to win Game 7, do you know how many takers I would have gotten on that wager? None. I don't know how he did it, but he played a hell of a game," Macauley recalled. "It was unbelievable but magnificent."

Almost taken for granted were the usual great clutch games by both Pettit and Hagan. With 28 points and 20 rebounds, Pettit led the way. Hagan followed with 18 points and Lovellette added 16.

"So after the game was over I go on TV to be interviewed and I'm asked, 'How do you think we'll do against the Celtics (St. Louis was 3–6 vs. Boston that year)?' I said, 'I think we'll do great. We're ready to go. I think we're going to win it!'

"As we were leaving for Boston that night my wife Jackie asked me, 'Do you think you can beat the Celtics?' I said, 'What? Are you crazy, without Slater we'll be lucky to win one game.'"

The team that played and beat the Celtics in '58 was not the troupe that Macauley was leading into battle in 1960. Sure Pettit and Hagan were there and Lovelette was a good tradeoff for Share. Missing, however, were Coleman, Martin and the coach himself, Macauley. In addition, McMahon had slowed considerably and was playing fewer and fewer minutes. It was up to a new cast, plus Ferrari, who was back from the service, but not contributing like he did the first two seasons.

As the Boston series began and the city was excited about another chance to dethrone the bad guys of Beantown, Kerner was holding to himself a terrible secret of something he'd done in Chicago en route to Game 6 of the semifinals. He would keep it a secret until the NBA Finals were over, though there is suspicion some players actually knew.

The Hawks were badly handicapped starting the series, down to only nine healthy players. Both Martin and McMahon were dropped from the roster,

Pettit was nursing an injured back and Ferrari had come back from injury. In this series, rookie Bob Ferry plus center Larry Foust and Dave Piontek, late season acquisitions from Cincinnati, were pressed into service.

The Celts had not only kept their team together for a few years, but added new firepower that would fuel the future success of those championship teams. Boston's future Hall-of-Fame roster included: Heinsohn, Cousy, Russell, Sharman and Ramsey, all veterans, plus the Jones boys, Sam and K.C. Another member of their squad doubled as a starting right-handed pitcher for the Milwaukee Braves, center Gene Conley.

The stats tell the story. The legendary backcourt of Cousy and Sharman had averaged 39 points per game in the season, while Heinsohn had led the team in scoring with a 21-point average. Russell had averaged an incredible 24 rebounds per game and the Jones boys were both on the way to the Hall of Famers.

"My biggest concern was that we didn't have anybody to play Russell," said Macauley. "Larry Foust our center had replaced the traded Charlie Share who had played Russell well. And even though Foust was a great player and could handle Russell, he was handicapped by a terrible heel injury that wouldn't allow him to play more than five minutes at a time. I do believe we would have won with a healthy Foust or with Share."

The series was a constant fight for the shorthanded Hawks. They were blasted in the opener at Boston, 140–122, but then scrapped to win Game 2, 113–103. Back in St. Louis, the Hawks couldn't put it together in Game 3, getting drubbed, 102–86, but again rallied in Game 4, 106–96, for a 2–2 tie.

The now best-of-three series had two games left in Boston. Game 5 was another green team slaughter, 127–102, sending the Hawks desperately back to Kiel. *The Globe-Democrat* newspaper headline blasted in bold type, "HAWKS ON ROPES, MUST TRIUMPH TONIGHT."

The injury-riddled Hawks got even worse news when they learned Foust not only had his heel problem that had caused him to have daily Novacaine shots just to walk, but in Game 4 team physician Dr. Stan London said the powerful center had fractured a bone in his hand and was done.

The always confident, if not cocky, Auerbach admitted, "We've got the edge, but anybody who lets up in this series is in deep trouble. The Hawks have been tough for us. We'll just have to see what happens."

Defense had held the Hawks in the playoffs. In their victories, the defense, especially the backcourt players, had been stalwarts holding down the production of superstars Cousy and Sharman. Cousy had become so frustrated he publicly stated he was considering sitting himself down the rest of the series. Too bad he didn't follow through on that hollow threat.

In Game 6, Macauley couldn't have been prouder of his team, and outside of the championship game in '58, St. Louis fans hadn't witnessed a more remarkable, heartfelt win with the club's back against the wall. The "Big Three" threw the party with a lot of help from their "secret weapon," Sihugo Green. The rafters were shakin' from the constant drone of the 10,612 packed into the Kiel like sardines.

A furious first half had the fans breathless. Boston was determined to end the series, but the Hawks were relentless. St. Louis led by eight after one quarter, 24–16, but by only a bucket at the half, 54–52. Then the game changed dramatically.

Globe-Democrat beat writer Bud Thies called the second half, "the one to be remembered always." About the players he wrote, "Cliff Hagan and Si Green played their greatest games as members of the Hawks." That's a mouthful in the case of the Hall-of-Famer Hagan who posted many magnificent nights. But under the conditions of having virtually no subs available and a championship at stake, the claim was valid.

In the Hawks' best third period in playoff history, the locals poured in 36 points, limiting Boston to a scant 12. Frank Ramsey had opened the half with

Boston's Red Auerbach, Bob Cousy and Tom Heinsohn contemplate Hawks' victory.

a game-tying basket to make it 54–54, but the trio of Lovellette, Pettit and Hagan rattled off 12 straight. Hagan took over from there as "Hagan gone wild" could have been the title of the period. He hit hooks, jumpers and fast break layups scoring 17 points alone in the period. When the sneakers stopped squeaking for the quarter break, the Celtics looked bleary-eyed as they stared unbelieving at the scoreboard reading, Hawks 90, Boston 64. It looked over, but was it?

Suddenly the Hawks began to play like they were in a "prevent" defense trying to run out the clock and not grinding on the offense. The Celtics lost, but would leave an indelible memory on the St. Louis fans. The champs were setting the tone for Game 7 in Boston.

The Hawks still led by 15 after Hagan hit a jumper with four minutes to play, but full-court presses, steals and 11 quick points had the Hawks and their fans down to their last breath inside a minute. Russell connected on a hook shot and a steal and a Heinsohn jumper made it 104–102. Finally, it was the secret weapon, Sihugo, who drew the decisive foul. He made the most important free throw of his life to cinch the win.

Before Game 7, sports editor Bob Burnes praised the fans and the city: "There was a crowd of 6,500 that had jammed into Washington U. just one Saturday before to watch the Hawks and Lakers, and then a pair of standing room crowds of 10,612 at Kiel for the Celtics' games. These Hawks figures are even misleading because the number of available seats doesn't tell of the interest in the games. The Hawks could have sold 25,000 seats for every game."

Incidentally, the Hawks had four players score all but four points in Game 6. Hagan again rocked with 36, Big Blue had 25 points, Lovellette chalked up 18 and Green had a career-high 21 points, including the final free throw.

Unfortunately, the Macauley miracles stopped in Game 7. Undermanned and overwhelmed by basketball's version of "America's Team" and a crowd of 13,909 Hawk-haters, an almost heroic 30–29 first quarter St. Louis lead was blown away by a 41-point Celtic second quarter. A lone basket by Pettit was surrounded by 14 Boston points and a never-to-be-threatened cushion.

The highlight of the night for the Hawks was a 60-foot shot that swished through the net by Hagan at the buzzer of the first quarter for the brief lead. Pettit played strong netting 22 points and grabbing 14 rebounds. Hagan slipped to 19 points, Lovellette again had 18 and Green finished a brilliant playoff series with a 17-point night. Boston, however, gave the St. Louis defense a sound whipping.

The Celtics won their second straight World Championship by cruising to a 122–103 win. Ramsey was the surprising leading scorer with 24 points. Russell and Heinsohn each had 22, while Cousy controlled play with 19 points and 14 assists.

Another fantastic season was over. The Hawks' popularity was at an all-time high, the team still had plenty of star power, veteran leadership and finally some continuity—and then Kerner's secret would rock the ship again as he had done after winning in 1958 when he fired Hannum.

After losing the seventh game in Boston Garden, Kerner asked Macauley to accompany him to New York for the NBA meetings the next day. Ed went to Catholic mass that morning at St. Patrick's Cathedral and when he returned to his hotel room there was a note at the front desk asking him to come right up to Kerner's room.

"As I walked into the room, Ben looked at me and said, 'Eddie, I've got a problem,' to which I answered, 'What's the problem?'

"He said, 'Do you remember I left the plane in Chicago when we went to Minneapolis before Game 6? Well, I met Paul Seymour in Chicago and hired him as my head coach for next season. . . . But I want you to remain as my coach."

"I was shocked to say the least," Macauley said. "We sat silently for a moment and then I replied, 'Ben, if you want Seymour as your coach that's the way it will be. Under these circumstances I wouldn't be comfortable coaching your team.'

"Frankly, it began to run through my mind that I would never want to be fired at halftime, and if I stayed, Ben was capable of doing either to me. I still had a contract and Kerner would have to pay me anyway.

"After I said 'no' to his request to keep me as coach and fire Seymour, Ben said, 'Then you'll be my general manager.' Since I didn't have a job and he owed me the money I said, "okay." Since Ben really didn't need a general manager he also added, 'You can also do the broadcasts and be the color man.' I said okay, I would like that—but that, too, never happened. Soon after a press conference, Kerner announced that the now-retired Dugie Martin would be the new color man for the radio broadcasts with Buddy Blattner, completely forgetting or ignoring his promise to me.

"He didn't want me to do it and now I was convinced there was no real place nor a need for me in the Hawks' organization though I remained with the general manager's title the next season. I never had a desk, never had an office and never went to work. But I did sign Lenny Wilkens to his contract and was there for Bob Ferry's deal."

On the way back to St. Louis, Macauley's head was swimming with the news. He realized then that Kerner thought they were going to lose Game 6 in the semifinals in Minneapolis, so he was ready to fire the St. Louis favorite. Then Ed and his gutsy ball club changed the script by upsetting the Lakers on the road and as the underdog stretched the mighty champion Celts to the seven-game limit in the finals. Kerner desperately wanted a retraction, but didn't get it from Ed nor did he deserve to be saved from public embarrassment.

The announcement in the press the next day muddied the waters for Macauley even more when Kerner put out a release that said Macauley was the new general manager and as his first duty he had negotiated a three-year contract for the new coach, Paul Seymour! Macauley never talked to Seymour and never negotiated any contract with the man. These quotes from Kerner in the *Globe-Democrat* couldn't have been farther from the truth.

The paper reportedly quoted Macauley as saying, "When Seymour became available I suggested he would be the ideal man to replace me." It further said Macauley was "elated over being able to get Seymour who has an excellent reputation as a coach," which was untrue.

It's not that Seymour wasn't potentially a good coach. He was a good name at the time, having played 13 seasons as an accomplished player with the Syracuse Nationals and four years as their coach. Instead, it was the level of disloyalty, unfaithfulness and deceit towards a popular player and coach who had

Standing along side Hawks van, center Larry Faust and forward Clyde Lovellette.

just won 89 games and lost just 48 (a .650 winning percentage) over a tremendous year and a half stretch, plus getting to the seventh game of the finals. To this day, Macauley ranks No. 1 in the Hawks' franchise list of coaches in winning percentage.

Seymour became the sixth coach in just the sixth year of the St. Louis franchise, a team that had been to the NBA Finals three of the last four seasons after finishing first in their division all four seasons! Gone from the glory days were guards McMahon and Martin, and of course, Macauley. But a future great new guard was about to be drafted and his signing was one of Macauley's last real duties.

The Hawks had drafted Lenny Wilkens, a slender 6-1 guard out of Providence, at the urging of Blake and the disdain of Kerner. But it was Macauley's job to get him signed. He met Wilkens, whom he had never previously met, in a New York hotel room to negotiate a contract.

"Lenny came up to the room and was very quiet," began Macauley. "If you've ever done any negotiating before, it's difficult to do with someone who doesn't say anything. I talked to him about what a great city St. Louis was, I told him how great our team was, what a great opportunity it was and how he could fit in and do a great job. All that went on for about 45 minutes.

"Lenny didn't have anything in mind as far as salary was concerned so I said we'll give you $7,500 a year and a $1,000 of that right now and he said 'that's fine.' I left for St. Louis and about a week or so later I knew it wouldn't work for me in the office so I left the Hawks. Ben paid my salary and I went into television work in St. Louis and that was that."

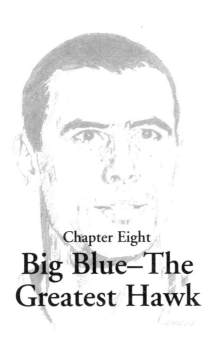

Chapter Eight
Big Blue–The Greatest Hawk

Before taking the story through the final eight seasons and four more coaches, the record needs to be set straight why the Hawks NBA franchise never made it in Tri-Cities, Milwaukee or even Atlanta to a large degree, but it had this marvelous run in St. Louis. Much has been said about Kerner's role, good and bad, but it wasn't Ben or the coaches, the Kiel or the fans. Winning, of course, helped make the success. But, in retrospect, it was all the losing, especially in Milwaukee, that allowed the best decision in the history of the franchise to be made—the drafting of Big Blue, the Bombardier from Baton Rouge, No. 9, Bob Pettit.

No St. Louis athlete before or after Pettit comes closer to the St. Louis model of the perfect athlete, "the perfect knight" Stan "the Man" Musial. However, in this city the best basketball player the fans had ever seen to rival The Man's dominance of the game, dignity and class on and off the field of play and the ability to rise to the occasion when his team needed him most was Pettit.

It's been said that when the new Busch Stadium was built in 1966, there was talk about putting not one, but two statues downtown to help support the sports tradition and upgrade the appearance of the city—the Musial statue, which stood outside the ballpark for its 40 years and is to be moved to the new Busch Stadium for its 2006 inaugural. But there was support for a similar honor for Pettit. Unfortunately, it didn't happen and there is next to nothing in St. Louis to memorialize this man or the team that gave the city a national champion image.

Think about it. If Pettit were not a Hawk, there would not have been division titles, conference titles and an NBA championship in St. Louis. Kiel would not have been filled to the rafters and a glittering era of roundball history would not have materialized without him.

By the way, Baltimore did snare St. Louis' American League baseball team, the Browns, which became the present-day Orioles. On the positive side, Baltimore did the Gateway City one very large favor. Their basketball team, the Baltimore Bullets, a charter member of the NBA in its inaugural season of 1947–48, made the decision to end their nightmarish existence 14 games into the 1953–54 campaign when they were 3–11 and headed for the worst record in the league. Their departure in midseason gave the Milwaukee Hawks their chance to be the worst and finish last. The reward was the No. 1 pick in the ensuing draft that everybody in the country knew was Bob Pettit, Louisiana

Hall-of-Famer Bob Pettit.

State University's three-time All-American center.

Robert was clearly big man on campus for three seasons, romping his way through the rugged Southeastern Conference schedules against the likes of Coach Adolph Rupp's legendary Kentucky Wildcats. He set numerous team and league scoring records and was a leading rebounder as well. In one college game he scored 60 points and, as a senior, averaged a remarkable 31.4 points per game. At 6-foot-9, 210-pounds, Pettit was the real thing and an NBA sure thing.

In his first season he learned humility fast with the raggedy Milwaukee Hawks, playing only in front of his best friends at the empty arena. Milwaukee won 26 and lost 46, but the rookie forward–thanks to the presence of center Charlie Share for helping him–finished fourth in the NBA in total points scored.

Pettit averaged 20.4 points per game, was third in rebounds with 994, made the first-team all-league team and was named NBA Rookie of the Year.

Recognition of this special player grew quickly in St. Louis. He blew into town and was an instant crowd favorite with his grinding, exemplary style of play. In his first NBA season, Bob racked up more league-leading totals, was top scorer at 25.7 points per game and was the leading rebounder at 16.2 rebounds per game with a total of 1,164 to earn his first NBA Most Valuable Player Award. The points and awards kept coming for this modest single man.

Pettit's technique, like that of Musial's batting stance, was an unforgettable trademark. He rarely dribbled more than once, and discarded the set shot that he came into the league with in lieu of developing a hard-to-block, soft one-handed jumper raising himself exactly vertically a couple of feet off the floor every time. As soft as his touch was from 10 to 20 feet from the basket, he was a ferocious driver in the lane for the layup. Pettit would use his great strength to barrel down the lane and dare opponents to challenge him. It was often said he may have had the strongest pair of hands in the NBA and couldn't be outwrestled for a rebound or driving for a bucket.

He didn't have that super strength the first couple of seasons as teammate Dugie Martin recalls, who was then forging his all-pro career and racking up NBA titles in Minneapolis.

"When Bob first came into the league you could easily knock the ball out of his hands. But after he found the weight-lifting program he got strong as the devil," chuckled Martin. "And that's when everybody was telling players not to lift weights because they'd get muscle bound and lose their quickness. Pettit proved them wrong and as far as I know, was the first player ever to do it."

Said Pettit: "Alvin Ray was the strength coach of the Kansas City Chiefs and the San Diego Chargers in those days, and he was light years ahead of anybody else in things like isometrics and exercising for athletes. That's why Jimmy Taylor (running back Green Bay) and Billy Cannon (running back LSU) worked with him.

"I told Kerner what I was doing and he nearly had a heart attack," laughed Big Blue. "He said I wasn't going to be able to shoot well anymore, but I guess we proved him wrong."

As mentioned, Pettit was the Hawks' and the NBA's No. 1 draft choice, so how was it going from one of America's premier college basketball teams to the bottom rung of the NBA ladder? Bob says he didn't mind it at all.

"When I got to the Hawks, I was able to play every minute of every game, and it gave me a great education," said an appreciative Pettit, who turned 72 years old in 2005. "Today a rookie would get very limited playing time and take three years to develop. But no matter how poorly I played, I still played and could learn at a much quicker pace. I guess I learned the game well enough to get that Rookie-of-the-Year Award.

"My first training camp was in Detroit at Wade State University to which I drove in my 1951 Plymouth. Coach Red Holzman took one look at me and after a couple of scrimmages said, 'You're a forward, not a center.' It was a great move for me and the team because Charlie Share was the center, and by getting me outside I had the mobility to develop a jump shot.

"Then it was in May of that year that I got a call saying we were moving from Milwaukee to St. Louis, which was fine with me. I figured it was a lot farther south and I was pleased with that. I liked Milwaukee as a city, but it was cold, there was snow everywhere and the wind was always coming off the lake. That's where I got that big blue coat that Blattner made into a nickname for me. I had to have that thing because it was so cold."

Big Blue was quickly adopted by the inhabitants of his new hometown. The fans knew one of the greats in the game was in their midst. Pettit compiled a list of incredible statistics over his 10-year career. Look at what he did in the first five seasons in St. Louis: From 1955 to 1960, he held the following single-season NBA records: most points in a season, most free throw and field goal attempts, most free throws and field goals made, most rebounds, and highest average per game. Over his first seven years, he averaged 25.3 points per game, the best career per game mark in NBA history to that date. He epitomized success in his game.

"In his day, Pettit was the best power forward that there was, Elgin Baylor (Los Angeles Lakers star) included," said Boston's Red Auerbach. "Pettit could do more things than Baylor, because he could play some center and was a much stronger rebounder. Pettit was Mr. Clean, Mr. All America. He was a clean liver and a super guy, but very, very competitive. He would play all out 50 points ahead or behind. It didn't matter, that's the only way he knew how to play."

In the late 1950s and early '60s, player endorsements were offered to just a few, mainly the superstars. Of course, if Pettit wore it or drove it, you wanted one. He did ads for Yates Oldsmobile on Washington Avenue and drove an Olds '98 Holiday Sedan. Rawlings Sporting Goods used Pettit as their model for uniforms that they sold to teams at all levels across the country. An ad for the Wabash Railroad featured Pettit and some teammates disembarking from a train in the Hawks' program. Pettit was the man.

It was stated before how much Pettit thought of the St. Louis fans and their role in the club's tremendous success at home. Big Blue said you could you hear the crowd loud and clear on the court.

"You'd really hear them when we were behind, and if we'd catch the other team, then go ahead the place would go berserk," remembers Pettit. "The other team would often call timeout and it was so loud you could hardly hear each other in the huddle. That would get us even more fired up.

"Incidentally, the discussion of the blue topcoat brings to mind the equal

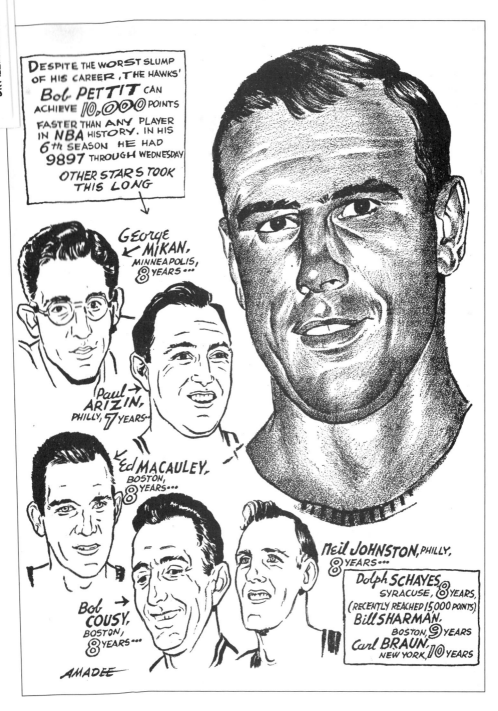

DESPITE THE WORST SLUMP OF HIS CAREER, THE HAWKS' Bob PETTIT CAN ACHIEVE 10,000 POINTS FASTER THAN ANY PLAYER IN NBA HISTORY. IN HIS 6th SEASON HE HAD 9897 THROUGH WEDNESDAY

OTHER STARS TOOK THIS LONG

GEORGE MIKAN, MINNEAPOLIS, 8 YEARS...

Paul ARIZIN, PHILLY, 7 YEARS...

Ed MACAULEY, BOSTON, 8 YEARS...

Bob COUSY, BOSTON, 8 YEARS...

Neil JOHNSTON, PHILLY, 8 YEARS...

Dolph SCHAYES 8 YEARS, SYRACUSE, (RECENTLY REACHED 15,000 POINTS)
Bill SHARMAN, BOSTON, 9 YEARS
Carl BRAUN, NEW YORK, 10 YEARS

AMADEE

intensity of our owner, Mr. Kerner who would sit in the first row and cheer or writhe with each passing play," added Pettit. "At one point in time in those early years, Kerner came into the locker room after a victory and proclaimed, 'If you guys win five in a row, I'll give everybody a new sport coat.' So we win five in a row, after which he says, 'If we win six in a row, we'll get new slacks.' We won the sixth, so he ups the ante again and says, 'At seven in a row we get topcoats, but at 15 in a row, everybody gets a new car!'

"That got our attention real good, but winning 15 in a row at that time in the NBA would be like making a hole in one a charity golf tournament to win the car. It wasn't going to happen although I think we got to ten. Then the league stepped in and told Ben he couldn't give individual incentives like that."

Those two seasons, the dramatic loss in Game 7 in 1956–57 and the championship season of '57–'58 set the tone for this storied franchise. And, above all, it was Pettit who gave them the foundation and who struck the most fear in the hearts of opponents. In the first of those two years, there was his heroics while coming back quickly from a broken arm to lead the Hawks in the playoff run. The next year climaxed, of course, with what is still today probably the greatest individual performance in a championship-deciding game in all of NBA history. Pettit's 50 points in Game 6 to win the NBA title by just one point over the Celtics at Kiel Auditorium is a feat never duplicated—not by Wilt Chamberlain, any of the Celtics, including Larry Bird, or yes, even the magical Michael Jordan. Not by anybody.

Was Pettit aware as the game progressed, the type of scoring numbers he was putting up in this very close contest?

"Most definitely. I could always think in my mind the number of points I had, and for some reason on that night I knew every minute of the game," Pettit said. "I felt it that night.

"I was playing well in the game and by the fourth quarter, could almost score at will. The team recognized it and they were so unselfish. It made it so much easier playing with a group of guys willing to set picks for you, to come off that pick and there comes a perfect pass at the right time. Then other times, I could run the baseline and someone would see me and hit me with a perfect bounce pass for a layup.

"Then I also scored a number of points by getting rebounds on the offensive board. That's probably where I scored a lot of the points that night. The Celtics had put a 6-5 player, Lou Tsioropoulos, on me with Bill Russell injured, and I could shoot over him. He was pretty physical and I had a lot of bruises, but also a lot of free throws."

Repeating the story, Pettit had 31 points in the first three quarters, and then with about six minutes to play in a two-basket game, Pettit wasn't bashful about asking the coach and the team to "get him the ball" the rest of the game. Outside of a Martin layup, Big Blue dazzled the Celtics and the delirious St. Louis crowd with 19 of the final 21 points. The biggest of all was the tip-in of a missed Cliff Hagan shot with 15 seconds to play to seal the deal.

This time the always glib and colorful Blattner was truly lost for words after the Game 6 triumph, "It was the greatest performance I've ever witnessed in all my years in baseball or basketball," he said.

"Because Bob was never vocal about anything, it was like okay, this is what I'm paid to do. But boy, you knew out there on the court he was taking personal responsibility for closing out the championship. He wanted the ball and he would take the responsibility win or lose. He was the hero. That was just his job."

Macauley, who did more watching than playing in the that final game, remembers it succinctly: "Bobby Pettit played one of the greatest games, put on one of the most clutch performances in a championship setting ever seen to this day in pro or amateur sports.

"Something every athlete dreams about is wearing a championship ring and I know everyone on the team had plenty of contributions along the way. But I don't care what anybody else thinks, I know I wear this championship ring thanks to Bob Pettit."

In an interview, Pettit gives his perspective on the Hawks' history and his answers reveal the humble but very proud qualities of the man.

Q. In the second season in St. Louis, the team jumped up in the second half to win their first division title, two playoff rounds and the near miss seventh game loss to Boston. What do you remember?

BP. I remember that late in the year coach Alex Hannum switched Cliff Hagan from guard to forward, and that became a major move that really helped the team and deflected some pressure off me.

Q. What about the acquisitions of Slater Martin and Jack McMahon?

BP. It was really those deals that had

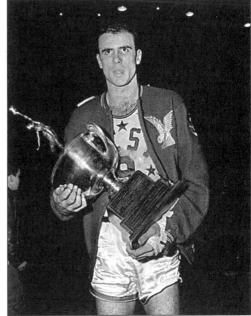

Bob Pettit wins 1958 MVP award for NBA All-Star Game.

given Hannum the chance to get Cliff out of the backcourt with Charlie Share at center and Jack Coleman also at forward along with Ed Macauley. We had great depth at every position.

Q. You have a story about the All-American Frank Selvy from Furman who was acquired by the Milwaukee Hawks in your rookie season.

BP. A quick little story. As seniors in college, Frank and I were the Nos. 1 and 2 scorers in the country in 1953–54, he at Furman and me at LSU, both averaging about 30 points per game. I go into Georgia Tech, score 45 points and think I had a pretty good night, when I find out that Selvy had 100 points the same night against Presbyterian College, I think. So that was the end of the contest. He ended up averaging 40 points per game!

Q. Individually, what was your best year in the NBA?

BP. My personal best was our team's worst season, '61–62 when the team lost 51 games to finish fourth. I averaged 31 points and 18 rebounds per game. I ended up being the head coach for the last six games and we went 4–2 for my coaching career. That was it.

Q. Speaking of rebounding, you once averaged 20 per game. Did you take a lot of pride in your rebounding ability?

BP. Absolutely. More than my scoring. In fact, after I got a stat sheet at the end of a game, rebounding, not points, was the first thing I looked at.

Q. Before Bill Russell came, you led the league in rebounding in '55–56?

BP. Yes, when Bill came he took over but I stayed up there. I averaged over 16 rebounds per game for 11 years, that was the third highest in history behind Chamberlain and Russell.

Q. You still hold the Hawks (St. Louis and Atlanta) all-time rebounding record with 12,851 or 16 per game and had 39 rebounds in one game.

BP. I felt my offensive rebounding gave me on the average of six points per game every season. I'd either get the rebound and make a basket or get fouled and go to the free throw line about 10 times per game. I had a science to my offensive game, things that I did to get inside the lane. But the important thing was to go to the basket every single time. I had 27 rebounds in one All-Star Game, a record that still stands.

Q. Who defended you the best in the league?

BP. It was Mel Hutchins of the Ft. Wayne/Detroit Pistons originally and later on Tom "Satch" Sanders of the Celtics. Both of them played me very tough all the time. But I took great pride in everything.

Q. Where was your most favorite and least favorite places to play?

BP. Detroit at the old Olympia Auditorium was like an old drafty barn and I think you were playing over the ice. There was always only about 1,500 people there and no atmosphere to motivate players. Playing in New York and Los Angeles with all the people and excitement was fun. There was lots of energy in the crowds, but nothing could touch our Kiel Auditorium. They loved the Hawks.

At the free throw line, Pettit was unique, too. He'd stand feet side-by-side, knees bent, and when he rocked back to shoot he'd cradle the ball in his large right hand and push it to the basket with the rest of his body coming up in a rigid position—and then swish!

Bob Pettit's trademark foul shot technique.

"I don't think he was quite as good Bill Sharman, who was the best, but he was darn proficient," remembers Macauley. "When the score was tied and the game on the line, he was ice water.

"He scored 20,880 points in the NBA and never once dunked the ball although he could have easily," said Macauley. "It was always a soft layup."

One thing Pettit emphasized was the quality of players in the league because there were so few teams. Ft. Wayne had George Yardley, Mel Hutchins, Andy Phillip and Larry Foust. Rochester had the great Maurice Stokes, Jack Twyman and eventually Oscar Robertson and Jerry Lucas. New York had a good team with Carl Braun, Sweetwater Clifton, Harry "the Horse" Gallatin (a Hawks' coach) and Richie Guerin (Hawks' coach).

The Celtics players have been mentioned throughout but don't leave out the Philadelphia Warriors with the likes of Neil Johnston, Larry Costello, Joe Grabowski, Jack George and Wilt Chamberlain.

Bob went back home in the summer to Baton Rouge, La., where he worked in the family real estate business. He'd work out with weights and work in the office. He met his wife, Carol, in Hawaii and to this day they've stayed in New Orleans.

After retiring at the end of the 1964–65 season, one nagged with injuries that limited Pettit to 50 games and a career low 22 points per game, he returned to Baton Rouge to become vice-president in charge of business development for a bank. He had told Kerner two years earlier that he would be leaving the game in 1965. He was still playing at a high level and could have hung around a couple of more seasons, but he reasoned in the long run, he would leave with his reputation intact and get started in his life's work.

"I think I made $55,000 my last year in basketball," Pettit said. "I inched my way up. It was never in quantum leaps. But that was good money then, and I was as happy as could be. Carol and I would be married in June of '65, and my last couple of years my in-laws would come up for a weekend to watch us play a couple of games.

"I worked for Baton Rouge American Bank from '65 to '69, and then I quit because I wanted to do something else. In the meantime, the chairman of the board who had hired me had put together a bank in Metairie, La., and I

High-scoring Boston forward Tom Heinsohn attempts driving layup over outstretched arms of Hawks Bob Pettit while Jack McMahon looks on.

became one of the eight-member ownership group. After that he eventually offered me a chance to buy the bank, a deal that he would finance 100 percent for me. So I went home and told Carol we were moving to New Orleans.

"We had a beautiful home in Baton Rouge, so two big tears rolled down her cheek, but she ended up loving the move and the home in New Orleans."

Pettit had come a long way from Baton Rouge High School where he sat in the stands, not on the bench until his junior year. Bob has always said it was the best thing that could have happened to him. He was cut from the squad twice, which helped him form that great determination and desire to overcome the obstacles in front of him. What he lacked in athletic ability he replaced with hard work.

The Pettit family reunion, June 2005. Front row, L to R: Mary Pettit, Leven Greene, Bobby Pettit IV, Crosseand Pettit. Middle row: Carol, Bob and Conway Pettit. Back row, L to R: Landon Greene, Peyton Pettit Greene, Lydia Greene, Lucy Jane Pettit and Robert Pettit III.

In his NBA encyclopedia biography, Bob tells what it took to finally make it as a 6-4 junior in high school. He didn't grow to his NBA 6-9 stature until his college days.

"Basically getting cut made me more determined," he said. "I'd go home and practice two or three hours in the afternoon just shooting around at a goal in our yard. When I did start getting more coordinated and got bigger, I was suddenly ahead of a lot of fellows who had been further advanced, but hadn't had to work at it and didn't have my drive."

At the 30th reunion banquet of the St. Louis Hawks in 1988, Blattner summed up the life of the greatest Hawk player.

"Pettit was one of the brightest young men as a professional athlete that I had ever known. He was gracious. He was humble. He was all the things you like someone to be. And of course, he possessed exceptional talent for the game. He had all the attributes I wish for a son, and he was a joy to be around.

"Pettit was a good businessman and always the leader of the group, not the follower. He wasn't vocal, but led by his deeds. He never, ever talked about his accomplishments, and in fact, when writers or others would say to him, 'Bob, you played a great game,' he would usually answer, 'Well, what about Macauley, he got those big five points when we really needed them.' That was Bob Pettit."

The incomparable Bill Russell has great praise for No. 9, whom he battled four times for championships and dozens of times over the seasons.

"Bob made the words 'second effort' a permanent part of this sport's vocabulary," said the Hall-of-Fame center. "He kept coming at you more than any man I ever played against in pro basketball."

Lenny Wilkens, later a teammate and fellow Hall of Famer, described Pettit as "a power forward who wasn't just a bull on the boards but could really score at a tremendous rate." You couldn't find forwards who could score much in those days.

Bob won two Most Valuable Player Awards, two NBA scoring titles, one rebounding title and was always among the top five rebounders. He owns a championship ring and had the famous 50-point game in the finals. And, oh yeah, he is the only player in NBA history to this day to win three Most Valuable Player Awards in the All-Star Game. Add them all up and they are the right ingredients for his first ballot Hall-of-Fame selection in 1970. He was also named to the 25th and 35th anniversary all-time NBA teams.

"The highlight of my career in St. Louis was winning the world championship and scoring the 50 points in the final game," Pettit said in summary. "Looking back at college and then the pros, I am pretty proud of what I was able to get done. It was a good career and I guess not a lot of guys have done much better."

Certainly an understatement. But in typical Pettit style, he stopped short of being totally satisfied with his basketball past. One could also predict what he said next.

"You know I was never totally happy or satisfied with the way I played," he said. "I always felt there was room for improvement."

Hawks' fans would say forget the humility and scream it at the top of the St. Louis Arch. There would not have been four trips to the finals and one golden ring were it not for the main cog in the wheel, Blattner's Big Blue, the Bombardier from Baton Rouge, No. 9 Bob Pettit.

Chapter Nine

Lil' Abner and the Texas Tornado: Cliff Hagan and Slater Martin

Sure, drafting Bob Pettit and trading for an established NBA superstar in Ed Macauley were two astute moves by the Kerner-Blake combo. In the end, however, and just as important to the creation of the championship mix, was the luck of having Cliff Hagan as a "throw in" of the Macauley trade and the cunning move of slipping veteran star guard Slater "Dugie" Martin off the roster of the Hawks top division rival and onto the St. Louis list without Minneapolis even knowing what happened until it was over.

Both occurred during the Hawks' second season (1956–57) and together they solidified the last two positions in the starting lineup, Hagan at forward and Martin at point guard. In the glib and colorful broadcasting style of Buddy Blattner, the duo became "Lil' Abner" and the "Texas Tornado"— Hagan for his jet black hair and handsome countenance akin to that of the newspaper cartoon character, "Lil' Abner," and Martin for his scrappy, tough style and hometown Texas drawl. To the NBA, they became two Hall-of-Famers.

Being a St. Louis Hawk was not envisioned by Hagan as he moved through his collegiate career with America's most famous college basketball program at the time, the Kentucky Wildcats. In those days people often went to school at mid-year, which Hagan had done in grade school, high school and college. He sat out a year in basketball, the 1952–53 season, when his Wildcats were suspended from play by the NCAA for charges that included illegal payments to athletes, academic irregularities, recruiting violations and gambling.

Three stars of Coach Adolph Rupp's 1949 Kentucky team admitted guilt and were arrested for point shaving. Hagan had nothing to do with those charges that occurred on teams before his time at Kentucky. The only punishment the NCAA could give a school, however, was to its current team.

Boston Celtics star Frank Ramsey and Hagan were teammates at Kentucky. Both were All-Americans waiting to be drafted after their 1954–55 senior season. As it turned out the Celtics drafted three Wildcats—Ramsey, Hagan and Lou Tsioropoulos. The trio looked forward to the draft because the NCAA in their ultimate wisdom, banned the three from postseason play after that perfect 25–0 year. They had all graduated the year before during the suspension, but had enrolled in graduate school to play this last season.

The frustrated players were told they couldn't play in the postseason right at the end of the season before the Southeastern Conference Tournament. With vengeance in mind, the three ripped through the tough competition of the tourney, including a hard fought win over Pettit's Louisiana State Tigers to win the title. Then Kentucky threw it back in the NCAA's face by declining their NCAA Tournament invitation. Hagan, a career 19-point per game scorer, set an SEC single game record one night that year against Rice, scoring 51 points.

Once the SEC tournament was over, the trio focused on the NBA draft and as Cliff said, "We were really happy to be drafted. Very few pro games were televised, but we did see the Celtics often, and then suddenly we were all drafted by them, which was exciting."

However, as an ROTC student, Hagan and company had a two-year commitment to military service to fulfill first. General William Garland at Andrews Air Force Base knew the players and would have them transferred to the base to play basketball. A bunch of All-Americans, including Hagan and Tsioropoulos, were on the team and won the worldwide Air Force championship both years.

"Ironically, in one particular game a guy named Richie Guerin was on the Marines team, and on free throws he would line up behind me and lean on me," remembers Hagan. "I'd had enough of it and asked the referee to get him off my back which he didn't do. So I got him off my back myself, which also cut open his eye. He had to leave the game to get stitches. Years later he's an NBA star with the New York Knicks, gets traded to the Hawks and I never get the ball passed to me again!

"Anyway, I'm looking forward to getting out of the service in the spring and report to the Celtics for the end of the season when I get a call from Coach Red Holzman of the Hawks. He tells me Boston had just traded my rights with Ed Macauley to St. Louis. I was immediately very depressed.

"St. Louis wasn't winning, Boston was on the verge of winning big and both my friends were there. Then to top it off, Holzman asks if I can play guard to which I say no. Then he said, 'Well we need you to play guard.' Bottom line I was not happy at all coming to St. Louis."

The next item on the agenda was to negotiate a contract with Kerner, which only deepened Hagan's disappointment.

"Ben was not known for paying good salaries and he gave me an embarrassing offer," Hagan said. "I was really upset on the way to the airport and he said if I made the team he would give me a $500 cash bonus, so I signed the contract.

"A week later I reported to St. Louis and went up to Knox College in Illinois for training. Holzman ran our feet off giving me terrible blisters. We were there two weeks and they were cutting players left and right. They went on an exhibition tour to Mexico City, but the Mexican team never showed up. We played each other in an intra-squad game instead and I got 40 points.

"But I guess coach didn't like it because I was thinking like a center and would go for the rebound while my opponent would be alone breaking the other way. He knew I couldn't play guard, further complicated by a knee injury that disabled me for almost two months.

"The good news was that Kerner couldn't cut me while I was hurt or I might have been gone. As the season started I would only play if we were 20 points ahead or behind. That lasted until Pettit broke his wrist in February and I was the only guy on the bench who could really play forward. I guess I did pretty well because I never left the starting lineup."

One thing about Kerner's one-year contract policy was that players were always hustling to earn another year. Hagan, like Pettit, Macauley, Martin and other Hawks were blessed on the one hand to have played in this golden age of pro basketball with so many all-time greats. But they were cursed on the financial side stuck in an era of financial hardship for owners of these teams in this still very young sport.

On the court, the magnitude of Hagan's scoring, rebounding and defensive prowess has been documented throughout game stories. In 10 NBA seasons, he scored 13,447 points in 746 games for an 18.0 points per game average. He was money in the playoffs, where in 90 games he racked up 1,834 points for a 20.4 points per game average, including a .453 percentage mark from the field and 80 percent performance at the free throw line. He appeared in five NBA All-Star games and was twice named second team all-pro.

In the 1957–58 championship season, just Cliff's first full year in the lineup, he was spectacular. Pettit may have won Game 6 and the series finale with his stunning 50 points, but the leading scorer of the entire playoffs was Hagan. He played the second most number of minutes only to Pettit, and scored almost 50 points more than Big Blue. Hagan scored 305 points, shooting a

whopping 50 percent from the field, for an average of 27.7 points per game. Pettit averaged 24.2 and Martin was next at just 11 per game.

"They thought I was a money player but I don't recall ever seeing any money bonuses for playing better in the playoffs," laughed Hagan. "I don't really have an explanation for why I excelled in postseason, but sometimes, you got lucky with who you were playing against in the playoffs. It would be the same guy for several nights in a row and if you had his number you could really produce.

"I would get points off fast breaks and I was pretty good at dishing off the ball, too. I often led the team in assists because a lot of our set plays were for Pettit and I was the feeder many times. He'd score and I'd get the assist."

In what the NBA called the "select circle" for a season, a list of the top single-game scoring performances each season, Hagan was always tabbed for a few highs. In the 1957–58 title year, he scored 40 points in a game three different times and 41 once, all four marks were in the league's top 20 individual high games of the year.

"I think I got a $1,000 raise for that season," he recalled with a chuckle.

One of the keys to his scoring ability was that remarkable hook shot performed with the grace of a dancer and uncanny accuracy. Where did he learn that picture book pose?

"A high school kid in Kentucky name of Bob Lavoy was about 6-7 and he'd get that ball out there in the palm of his hand, straighten out his arm and arch it to the basket," described Hagan. "I couldn't believe how good he was at it and how you couldn't reach it to block. I started doing it myself and just did it on my own through high school where I got some attention from a coach at the University of Kentucky during a spring break trip.

"His name was Coach Webb and he told me that when I was ready to go to college to come see him, so I went back and really worked hard on the hook. I could shoot a 10-foot hook shot with either hand, and eventually in college, started taking them from the free throw line or even from the head of the key.

"I learned to shoot it on the fast break fading away as I neared the basket instead of going up with someone who might block my shot. The secret of basketball is getting the shot off, isn't it? You surely can't score if it's blocked. I remember scoring 43 points one night in St. Louis against the Celtics and Bill Russell with hooks and reverse layups."

A little Q. and A. with Cliff Hagan gave an introspective into the thoughts and opinions of this Hall-of-Famer—stories that unfolded around the ever-changing, but always competitive Hawks up to his departure from the floor and to the broadcast booth in 1966.

Q. Your recollections of the final moments of the '56–57 Game 7 loss to the Boston Celtics when Alex Hannum threw the ball the length of court?

CH.   Of course we were down by two points in the second overtime with just a few seconds to play when in the timeout Alex sets up this wild play. First he takes me out of the ball game and puts himself into the lineup, which I really didn't like. Then again, we didn't call Hannum "Iron Head" for nothing. As you know the play throwing the ball off the backboard at the opposite end of the court right into Bob Pettit's hands almost worked but Bob missed the shot and Boston won. We called him Iron Head because he was so stubborn. But to be honest, you needed someone who was stubborn to do things his way or the highway.

Q. What about Bill Russell's play and impact on that series and later?

Cliff Hagan layup over Boston's Tom Heinsohn.

CH.   That was the Celtics first championship, which didn't really impress us. Russell had reported that year after the Olympics. He had won championships at the University of San Francisco, but he was a big guy who couldn't shoot the basketball. He could rebound and block shots, because he was quicker than the standard tall, slow, lumbering centers of the day. Today every team has a Russell on it.

Q. What about the Hawks' center Charlie Share and his role?

CH. Because of the attention Pettit, Martin, Macauley and I drew, people didn't give enough credit nor remember as much about Charlie. He deserves a lot of credit because he blocked, passed and rebounded for the rest of us to shoot. He was very important to our success.

Q. What do you recall about the players around the league you played against?

CH.   I had to guard a lot of fantastic ballplayers, usually the best forward on the opposing team because I was a little quicker, smaller and mobile than Pettit. When I'm asked who the best player I had to guard was, I answer without a doubt that it was Elgin Baylor. He was one of the first guys who at 6-foot-5 could put the ball on the floor, go to the basket, had an inside and outside game and had unbeliev-

able moves to boot. He had that move across the free throw line where he would sort of hang in the air and flip that jump shot. If you got in front of him, lead him and don't try to follow him up he was very clever at knocking your hands down, getting the shot off and you get the foul. For some reason I didn't have the reputation as a "defensive guy," but I always got the tough ones to guard.

Q. Your thoughts on the guards that ran the championship club and all those early division winners, Slater Martin and Jack McMahon?

CH. Martin and McMahon were throwbacks to the old time guards. Neither had a jump shot. Jack had a two-handed set shot and not much of a layup but was a great passer, particularly on the give-and-go play. Martin had a one-hand push shot, was quick and could really dog his opponent on defense. He was a fiery floor leader who gave the team confidence. I remember in training camp Kerner didn't want McMahon on the team, but those two guys were so unselfish and made us go. I just wish I would have listened a little more to McMahon learned to go without the ball, because he loved to hit you with a pass for a reverse basket. Against the Celtics Martin and McMahon would always hold those two great scoring guards, Bob Cousy and Bill Sharman, below their point average.

Q. Tell us about your early contracts and what you did to make ends meet?

CH. That first season I went to graduate school at Washington University and got my Masters Degree thinking I'd end up going into coaching or teaching. The third season, Share and I began working in the Hawks' office selling tickets in the summer. I might have been paid $50 per week. My highest salary in the NBA was under $30,000 a year (he'd make $10 million today). Ed Macauley was making two or three times my first-year salary, so I'd have him buy the newspaper and then I would read it. I couldn't afford it.

Q. Cliff, you always had the "clean cut," All-American guy image with the fans. You even did the Adams Dairy commercials with your whole family.

CH. I was a teetotaler, never had a beer, a cigarette or a mixed drink. I was Mr. Clean, even through the military. The only time I had a drink was after we won the championship and the guys told me to have a champagne cocktail.

Q. When Ed Macauley was being fired in the middle of the conference semi-finals against Minneapolis with the team down 3-2 going into Minneapolis in 1960, how did the team react?

CH. We had heard whispers through the newspaper reporter that because we were trailing and expected to lose the series, Macauley was losing his coaching job. We didn't know Ed wasn't aware of the story, but before Game 6 we got together as a team. I was really mad, and we went out and beat those suckers on their own court after which we went up to Ed and said, "We did that for you, coach," never realizing he didn't know what we meant.

Q. Take us to the end of your Hawks' career?

CH. I played for Coach Paul Seymour and we had a great club, but didn't win the postseason. I stayed through Richie Guerin as coach and finally quit in 1965. I did one miserable year on television with Jerry Gross and unfortunately had to leave St. Louis after 11 tremendous years for an opportunity in the American Basketball Association as a player-coach.

Hawks visit Hollywood set. Top, L to R: Slater Martin, actor Tony Perkins, Bob Pettit. Bottom, L to R: Cliff Hagan and Al Ferrari.

Hagan got three years at $30,000 each to coach the Dallas team in the new league where NBA stars were jumping for the money. Rick Barry had gone to the Oakland team from the San Francisco Warriors, and Cliff even ran up against his old teammate, Slater Martin, who crossed his path as coach of the New Orleans franchise.

"Ironically, I played in my first game after not playing for a season and scored 40 points. But it was easier when you were also the coach and the players thought they better pass you the ball all the time," laughed Hagan. "We made the playoffs my first two seasons, and even though I'd never coached anything before, the writers selected me as the "Professional Coach of the Year" in the state of Texas. But you know what, I really wasn't cut out to be coach.

"I couldn't stand players who didn't take the games seriously, and would come into the dressing eating popcorn or drinking a soda. I couldn't understand how guys on the bench weren't ready to come into games. They weren't ready to take a pass, take a shot or know what was really going on in the game. Things had really changed for the worse so I retired from coaching after Christmas 1969 and went back to Lexington, Kentucky, back to my beginnings."

Hagan went from a developer, developing the Lexington Mall, to a bank vice-president of development, to the assistant athletic director and then athletic director of his Kentucky Wildcats. He also opened 12 successful Cliff Hagan's Ribeye Restaurants in Kentucky and North Carolina.

It was evident early on that Lil' Abner with his familiar No. 16 (after beginning with No. 6) was destined for success, an irreplaceable piece of the Hawks' championship wheel.

Pettit and Hagan, the one-two punch were rookies with the Hawks, born and bred from Day One in the NBA. However, the player the Hawks received to provided the ignition switch to the St. Louis machine was a proven NBA all-pro with seven years experience and no less than five championship rings. Martin had a four-year run of success as the general of the Hawks' platoon.

In Chapter 3, the devious yet cunning way Martin got to the Hawks was laid out as one of the Kerner-Blake tandem's most ingenious moves. Veteran leadership is what the team lacked and Slater was the perfect partner for McMahon. The Hawks of the previous season couldn't dribble the ball down the court—McMahon included.

"Everybody pressed St. Louis and it was pretty easy pickins' for awhile," began Martin. "When I got there in December of 1956 I told the team just give me the ball and get the hell out of the way.

"When Mr. Kerner acquired me he asked if I thought we could win a championship and I said sure we could because we've got Bob Pettit. But it might take a couple of seasons, which turned out pretty prophetic."

Martin said that first year team was really pretty good with Macauley, Coleman, Share, Pettit and Hagan. They melded very well. Martin's job was to net assists for the scorers, but he was dangerous offensively as well, pumping in 10 points per game.

"When last-place Rochester beat us the last game of the regular season, it forced a three-way tie and we had to play Ft. Wayne and then Minneapolis to win the division," said Martin. "We had to play at Washington University, but that became a real home-court advantage for us. The fans were so close they might as well have been sitting on the bench and when a ball went out of bounds, a fan would just catch it! They were great because they would holler and scream at the Pistons and they could hear every word."

Dugie drifted onto another subject, shaking his head as he talked about the transportation mode for the team in those days. The mention of Ft. Wayne reminded him that Fred Zollner, their wealthy owner, could afford an airplane for his team, while the Hawks and everybody else rode the train.

"We rode the train the evening before games in the East just to get there in time. We slept in those little berths, which was fine for me but not for those tall fellows," said Martin. "Those big guys had to sleep with their knees bent. I remember big George Mikan with the Lakers (6–11) wanted to stay with me

Hawks team boarding Ozark Airline flight

because I was small and I could get up on top so he could have the lower berth. Then he would put suitcases at the end of his bed to elevate his feet, which hung over the end of the bed."

In contrast to his fierce competitive nature on the floor, Dugie was a quiet guy, according to his teammates. He doesn't recall a lot of detail about some of the significant games or moments, but he has a few one-line memories. About Game 4 in the first Boston championship series in the 1956–57 season, he had blotted out the memory of the five-point loss in St. Louis, a real turning point in the series. But when told that Bob Cousy had 31 points in that game he said: "Whew, I didn't do a very good job guarding Couz, did I, so I figured I better do something fast."

When told Cousy was held to just 15 points in the Game 6 in St. Louis' win that sent the series back to Boston tied 3–3 Martin said:

"That was more like it, I owed that effort to the ball club. Then I remember in Game 7 it looked like we had lost when Cousy went to the free throw line with 12 seconds left and they led by two points. But he missed the free throw and we got the ball. I told Cousy while he was shooting that he had steel arms. It was very unusual he would miss, but we lost on the missed shot by Pettit anyway."

About the last shot by Pettit, what did Slater think about the floor-length pass by Hannum off the backboard to keep the clock from starting since there were only a couple of seconds left in the game?

"When he said that was going to be the play in the huddle during the time out, I thought he was absolutely nuts! How's Alex going to throw the ball the length of the court in this pressure-packed situation and hit the backboard? Hell, Hannum couldn't spit in the ocean if he was on the beach!

"I was standing near him on the court when he heaved the ball and I was surprised he hit something in the building much less the backboard. Give him credit. He did what he said he would do."

Martin summarized Hannum, whom he had recommended for the coaching job over himself, this way:

"Hannum couldn't shoot it from no place. He threw that length-of-the-

Celtic Hall-of-Fame guard Bob Cousy makes razzle-dazzle pass to forward Tom Heinsohn as Hawks Slater Martin (#22) and Ed Macauley attempt to defend as Boston's Bill Sharman (#21) watches.

court pass like a baseball. He was a big, strong man, strong as a bull. He was a carpenter in the off season, built houses and was hard as the nails he drove in. Hannum drank like a fish, but he could get us going."

Martin's leadership was a critical factor in the championship season, but you'll never hear it from him. He had little to say about the final series with Boston except to recall how they were pressing the heck out of him with the few seconds remaining in Game 6 with the Hawks ahead, 110–109. He wanted to keep the ball in his possession to insure the victory and not gamble a pass but. . .

"I couldn't keep the basketball and not get fouled. So I reluctantly passed it to Macauley and he shocked me by throwing it up in the air with a couple of seconds left," says Martin. "I think the place went crazy at the buzzer and we were World Champions."

It might be true that the first great guard rivalry spoken about by people covering basketball at the time were the battles between Martin and Cousy.

They were two tough, stubborn athletes who could shoot, pass, dribble and play defense. Cousy was 6-1 and 175 pounds from Holy Cross and came into the league for the 1950–51 season. Martin was a shorter 5-10 and 170 pounds from Texas and entered the league in 1949–50.

Their career numbers stacked up this way. Cousy average 18 points, seven assists and hit 80 percent of his free throws over 13-plus seasons. Martin averaged just short of 10 points per game, four assists and shot 76 percent from the line. Cousy played 13 years, played in 13 All-Star games, was All-NBA first team 10 times, led the league in assists eight straight years and won six world titles. Martin played 11 seasons, played in seven All-Star games, was a tenacious defender and ball hawk, and won five world titles.

Cousy was a proud man who always said: "Nobody can beat me one-on-one, but the guy I disliked playing against the most was Slater Martin. At that time in the late '50s, the St. Louis Hawks were easily our most intense rival. Nothing epitomizes that rivalry any better than the match-up of me against Martin. His skills matched mine very well, and he had the speed and quickness the bigger guards didn't have to keep up with me. I always had to tell our big men, 'You better set a lot of picks for me to shake loose from Martin.'"

Martin expressed his sincere thanks to Cousy for the kind words and returned the praise to his most fiercely contested rival.

"Couz was so tough. He could do anything with the damn ball. He was truly the first 'magic' in the NBA. I used to call him 'Mandrake' after the magician. He was a great and smart ballplayer who could pile up the assists and points. He had the guts of a burglar. He could shoot 10 times, miss 10 times and shoot 10 more times and he might make them all!

"Bob had an unusual shot, that little old fade-away jumper, and a set shot that was hard to get up on. He was just a fabulous competitor and it was always fun to play him."

Winning five national championships puts Martin in a special category of NBA players, but he doesn't hesitate to single out the most satisfying of the five.

"I clearly enjoyed the win over the Boston Celtics because we were the underdogs. The games were so competitively. You had the arrival of big crowds and national television that made it all special," he said. "The Hawks? Well, we just put it together, but Pettit made us win. If you want to know the truth we wouldn't have won a damn thing without him."

Martin found Kerner to be tough, but entertaining, and he was really fond of him. He liked a guy who was his boss but would sit down and play cards.

"Mr. Kerner used to play poker with us all the time, he loved to play poker," said Martin. "He would often play in a hand with Pettit alone. Pettit would never show his cards unless somebody called him. If you wanted to see his cards, you had to pay."

So could you beat Kerner at poker?

"He was a pretty good player, but he would raise at the wrong time. He was just getting in the pot.

"However, Kerner cared about the team and always wanted to improve it. He made us dress up by buying us sport coats, a gray blazer and gray trousers. He wanted us to look good when traveling."

Slater wanted to add about the Hawks' great broadcaster, Buddy Blattner. To a man, the Hawks' players of the early era agree Blattner is deserving of basketball Hall-of-Fame recognition.

"Buddy was first and foremost a real gentleman. He always worked from notes and was well prepared for the game," said an admiring Martin. "He'd talk basketball, baseball and table tennis. You know he was a national table tennis doubles champion. I'd sit down and have a drink with Buddy all the time. He gave me the nickname 'Texas Tornado.'

"Buddy gave the team a personality. He really built the image of the Hawks. When he said over the radio, 'There walkin' the wrong way,' everybody in St. Louis knew the foul was against the Hawks. Today marketing departments of several people do nothing but build the team's personalities and image. But back then, Blattner was a one-man band on the radio with his own dictionary of terms identifying and humanizing us players to the fans. Buddy was the very best."

It didn't really matter to the feisty Martin where the games were played, but he does remember some of the nuances of the various NBA venues starting with St. Louis.

"I liked Kiel Auditorium as a home court," he said. "Kiel had a sticky floor, which I liked to play on. Some floors in the league would be a little slick, but on a sticky floor you could stop and start, turn and twist. Then Kiel was loud when it needed to be.

"When you're concentrating on the floor you really don't hear the crowd, but I could hear the Murderer's Row group of people sitting with Mr. Kerner at center court and the first row under the basket. They would work hard at getting under the skin of our opponents and they were good at it. Players remember when they would run off the court after a ball, the crowd was so close they would collide and they could count on getting an extra elbow or arm thrust into their mid section by a fan."

Speaking of fans, it wasn't while he was a Hawk, but instead while a guard on the Lakers that he recalls a funny moment in one of those NBA doubleheaders where four teams went into a city to play on the same night. Boston was playing New York in the feature game at Madison Square Garden and the Lakers played Detroit in the first game.

"Near the end of the game we (the Lakers) were ahead by seven or eight points and Detroit was throwing in the ball. As I was running down court on defense I thought maybe I could steal it," explained Martin. "As I turned

around the guy threw it right to me, and as I ran off the floor I just threw it, a hook shot, and it banked off the backboard and went in from way out. The fans were going crazy and I didn't know why because we won by eight or ten points and neither team was at home.

"When I came out of the locker room to watch the second game, the fans gave me a huge ovation. They just clapped and again I didn't know what in the hell they were so happy about. The public relations man for the New York Knicks came over to me laughing, 'Your shot beat the spread, you beat the betting line, and now they all want to go double up on the second game.' That's something you're never aware of while playing.

"The hardest place to play was Philadelphia. We didn't like the city or the arena. Besides Kiel, the Garden in New York was the best place to play," continued Dugie. "We also played in some very interesting arenas in the early days in places like Oshkosh, Wis., Sheboygan, Mich., Waterloo, Iowa, and the Tri-Cities (against the first Hawks' team). They were just high school gyms."

Dugie had a few random thoughts about his Hawks' days, which overall he considered his best experience in the NBA. He began with the experiment the NBA tried with a 12-foot basket.

"I was playing in Minneapolis and we were hosting the Milwaukee Hawks when the league tried out this 12-foot basket in a league game and it was horrible," laughed Dugie. "I couldn't make a layup. Two extra feet made it a long, long way up there. When you tried a set shot and hit the rim, you needed to run back to center court to retrieve the basketball. It was just stupid and it went away after one game."

As well as Kerner put teams together, promoted the games and got fans to come to the building, why couldn't he win more championships? Dugie says the revolving door of coaches hurt the team the most.

"It was a fetish of Kerner's and a real detriment to the team," said Martin. "He should have kept Hannum for a long time. All Alex wanted was a well-deserved raise. When he made me coach I told him I had to still play a lot and couldn't stay up with all the substitutions the other team would make. It got to be a real pain in the butt. I didn't like it a bit."

What about the three-point shot? If it would have been a rule back then, would you have scored a lot more points?

"I wouldn't have paid any attention to a three-point shot rule," he said flatly. "I didn't take that many shots, six or seven a game, and most of them were driving the lane. My job was to bring up the ball, set up the offense and pass the ball for the real shooters, Pettit and Hagan. That was the whole story and it was a great ride."

<blockquote>
Chapter Ten
</blockquote>

From Len Wilkens to Richie Guerin

A s the Hawks entered into their sixth season in St. Louis, now firmly entrenched as a premier NBA franchise with a rabid local following, a third professional sports team announced they were transferring to the Gateway City. Perhaps the Hawks success as a compliment to, instead of a competitor, of the baseball Cardinals encouraged the new rivals to make the move. The team, of course, was the National Football League's Chicago Cardinals, who announced on March 13, 1960, that they were officially transferring to St. Louis.

The football Cardinals would compete for the sports dollar with the Hawks more than baseball since their seasons crossed over for three months. However, tickets to basketball games were a bargain in comparison to football. The St. Louis newspapers wrote articles about the high price of tickets, which were $4, $5 and $6, putting St. Louis in the upper echelon of NFL ticket prices in the NFL. The team claimed the size of Busch Stadium (the former Sportsman's Park), which had a seating capacity of only 32,000, the smallest in the league, was the cause for the high prices. Still, they sold like hot cakes despite the grumbling.

Tickets for the Hawks' games now seemed very reasonable, especially for a team that had met with so much success so quickly. They had made the playoffs in all of their five seasons, advancing to the conference finals four times and the NBA Finals three times. General admission tickets were just $1.50

with reserved seats going for $2.25, $2.75, $3.00 and on the floor for $3.50.

The football Cardinals would go 6-5-1 that first season. At the gate, they averaged just over 23,000 fans per game (9,000 under capacity) with a single-game high attendance of 26,000 recorded that first year.

Still, the arrival of the NFL meant shrinking newspaper space and air time, which the Hawks and the baseball Cardinals had to share with new Grid Birds. Kerner had left Milwaukee in '55 because a new pro team, the Braves, was bumping his team off the front page of the sports section and garnering a lot of the sports fans' time and money. The Big Red, as the new football team was nicknamed, would become a fixture in the city though the Hawks would remain the far superior team on the field of play.

In addition, the unpopular and unwarranted firing of Macauley by Kerner robbed the Easy One of another opportunity. As Western Division champions in the 1959–60 season, the head coach of the Hawks was entitled to coach the Western Division in the NBA All-Star Game in the ensuing season. Macauley had played in the game seven times.

Paul Seymour took Macauley's place as the Hawks' new head coach and of the West squad. The West won the All-Star Game that season, 153–131, with the Hawks' Pettit leading all scorers with 29 points, while teammate Clyde Lovellette had 21. Ironically, the All-Star Game was played at the place Seymour had called home for 13 seasons—Syracuse, N.Y.

There were feathers to smooth with the club's veterans who were angry at Macauley's release. But Seymour managed to get them on the same page and even inherited a new weapon that would ease the transition in the backcourt after the retirement of Slater Martin.

According to the stories, Seymour had watched Providence College guard Len Wilkens play in an all-star game, and told super scout/G.M. Marty Blake to strongly consider drafting him. The youngster was a quiet kid who wasn't impressive to look at, wasn't considered fast, but was clearly "sneaky quick" said the scouts. The signing of Wilkens was discussed previously as Macauley's final real duty.

Seymour was not without coaching credentials, it was just the manner in which he was hired. Seymour had 13 good seasons as a player at Syracuse where he was known for his "stick-like-glue" defense and brilliant floor play on offense. He also managed to average up to 14 points per game for a couple of seasons, and was a three-time NBA All-Star.

As coach of the Nationals for four seasons, he took the Syracuse teams to two second-place and two third-place finishes. His teams reached the Eastern Division finals in two of the four years always running up against the brick wall of the Boston Celtics.

The Hawks were still a very good ensemble headed by the big three of Pettit, Hagan and Lovellette. Veterans guards Ferrari and McCarthy were still

Hawks superstars Bob Pettit, Cliff Hagan and Len Wilkens sign contracts for smiling owner Ben Kerner.

around with the rest of the members, Green, Foust, newcomer forward Woody Sauldsberry, rookie Fred LaCour and Dave Piontek. Sauldsberry was noted for his unusual "line drive" jump shots that looked like laser beams and would bang off the rim and ricochet all the way to near center court sometimes.

Wilkens, meanwhile, would become the club's new adhesive, but not until he, too, could overcome the skepticism of an owner who didn't support his drafting in the first place.

"No, Ben didn't want Lenny, but then again, there were a lot of guys Ben didn't want," laughed Blake. "We held our rookie camp out of town and Lenny showed up and frankly didn't play very well. Benny kept bugging me saying Wilkens can't shoot, he won't score, get rid of him. I kept saying relax, it's July not October."

Wilkens memory of the rookie camp echo those of Blake. It was a good thing for the Hawks he already signed a contract, because Lenny had turned

down an offer to play for the Industrial Basketball League for $9,000 and could have just said the heck with it after Kerner's griping got back to him.

"I heard that somebody, apparently the team owner, was telling people I was a terrible player, and I guess I wasn't very good at the time," said the now retired star player and coach. "When the team asked me to come to summer camp, I had just sprained my ankle pretty badly. When I got there, I was really hurt but didn't want to tell anybody about it and there wasn't a trainer around. I just tried to play through it and didn't fake it very well.

"We went back to St. Louis and opened camp at Concordia Seminary in Clayton where I guess I still didn't impress Mr. Kerner," continued Lenny. "I wanted to get the ball up and down the floor quickly and the Hawks were really a 'walk-it-up' type of team. He didn't like my style of play and he was looking for someone to replace Martin. You just can't expect a brand new rookie to walk in and replace the style and success of a perennial all-pro and Hall of Famer like Martin in a day."

Wilkens didn't doubt his ability from day one. After all, his college credentials included an National Invitation Tournament game in 1960 against guess who? The St. Louis University Billikens with Lenny's Providence Friars coming up the victor, 64–53. Kind of spooky, isn't it?

The 1959–60 season began and the club got off to a strong start. After splitting the first two games of the year, the Hawks reeled off five straight victories to go to 6–1 and by Thanksgiving they were 12–4. Wilkens, though, wasn't much of a factor because his playing time was sparse.

"I wasn't getting hardly any playing time, just a minute or two per game, and every time I made a mistake I'd come out," said Wilkens. "I remember vividly one practice, we were in New York to play the Knicks. I had a real good practice. Afterward, Seymour, who used to call me 'Rook' came up and said, 'Hey, Rook, how come you don't play like that in a game?'

"I turned around and said, 'How would you know? I'm never in the game.'"

After Wilkens thought about his remarks, he figured he'd never get in a game again. Meanwhile, in the locker room after the practice Lenny was getting dressed and ready to visit his family at home in New York when the coach came over and sat down with him and started talking.

"So Rook, what's on your mind?" asked the coach.

"Coach, every time I get into a game and make a mistake I'm immediately taken out. But other new guys make mistakes and they continue to play. What's the deal?" asked Wilkens.

Seymour responded saying, "You might have a point there." Then he left.

"However, at the game against the Knicks in the Garden that night Coach Seymour called my number early," said Wilkens. "I immediately got the ball and saw Cliff Hagan cutting for the basket, and I fired the ball right over his head into the stands! I said to myself, 'Oh crap, now I'm really out.' But for the first time coach let me stay in and I wound up getting 14 points with eight assists. The next game I became a starter."

Seymour inserted Wilkens over Kerner's angry objections. Kerner instead wanted the rookie benched long term. But when Lenny produced the points and assists plus made several steals, the arrogant Kerner took credit for making Seymour play the rookie.

"Kerner stood at mid-court after we won puffing a big cigar," said Seymour. "He bellowed out to anybody who would listen that he wouldn't trade Lenny Wilkens for the whole Knicks' team and $50,000!"

The Hawks continued to roll. The high-powered offense was producing a lot of points, 132 against Syracuse on November 24, 139 on the road against the Knicks, and a humiliating 143–110 romp over the Detroit Pistons on December 6.

After a pair of victories over the Los Angeles Lakers and a 105–99 victory finally against the World Champion Celtics on December 28, the Hawks' record was a lofty 23 wins and just 9 losses.

Wilkens had to prove himself to his teammates as a rookie, but it wasn't long before they realized how effective he was running the team. Pettit prospered under the new floor leader, posting his second best points per game average (27.9) and posted his best overall season ever in the NBA. Big Blue set career team marks in eight categories including: games played (76), minutes played (3,027), field goal attempts (1,720), field goals made (769), field goal percentage (.447), rebounds (1,540), assists (262) and total points scored (2,120). He was fourth in total points in the league and third in rebounding.

"The first guy I won over was Bob Pettit because he was the key guy," said Wilkens. "I knew if I made sure he was going to get the ball as much as possible, I would be accepted by the club."

Hagan and Lovellette saw good times as well. Lil' Abner averaged 21.8 points per game and finished second on the club in assists with 381, which was ninth best in the league. Lovellette stood toe-to-toe with Cliff, tallying 21.9 points per game, the second best season in his distinguished NBA career.

The Hawks rolled through the second half of the season just like the first. They began on December 29 at 23–9 and ended on March 1 off a scintillating 110–97 thumping of the mighty champion Celtics in the Boston Garden for a 46–27 record. Along the way, St. Louis had showed unusual prowess against the now two-time defending champs, winning four times in seven tries.

The regular season ended on March 11 with a Hawk 130–87 massacre over the Philadelphia Warriors, to wrap up the best season in franchise history. The regular-season record of 51–28 would stand as the best until the franchise's final year in St. Louis. Seymour's team had jelled thanks in no small part to the precise play of the sinewy, quiet man from Brooklyn, N.Y. He played bigger than his 6-0, 180-pound frame.

"It turned out to be a pretty good year for me even though I didn't shoot much because the coaches didn't have many plays for the guards," said Wilkens. "Then again with Pettit and Hagan, why would you? I still broke the team record for points by a guard with 890."

Though the Los Angeles Lakers finished a whopping 15 games behind the Hawks in the Western Division standings, that club led by Baylor, West, Hot Rod Hundley and Rudy LaRusso was gaining momentum every game. St. Louis had overcome a 3–2 deficit just the year before when Macauley's team rallied to win Games 6 and 7 to get to the NBA Finals. This challenge for the Seymour crew would be just as tough.

The Western Division finals began in St. Louis on March 21, 1961, and the Lakers took charge. In fact, L.A. won Games 1, 3 and 5, two of which were played in St. Louis. With that kind of road playoff success, victory seemed a likely scenario for the Lakers. But again down three games to two and on the road in L.A., that old St. Louis playoff magic popped up once again. In a thriller, the Hawks nipped the Lakers, 114–113, to push the series to a Game 7 at Kiel for the second consecutive year.

Local fans were treated again to another spectacular series-ending contest. Three of the first six games were decided by four points, including two one-point affairs. Game No. 7 was no exception. The Hawks would post a breath-taking 105–103 decision to eke out a 4–3 series victory, moving into their fifth and what would turn out to be final NBA Championship Series.

"The playoffs in the first year were a great experience for me because we had so many crucial situations in the Lakers' series," said Wilkens. "In Game 4 we were down two games to one and on the verge of losing again on the Lakers' floor. I'll never forget the ending. We were down one point so we drew up a play for Pettit. But Bob missed the shot, and the ball fell to me.

"There were about six seconds left when I got it, so I drove to the basket where both Elgin Baylor and Jerry West grabbed my arms as the buzzer sounded. A foul was called and with no time on the clock I went to the free throw line all alone. Don't think my knees weren't shaking. I took a deep breath, the crowd was roaring for me to miss and I made both shots to win the game, 118–117. That made my season."

That series took a big toll on the team's energy as the Hawks prepared to again battle the giants from Boston. The Celtics had gone 57–22 during the regular season and had buried the Nationals in a ho-hum five-game Eastern Division semifinal series. They were just getting better each year with their roster of All-Stars: Russell, Cousy, Sharman, Heinsohn, Sam and K.C. Jones, Sanders, Ramsey, Jungle Jim Loscutoff, the baseball player Gene Conley and Gene Guarillia. The juggernaut was chugging along at full speed.

The finals started April 2 in the Boston Garden, the night following the dramatic St. Louis win over the Lakers. Tired from the travel and mentally exhausted from the stress-filled semifinal series, the Hawks were no match for Boston and took a 129–95 drubbing in that first game.

What was different in this series as opposed to the other three championship rounds played by these two dominating teams was that the Hawks didn't win either of the first two contests. They were competitive in Game 2, but fell 116–108 defeat.

"This was my first experience in the championships so I wasn't sure what to expect, but I did know the Celtics were a great basketball team," said Wilkens. "I thought we competed every night, but with the exception of Pettit and Hagan, I didn't feel the rest of the team had much confidence in their ability to play with and beat Boston. It still was a thrill as a former Providence College guy who heard stories about the Celtics all the time."

Kiel cooking was good for the home team in Game 3, but the old magic wasn't there in Game 4. The only win of the series was a tough 124–120 victory in the third game. The next night, however, reality set in. Boston was dominant in carving out a decisive 119–104 triumph under the Kiel lights to take a 3–1 series lead. The finale in Boston was academic as the Celtics rolled over Pettit, Hagan and the underdog Midwesterners, 121–112, for their fourth world title in five seasons.

Despite the rout in the finals, Seymour still had had an excellent first season as head coach. The team had some personnel changes to adjust to and had to adopt yet another new playing system. However, after a year it was apparent the relationship of coach and owner, Seymour and Kerner, was not a match made in heaven. Kerner would try to force his ways and ideas on his coach and Seymour would have none of it. Seymour followed his own instincts and beliefs and let the chips fall.

What happened next was not the failure of coach or owner particularly, but a set of circumstances that caused the club to unravel. The NBA was changing, also, with new, young stars emerging and one new franchise being born as the league continued to expand to the largest U.S. cities.

The "original eight" had included medium and small markets, but that had begun to change after the Hawks moved to St. Louis. Now it was happening again. The Rochester Royals shipped out to Cincinnati, Ohio, and the Ft. Wayne Pistons moved to Detroit, Mich. Only Syracuse, N.Y., remained as a city with less than one million people.

Jumping back into professional basketball after losing its Basketball Association of America team in 1950 was the sprawling Midwestern commercial center, Chicago, Ill. The Chicago Packers were brought into existence and added to the NBA's Western Division with the Hawks. They were the league patsies in the beginning, going just 18–62, but they did boast of having the NBA Rookie-of-the-Year in 6-11 Walter Bellamy, who averaged 31 points and 19 rebounds per game. Incidentally, Bellamy would spend the next 14 years in the league, including five with the Atlanta Hawks, before landing in the NBA Hall of Fame in 1993.

St. Louis had won 51 games, won the division by 15 games and were the clear favorite to repeat again. But the problems began in the off season with the odd draft of a small-college guard named Cleo Hill. He was Seymour's pick out of Winston Salem Teachers College along with second-round pick Ron Horn, a 6-7 big man from Indiana University, who was joining the club after a year in the service.

"Cleo Hill was Seymour's guy and he had put all his chips on this player coming through," said Hagan. "We still had Johnny McCarthy, Si Green and of course a young budding star in Len Wilkens, but he wanted Hill in the top group and I never did understand why.

"He was a guard and a guard's got the ball all the time. I mean he must have thought he was the second coming of Bob Cousy—which he wasn't."

Ferrari the son of a New York City chef, who had played so well in those first years in the second half of the 1950s, remembers vividly the Hill acquisition and the catalyst to failure it was for the team.

"The problem with the drafting of Cleo Hill began and ended with Coach Seymour who was quoted in the local newspapers saying, 'Hill is the guy who can lead us out of the wilderness.' We players went crazy. We had just won 51 games, gotten to the finals again and stretched the powerful Boston Celtics to seven games just the year before and this kid needs to lead us out of the wilderness?!

"Seymour had set this kid up to fail. The story created a bad atmosphere around the team. Hill was not the brightest kid on the block nor was he a great player. Seymour tried to make him a great player when he just couldn't play at this level. He was a great small college player who couldn't cut it in the pros.

"Unfortunately, some people took our team situation with Hill the wrong way and began to conclude that their were racial undertones on the team. Hill was a black man, which caused a lot of finger pointing on the ball club. It wasn't true. Len Wilkens, an African American, had just finished a spectacular season as our backcourt leader replacing a Hall-of-Fame guard in Slater Martin. But like it or not it all contributed to us going down the chute for the season."

In Seymour's defense, the need for a standout guard to start the season was real because Wilkens had been called to military service because he had been an ROTC student at Providence. But Hill was not the answer and Wilkens, after creating all that positive new chemistry the year before, would only play 20 games all season.

"I was an officer and they let me fly in to see the first game of the season, and I even wore my Hawks' uniform," said Wilkens. "This rookie named Cleo Hill had 20 something points, but he also always had the ball. I heard the players were upset even to the point that Seymour had to fine a couple of them for supposedly not passing the ball to Hill."

At mid season of what was becoming an awful year, Lovellette, averaging 20 points per game, tore his Achilles tendon and was out for the season with more than 40 games to go.

"I felt it go in a game at Philadelphia and I knew right away I was done for the year," said Lovellette. "It just further complicated an already tough season."

The great pros that they were, Pettit and Hagan worked overtime at trying to reverse the team's fortunes. Big Blue had his best scoring season, averaging 31 points per game, and Hagan added 22 points per game. But the two superstars couldn't overcome the rest of the club's shortcomings.

Chaos reigned as Seymour, hailed as a great coach the season before, was fired after just 15 games because Kerner recognized the magnitude of the Hill problem. He hired Fuzzy Levane as Seymour's replacement, a journeyman player from the late '40s pre-NBA era, but he couldn't stop the bleeding. The Hawks went a ragged 20–40 before Levane was dismissed as coach with six games left in the season.

Those six games were coached by Pettit as a player-coach. He did win four of the six but had no interest in continuing the coaching role. The final record for the year was a stunning 29 wins against 51 losses and fourth place in the five-team division. Thanks to the expansion team in Chicago, the Hawks didn't finish in last place.

"The 20 games I played in the 1961–62 season were mostly weekend games on a pass from the military," said Wilkens. "When I came to play for the Hawks it was a very different team from the one I played for my first year. Lovellette wasn't playing and we had new guys like Barney Cable (forward from Chicago), rookie Bobby Sims and Larry Foust, who was only playing sporadically with injury. The coach was Fuzzy Levane and I can tell you a funny story about Levane that was told to me by my Providence College coach Joe Mulaney.

"Fuzzy Levane was the coach of the New York Knickerbockers and I guess he stuttered a lot. Joe was saying that when Levane came into the huddle for a time out he stuttered so much that his guard Carl Braun used to take over and tell the players what to do. Then one time Fuzzy got a little upset.

"When Carl started to tell the team what to do in the huddle, Levane stuttered, 'W-w-w-w-wait a m-m-m-m-minute, I-I-I-I'm the c-c-c-coach. I-I-I-I tell them w-w-w-what to do!' Braun said, 'Okay,' but as Levane tried hard to get his words out the clock was running down for the time out and finally he just said totally flustered, 'C-C-C-Carl, you tell them w-w-w-what to do.'

"Now here's the first time I'm meeting Fuzzy knowing this story. The team was playing in Cincinnati and our announcer Jerry Gross picked me up at the airport and took me to the hotel. I was set to play for the Hawks that night but I knew nothing about the team. As we come into the lobby there sat Fuzzy waiting for me and I was introduced to him.

"As he started to stutter 'H-H-How are you?' I rudely started to laugh. Levane says to Gross, 'W-W-W-What's wrong with him?' I apologized but I couldn't help myself initially because all I could think of was that story in the huddle during the timeout and the clock running down.

"Fuzzy and I did become very good friends and he really was a wonderful man," said a humble Wilkens. "It's a shame he couldn't get the team turned around, but at the time nobody could do it."

The worst season in franchise history was over and it signaled the end of a fantastic era for the Hawks, who had four appearances in the championship round and a near miss fifth in five seasons. It could be argued today that the Boston Celtics of that time constituted the best team in NBA history and St. Louis' upstart Hawks had given them an unforgettable challenge to the throne for all those years.

For Kerner and Blake the challenge for the future was clear. Pettit, Hagan and Wilkens were the established core but it was time to search for new personnel to compete with the likes of the Lakers' tandem of West and Baylor, Philadelphia's monster of the middle, Wilt "The Stilt" Chamberlain, the Celtics dynasty and the incomparable Oscar Robertson at Cincinnati.

Once again Hawks' management made some astute decisions in drafting players, proving the value of Blake's somewhat unprecedented player scouting techniques. If you don't pay a lot of money to players, which Kerner couldn't and didn't do, then you'd better find some sleepers in the draft that other teams don't know much about. That's when Blake was at his creative best and Kerner would usually grant his wishes.

"Before we moved to St. Louis, nobody ever scouted," recalls Blake. "I took my first trip on a bus from Milwaukee to Ft. Leonard Wood near Waynesville, Mo., to see Al Bianci and Sam Jones play basketball. It cost me $28 and I don't think Benny ever reimbursed me for it. Other NBA teams didn't know what we were doing. I decided to do what we used to do in baseball where I started scouting by making files on all the players in college. I started calling them, using other people's phones because Kerner was on the brink of bankruptcy. This was before the move to St. Louis.

Back to the spring of 1962, Blake had to find some players capable of bringing the Hawks back to the top echelon of the NBA fast. St. Louis fans were used to winning and the impatient Kerner didn't want to return to those days that he had experienced before and risk the loss of his following.

"I'm the one who dug up all those players we drafted and nobody but me was out there in the field really scouting players," said a proud Blake sitting in his hotel room at the 2004 NCAA Final Four in St. Louis. Wearing a retro St. Louis Hawks T-shirt, he poured over the current crop of college prospects as the NBA's super scout now some 40-plus years after his Hawks' beginning.

"We needed a couple of good players badly to complement Pettit, Hagan and Wilkens in '62, so I'll tell you how I found Zelmo Beaty," he said. "I was doing a story for Esquire Magazine and I had to go to a town called Cut and Shoot, Texas. The story was about a boxer named Harrison who was a heavyweight fighter about to fight some big name boxer like Rocky Marciano.

"When I got there his father had this old chicken ranch and a boxing ring in the yard where his son was boxing. The old man asked me what I did for a living and I said I was the general manager of the St. Louis Hawks pro basketball team. He answered by saying he wanted me to see this big high school kid play ball so he gets his flat bed truck for the trip into town with me and a couple of chickens riding in the back with his son.

"There I saw Zelmo Beaty playing a pick-up game as a high school senior in a segregated park. I got to meet his coach, Dr. Leroy Moore. So later I knew about Zelmo when he went and starred in the NAIA at little Prairie View A&M. He was 6-9, powerful smart and I'm the only guy who knew about him. We could sign Zelmo."

With the center slot solved Blake searched for depth at forward and guard and found a pair both in the draft and by dealing. Blake drafted guard John Barnhill from Tennessee State University in '59, but in a strange turn of events, Barnhill decided not to play and stayed an amateur to get more experience. The additional preparation paid off and Barnhill was a better player when Blake grabbed him out of a new league, the American Basketball League, where he was selected as the Most Valuable Player after averaging 11 points per game.

Hawks center Zelmo Beaty during college career

"I just wanted to get a college degree and coach in high school, an opportunity offered to me in my senior year, but I had to tell the high school in Tennessee that it wasn't enough money," said Barnhill. "Then they said I could also be the assistant baseball coach as well as basketball and they could pay more. But it still wasn't enough to live on so I went into the service.

"I only had to serve six months after which I followed my college coach, John McLendon, to the Industrial League in Cleveland and then to the American Basketball League. That's when Marty Blake showed up to a game and asked me to come to the NBA and play for the Hawks. Frankly, I didn't come then because I had heard the Hawks were very prejudice towards African-Americans at the time. He kept asking and finally I decided to come and see for myself. It all worked out great and I enjoyed St. Louis and playing for the Hawks."

A second guard was a fourth-round pick, and again from a smaller institution. It was one that Blake could easily get down to see. Just three hours from St. Louis in Carbondale, Ill., was Charley "Chico" Vaughn, a 24.5 points per game scorer for the Salukis of Southern Illinois University. He had a slingshot for a jumper and was an aggressive player both ways.

In the summer before the 1962–63 season, the Hawks made a move that would pay off in the upcoming season by dealing Shellie McMillan, a forward who stayed less than a season with the Hawks, and Ferrari to Chicago for the rights to Ralph Davis (who never played) and Kansas' Bill Bridges, who was playing in the rival American Basketball League.

Late in the 1962–63 season, the Hawks were ready to exercise the rights for the burly, talented 6-6, 235-pound Bridges. The American Basketball League was making a run at the NBA. Bridges had decided to play for the Kansas City Steers to play for ex-Hawk star and now ABL head coach Jack McMahon. The Hawks' front office sent their public address announcer and friend Jack Levitt to Kansas City to nab Bridges.

"Ben Kerner calls me up and asks me to come down and see him one day, and tells me the story about this good player he's interested in named Bill Bridges," said Levitt. "Ben told me the league was going to fold and we needed to sign Bridges. He said to go to K.C. for tomorrow's game and I said okay.

"I get on the plane to Kansas City and upon arrival I call McMahon and tell him I need a ticket for his game that night. He asked me why and I said you're league is going to fold and I want Bridges. Almost in shock he said he knew nothing about the league folding, but gives me the ticket.

"As I watched the game, there's no doubt Bridges is a great player, but he's limping badly, favoring his knee. After the game, I start talking to him under the basket and show him the contract I had in my hand. I told him I didn't want to be doing anything underhanded or out of line, but the league was going to fold and he would be playing for the Hawks in the NBA. That changed the whole conversation.

"All of a sudden Bridges perked up, told me his knee was okay and sure enough, shortly after the league folded and because we had his rights, he signed. Bridges always had the knee problem and it really held him back from greatness as a player, but he wouldn't have the knee operation ever. Now we did have a helluva team again with Pettit, Hagan, Wilkens, Beaty, Bridges and Barnhill."

The revitalized Hawks were given a new coach, their ninth in St. Louis, by signing Harry "The Horse" Gallatin, a Hall-of-Fame player for the Knicks and Pistons. Gallatin signed a two-year contract in March 1962, receiving the highest contract ever paid to a St. Louis coach. He came after having coached the four previous years at Southern Illinois University where Chico Vaughn played.

Hard-nosed forward Bill Bridges

Gallatin had local roots and fit the bill for Kerner who seemed mesmerized by former great ballplayers in the league. They were his favorite coaching material. He was a native of Wood River, Ill., just outside of St. Louis, and was a first-round draft of New York in 1948. He played 10 seasons in the league and was known as an "Iron Man," playing in 682 consecutive games and averaging 12 points and 13 rebounds per game. He played in eight NBA All-Star Games and was a first team All-NBA player in 1954. That met Kerner's qualifications to be a coach.

The Gallatin era and the new flood of stars on the Hawks began on a high note, but as the days went by and unforeseen struggles recurred, the unsettling style of Kerner would keep the Hawks in transition throughout their remaining days in St. Louis.

Chapter Eleven

The Roller Coaster Years

The worst season in franchise history was fresh in the Hawks' memory as the 1962–1963 campaign approached and St. Louis fans were hoping it was an aberration. A combination of key injuries, the unfortunate loss of a star player to the military and lack of team unity over the Seymour-Hill issue could have been the blame for the troubling year.

Around the NBA, the Lakers had made their abrupt, but lucrative move from Minneapolis to Los Angeles in the 1960–61 season, and now an East Coast franchise dating back to the first days of the Basketball Association of America was taking the bus out of town. The Philadelphia Warriors and their No. 1 attraction, Wilt Chamberlain, took a one-way ticket to the Golden Gate setting up shop in San Francisco, Calif. Meanwhile, after two last-place finishes, the Chicago club decided that changing their identity might change their luck. Thus, the "Packers" became the "Zephyrs."

Of interest to the Hawks, their fans and all NBA followers was the announcement of the retirement of 34-year-old Bob Cousy, perhaps the greatest ball magician of all-time, from the Boston Celtics. Couz said this would be his last season of leading the now four-time champion Celts. They were introducing a bright, young star to their championship lineup by the name of John Havlicek.

Another season, another coach for the Hawks, this one came from the

Hawks coach Harry Gallatin (1962–1965)

college ranks. Harry Gallatin, a four-year veteran of the hardwood in Carbondale, Ill., where he coached the Southern Illinois University Salukis, was coming to the Hawks, who had nowhere to go but up.

"It seemed that when I came in as coach, things on the team were kind of loose, with everybody going their own way and not really contributing to the team effort," analyzed Gallatin. "I wanted to immediately bring everyone on the same page, including basic conditioning and fundamentals. I even put together a program of isometrics that had the players thinking, 'Boy, this guy Gallatin is from outer space.' But we had used them so successfully at the college level at SIU that I wanted the pros to try it. We also had documentation about how many injuries the exercises had prevented.

"It wasn't unusual for someone to see the players running up and down the steps at Kiel with a player riding piggyback on their backs during practice. We needed to be stronger and quicker.

"I was fortunate to have three new players come in at the same time as I did, so they were my guys learning my way," continued Gallatin. "Charlie Vaughn played for me at Carbondale, and I remember the importance of drafting Zelmo Beaty. I told Mr. Kerner that before we commit to a player, I need to go down and play one-on-one with the player prospect. I went down to Prairie View A&M and played with Beaty. People kept saying, 'Who is Zelmo Beaty?' But what a great choice he turned out to be."

Added Wilkens: "When I got back to the team I find it's changed quite a bit and for the better. I couldn't get there for training camp because they had canceled all leaves in the military. What I noticed when I did get there was a more unified team and a coach with bulldog tenacity. If Harry made up his mind about something he wasn't about to change it. Harry had coached Vaughn in school, Barnhill was already in place and I thought the three of us got along real well."

"The Boomer" Lovellette was traded to Boston making room for Beaty at center. Ultimately, the backup to Big Z was Gene Tormohlen, a bruising 6-9 center swiped from the fast-folding American Basketball League. Nicknamed "The Bumper" for his rough, tough style by Blattner, he was Barnhill's team-

160

mate with the Cleveland Pipers, which was among the top amateur teams in the nation. The burly middle man had averaged 14 points and 15 rebounds per game at Cleveland. He came to the team in early January.

As Wilkens worked back into Gallatin's system after easing out of his military commitments, the Hawks' starting guards were Vaughn and Barnhill. The front line of Pettit and Hagan was still producing plenty of points and rebounds, backed by Tormohlen and Bridges, both of whom came in January with more than half the season gone. Of course, Beaty manned the center spot and once again the Hawks had a talented team centered around their two Hall of Famers.

The season began and again it was clear that the Hawks were going to be winners more often than not. Skill wise, this was an excellent ball club anchored by the two superstars. Beaty was a solid replacement, a good scorer and better rebounder than Lovellette and proved to be more durable. Wilkens was becoming an NBA star. In addition, Barnhill and Vaughn added quickness, good defense and some important points. When Bridges arrived, youthful toughness was added to the forward rotation in the lineup.

"Coach Gallatin had like a hundred plays and I can remember him commenting that I would have to learn them all," said Wilkens. "All I saw was the ball going to Pettit, so I said to hell with all those plays, I know how to get the ball to Bob. Later, Harry was bragging about how I knew his offense!"

There was chemistry on the team all season long and there was consistency in the team's play. The nightmare of Seymour's second season was a fading memory and the fans at Kiel were filling the seats and loving the excitement again. Something to note and contrary to what some people believed, the transition of the Hawks from the last all-white team to win a national professional basketball championship to being half African-American was having no effect on fan interest. The business was all about winning, though keep in mind, the ball club's stars were still Pettit and Hagan.

As had been the case in winning seasons past, St. Louis was dominant at home and won the regular season series over six of their eight opponents. Only the two best teams in basketball, Boston and Los Angeles, claimed more victories than the Hawks in head-to-head play. Kiel Auditorium remained the domain of the Hawks and continued to represent a tremendous home-court advantage with the steady stream of customers to games. Gallatin's squad posted a 30–7 record at home, and four of those losses were to the Lakers (3) and the Celtics (1). Against the combination of San Francisco, Chicago and Syracuse, the Hawks were a glistening 14–0!

Gallatin's team went 48–32 and finished second in the West by five games to the Lakers, who were 53–27. Boston ran away again with the Eastern Division at 58–22, followed by Syracuse, which posted the same record as the Hawks. Pettit had another brilliant season averaging 28 points and 15 rebounds per game, putting him fourth in the NBA in both categories. He was named first team all-pro for the ninth straight time and played in his ninth straight All-Star Game. His 2,241 points lifted his all-time and league-leading career total for an active player to 17,566. Only the retired Dolph Schayes from Syracuse with 19,115 career points was ahead of Pettit.

The balance of the team was just that—a balanced scoring machine. Hagan's scoring production dropped from the 20s to 15 points per game, but that was in part due to the increased scoring coming from the guard position. Wilkens was often in the 10- to 15-points per game range, as was Barnhill (11 per game) and Chico Vaughn (10 per game). In addition, Beaty would supply another 10–12 points.

Postseason fever returned to St. Louis and a familiar foe faced the locals in round one. The Detroit Pistons finished third in the Western Division, but a distant 14 games behind the Hawks. It was no match with the Hawks winning the best-of-five series in four games, taking three games at home.

The division championship series with the heavily favored L.A. Lakers almost took St. Louis to a fifth trip to the NBA Championship Series, but they fell just short. After losing games one and two in L.A., the Hawks swept both home games to even the series 2–2. After each team won one more on their home court, it went to Game 7 in L.A. Gallatin's courageous bunch battled, but the Lakers pulled away for a 115–100 victory ending the Hawks strong run. Both Hagan and Beaty had played the final three games with significant injury problems

Now retired and living in the Los Angeles area, Barnhill remembers a critical play in Game 2 in Los Angeles that could have been the difference between winning and losing the series. Game 1 had been a spirited battle won in close fashion, 112–104, by the boys of Hollywood, so the Hawks knew they could play with the Lakers on their own floor. The Game 2 final score was a heartbreaking 101–99. Barnhill recounts the Game 2 disappointment.

"We should have won that game," Barnhill said. "I'll tell you why we lost. Remember Cliff Hagan was a better free throw shooter than me. We had the lead by one point late in the game and we're stalling with the ball. The coach wanted Hagan to have the ball if the Lakers are forced to foul instead of me dribbling around. Next thing you know Jerry West steals the ball from Hagan, runs down and makes a three-point play hitting about an eight foot jump shot while being fouled. The buzzer sounds as we get the ball inbounds and we lose. I felt awful for weeks thinking I was the guard and I should have taken control of the ball at the end of the game."

The Lakers took on Boston again in the NBA Finals. In Cousy's career-ending series, the Celtics dominated a very good Laker squad. The Celts held series leads of 2–0 and 3–1 before closing out the Hollywood kids four games to two. It was the Celtics' fifth world title and fourth in a row.

Encouraged by the achievements of the revised cast of Hawks, Gallatin entered his second season on the bench and St. Louis was thinking of getting back to the title round. The 1963–64 roster looked identical to the one that finished the previous season. The question was did the Hawks have enough firepower to get past L.A. and into the finals?

While Hawks' fans were looking for a return to the greatness that they enjoyed in the 1950s and early '60s, they were also getting used to a new broadcast voice. A significant marketing piece for the Hawks called it quits in St. Louis when Blattner resigned before the start of the 1963–64 season. It was a blow to the loyal listeners who had become Hawks' fans because of Buddy's exciting, colorful and familiar calls. No longer would "He's walking the wrong way" signify to the listener that the foul call was against the Hawks.

Blattner had taken the job as the voice of the Los Angeles Angels of baseball's American League, unable to resist a love of the game he had once played professionally. The opportunity to be in America's second-largest market didn't hurt either. At first he tried to combine the duties with Hawks' basketball, but the length of the season and carryover to the spring became an irritant to the Angels.

"The Angels became really irked at me for missing spring training games in the desert," explained the still-golden voice, who retired to the St. Louis area. "The Angels were playing in Anaheim as they do today, and were battling for recognition in L.A. against the Dodgers. The Dodgers had the great Vin Scully as their broadcaster, and here I was, the Angels play-by-play voice out in the Midwest doing pro basketball.

"I'd get phone calls from the bosses saying, 'Where the hell are you? Who do you think you are, you need to be here!' So I'd had no choice but to give up the Hawks broadcasts. It was a very painful decision."

It was also a personal loss for Kerner, his friend and long-time employer, and the owner knew it would be a marketing loss for his franchise on his most important medium of communication, KMOX Radio. Kerner's wife, Jean, spoke about the loss of Blattner.

"Ben's feelings about Buddy leaving were mixed," she began. "He was terribly upset to lose the best announcer in basketball and a friend he shared many things about the team with. On the other hand, he knew it was a great business opportunity for Buddy in his profession. He didn't have that much work here in St. Louis, just basketball. The Cardinals had Harry Caray, Jack Buck and Joe Garagiola, so there wasn't going to be any baseball work here."

Blattner's replacement was not a stranger to the broadcasts. Jerry Gross, who had been the color commentator for the Hawks' games, was promoted to the play-by-play position. He was a personable man with a pleasant tone and was in his fourth year of broadcasting the Hawks' games. Gross had even done some color commentary on Cardinals' games on radio and television and had done some pre and postgame Cardinals' shows.

Replacing Gross as color commentator was Al Ferrari, the former Hawks' player. After being traded by the Hawks to Chicago for Bill Bridges, Ferrari called it quits and was returning to St. Louis to begin life in a new profession.

Hawks broadcaster Jerry Gross

"I was traded by the Hawks to the Chicago expansion team for the 1962–63 season playing for a great guy and coach, old Hawk Jack McMahon, and we were pretty good," remembers Ferrari. "I played with Walt Bellamy, Terry Dischinger and Johnny Cox, but I hurt my knee. I had to come home and went to work for Lincoln National Life Insurance where I've been for 40 years."

With expectations running high, Gallatin was asked to describe his relationship after one season with the irascible Kerner, who had yet to have a coach longer than two seasons with the Hawks?

"Well, you know winning cures all ills and I thought the first season had gone fine," said the upbeat coach. "Mr. Kerner was a good observer. He questioned me from time to time, even had me come into his office on off days to talk about the team and personnel. He was one of the best owners as far as staying on top of what was going on with his team.

"There were times when I felt that maybe some of the questions were a little bit out of order. Ben liked to talk about the team so as coach I was pretty much in constant conversations with Kerner."

Kerner would ask questions such as, "Why did you substitute say for Cliff Hagan at the start of a game and why did you make other specific decisions on the court? Why didn't you call a time out when the opponent was on a big scoring run?"

"You needed to explain it if you wanted to get out of his office," said Gallatin. "Then once you explained your decisions, he would either nod and accept it or tell you it might have been done better another way."

As the season began and despite the solid success of the year before, Gallatin knew he would be judged quarter by quarter, game by game, and week by week in the executive tower. Just winning the division wasn't near enough. Kerner was consumed with beating Boston.

With Wilkens beginning to assert himself as a dominant guard in the NBA, the season opened with Barnhill and Vaughn splitting time at the off-guard position. Pettit, Hagan and Beaty controlled the front court. The tough boys who came in and spelled the scorers were Bridges and Tormohlen. The unit had chemistry and depth to challenge the league's best teams.

Then right before the season began, a major trade evolved that, while bringing a big name player to St. Louis, threatened to disrupt team harmony because it meant somebody would have to do more sitting and everyone less shooting. Was this deal made out of need or one made just because the star player just became available?

Richie Guerin, 31, the 6-4 eight-year veteran of the New York Knicks, came to the Hawks on October 20, 1963, in what was reported to be the largest cash transaction in the history of the NBA. St. Louis gave New York

$50,000 and a second-round draft choice the next season. Guerin was known as a scorer having averaged 21, 21, 29 and 21 points per game the previous four seasons as a Knick. However, New York failed to reach the playoffs in any of those years.

Born in the Bronx, raised in Queens and a player at Iona College, Guerin had the look, the accent and the rugged attitude of a pure-bred New Yorker. The Knicks hadn't won with Guerin in their lineup so they were ready to cut back his playing time in favor of youth. They had drafted Art Hayman, a youngster from Duke University, which didn't sit well with Guerin.

"I wasn't ready to start that phase of my career yet, and I told New York I would appreciate getting traded to a contender if they could make it happen," Guerin said. "We played two games and bang, I was traded to St. Louis."

A New Yorker in the '50s coming out to the wild west in St. Louis could have been a culture shock, but not according to the aggressive backliner.

"I enjoyed St. Louis right from the start," Guerin said. "After playing seven

Hawks player-coach Richie Guerin

years in the league you knew what different cities were all about and this move was okay with me."

But Gallatin's concept and Guerin's goals were not on the same page. A man who was used to being a go-to guy for points was asked to set-up the Hawks' future Hall-of-Fame front court of Pettit and Hagan. Frustration set in quickly and an uneasy atmosphere was building on a team that had jelled so well the year before.

"I felt I was being totally misused," said Guerin. "Gallatin was the coach and his plays were designed for his front court players. I said to Harry, 'I don't know why you got me in a trade if you don't intend to utilized my strengths. You already have Barnhill and Vaughn doing what you're now asking me to do.' So I went to see Mr. Kerner.

"Of course, Ben talked me out of asking for a trade and somebody told me to just go out there and improvise when plays are called. He said to start playing my own type of game, which I did and the rest of the season got better."

Richie may have thought it went much better and the final results of the season were close to the victories of the previous year. Gallatin, however, didn't have the same perception about how things were going.

"After really turning the team around the first season I coached, I thought the second season would really take off," moaned Gallatin. "But as we went along for a little while and everybody saw their role, we began to have dissension regarding playing time and who should have the ball."

Wilkens also noticed the difference: "I remember we started the season with a pretty good team winning games. Then we acquired Richie Guerin, a tough, hard-nosed player from the Knicks. We continued to play all right and then began to struggle when we had some injuries.

"One game in particular Coach Gallatin took me out, took Richie out and took Pettit out of the game at the same time in Boston because we had a solid 12-point lead. Boston makes a run and he rushes Pettit in, waits awhile and finally puts Richie and I in the game. Boston ties it and wins it by two points.

"Richie was enraged and he let everybody know it. He and Gallatin were feuding at the time, adding fuel to the fire. Soon after Hagan and Ritchie got hurt and suddenly you look over from the court to the crowd and you see Guerin sitting at center court with Kerner while the other injured players are sitting on the bench. You couldn't help but notice that as a player. When we went on the road Guerin was always playing gin rummy with Ben Kerner."

Certainly the fans didn't know what was going on and the team played well enough to finish second again in the Western Division with a 46–34 record, just two games behind the league leading San Francisco Warriors at 48–32. The Lakers finished third at 42–38 and would be the Hawks' victim 3 games to 1 in the divisional playoff round.

The Warriors were sparked by the tremendous play of its two towering stars, Chamberlain and rookie forward Nate Thurmond. Ironically, San Francisco was directed by a man who probably should have still been the coach of the Hawks. Instead Alex Hannum was guiding the Warriors to the Western Conference Finals against the Hawks.

It had to be a bitter internal battle for Hannum and Kerner, but neither let on publicly. The Hawks pulled together and surprised San Francisco, 116–111, in the City by the Bay in Game 1. The Warriors evened it in Game 2 and the teams split again in St. Louis, squaring the series a 2–2.

The teams again split the next two games, setting up a Game 7 in California. The Hawks stood proud that they'd taken one of the league's biggest physical teams and top team defensively (giving 102 points per game) to the limit. But Hannum got his revenge, advancing to the NBA Finals, 105–95. Pettit averaged his usual 27 points and 15 rebounds per game for the season, finishing fourth in scoring and fifth in rebounds.

"We could have won that series with San Francisco, but what happens all the time is that you're playing great and then all of a sudden you lose a game you should have won and it costs the series," Guerin clearly recalls. "We were up 2–1 playing Game 4 in Kiel all set to go up 3–1 with still another home game ahead in Game 6, when the Warriors rally and beat us at the buzzer 111–109 to tie the series going back to Frisco. It was frustrating."

While it looked like the club was on the right track after two near misses in the conference finals, things weren't all that rosy. The NBA was getting stronger and stronger, players were bigger and bigger and keeping up with the competition was a big chore.

"The last two seasons for me were fun, playing with guys like Len Wilkens, Zelmo Beaty and of course, Cliff (Hagan)," said Pettit, who had just finished another stellar season and who wanted to go out on a high note. "But attendance at our games had slipped from almost 10,000 every night to about 5,000, and I was ready to go on with my life."

The other great superstar in the city, Stan "The Man" Musial had taken off his Cardinals uniform for the last time and retired at the end of the 1963 season. Pettit was now following suit a year later. Without Pettit, winning now came more into focus for the fans. Adding to the competition, the Cardinals had become a championship-caliber team again, just missing the National League pennant in '63. The Redbirds followed that with their magical run in '64 that featured the greatest comeback in baseball history, roaring back from 6 1/2 games out of first place to win the National League pennant in 1964.

While the Hawks were set to take the floor for their 10th season in St. Louis after announcing the retirement of their all-time greatest player, the Cardinals were playing and winning the '64 World Series in a seven-game thriller over the powerful and star-studded New York Yankees, who were led by Mickey Mantle, Roger Maris, Yogi Berra and Whitey Ford. The football Cardinals, meanwhile, had gained a foothold with the fans of the fast-growing NFL team.

Competing with those fan distractions was Kerner's first concern, but Gallatin had his own worries trying to keep pace in the Western Division with a team that was about to be hit with a rash of injuries and on-court problems. Through the first 33 games, the Hawks were struggling at 17 wins and 16 losses.

One change off the court came in the broadcast booth where the Hawks' big sponsor, Anheuser-Busch, hired a new color analyst for both radio and television. A surprising but well received choice was Bill Sharman, the former star shooting guard of the Boston Celtics. Sharman joined the voice of Gross and Harry Caray on KMOX Radio and KPLR-TV, Channel 11. Sharman was hired directly by A-B chairman August A. Busch, III, and his duties included public relations work for the brewery.

A new lineup started the season, and though it had great promise, it didn't jell early. The guards were Guerin and Wilkens, the center was Zelmo Beaty and the forwards were Pettit and Bridges. Obviously now missing from the starting lineup on a regular basis for the first time since early in the 1956–57 season was Hagan, now playing the sixth-man role off the bench.

The season began and ended with M*A*S*H theme as a rash of injuries plagued the club throughout. Pettit missed 30 games, Guerin missed 23, reserve forward Mike Farmer was sidelined for 20 games, and Barnhill was out for 36 contests. In addition, Jeff Mullins, a much-heralded rookie from Duke who would later become a star performer with the San Francisco (Golden State) Warriors, missed 31 games. Also hampered for short periods were Vaughn, Wilkens and Hagan.

One of the injuries contributing to the slow start was Guerin's torn calf muscle, putting him out of the lineup for about 15 games. Continuing injuries to Pettit also reduced his playing time dramatically.

One positive amid the failures was another good draft choice by super-scout Blake, who selected bulky 6-7 230-pound Creighton University's Paul Silas, a ferocious rebounder who rotated through the front line with Bridges, Pettit and Hagan. The acquisition of Silas made the Hawks one of the strongest rebounding teams in basketball. Silas would play four years with St. Louis and 13 more years in Phoenix, Boston, Denver and Seattle.

Guerin describes what happened during that rough time for the club when he and Pettit were sidelined by injury.

"The team just wasn't playing as well as they could with the same basic talent that had won so much the year before," said Guerin. "You can get off to a bad start, but then get going and everybody forgets about it. But this owner never had the patience to wait anything out. Harry got blamed for whatever shortcomings we were going through at that particular time."

Said a disappointed Gallatin: "The teamwork we had created earlier just seemed to disappear. I don't know if the players thought we had done well and didn't have to work as hard or what. I was spending a lot of time on motivation and I just couldn't get the players to play hard enough."

Wilkens remembers the events leading up to yet another coaching change after a couple of excellent seasons and a slow start to Gallatin's third year.

"We went to New York to play the Knicks and Coach Gallatin was under a lot of pressure to turn things around," said Wilkens. "We'd lost a bunch of games and I'll never forget what he wrote on the board in the locker room. It said: 'It's not the dog in the fight that counts, it's the fight in the dog that really counts.' It fired us up and we won the game that night.

"Harry was a happy man on the flight back home, but whether he realized it or not he had an unhappy ball club on his hands. I guess management knew the deal because when we landed in St. Louis, G.M. Marty Blake was waiting for the plane. Harry never got back to the office I don't believe. He was fired on the spot and Guerin was picked to be the coach."

"There was so much unrest on the team during Harry's final days. There was a collective sigh of relief when Guerin took over, and our record the rest of the season is testimony to the improved atmosphere. Richie was a good politician and Bill Bridges had a great relationship with Guerin, which helped pull it all together," Wilkens added.

Bridges had problems relating to Gallatin. In the season's fifth game, a key early season contest against the Celtics played at the St. Louis Arena to accommodate what would have been an overflow crowd of almost 13,000, the Hawks were on fire. They

Cliff Hagan shows huge hands in palming ball.

maintained large leads of 10 to 16 points through much of the game.

However, in the second quarter, Bridges suddenly exploded in Gallatin's face, cursing him. Gallatin sent the big forward to the bench and when Bridges continued to insult his boss from his bench position, Gallatin came roaring to his seat and sent Bridges to the dressing room for the night.

The Hawks ended up blowing the giant lead and squandered the game, losing 119–117. Boston's Tommy Gun Heinsohn hit the game winner inside a minute to play. The Celts then sent out a young defensive fivesome to shut down attempts by Pettit and Hagan to tie the score. Beaty was spectacular scoring 30 points with Pettit chipping in 24 and coming off the bench after Bridges was ejected, Hagan pumped in 22 points. The game was one of the most frustrating losses of Gallatin's short season.

Merry Christmas and a Happy New Year, Harry, from "Uncle Bunky" as the *Post-Dispatch's* Bob Broeg fondly referred to Kerner. Coach Gallatin was dismissed from his post on December 27, 1964.

A highlight of the year came early while the club was in its doldrums. Pettit was in his 11th and final season, fighting off injuries and just trying to finish strong. On Friday, November 14, the 6–4 Hawks were taking on the 6–5 Cincinnati Royals. With Cincy up 43–34 just 1:20 seconds into the second quarter, Pettit made NBA history by hitting a jumper to become the first player in NBA history to reach the 20,000-point plateau.

After his trademark jump shot swished through the basket, the game was stopped and a ceremony was held, led by the Royals' team president Carl Rich. In his comments Rich said about Pettit to the thunderous crowd: "You've made basketball history throughout you're great career, but tonight you made history that future players will be trying a long time to emulate."

Standing at mid-court, Pettit received the game ball from Rich. Alongside Kerner, Bob's teammates, all of the Royals and a large cake from the fans of Cincinnati, which read: "20,000 points, Congratulations Bob." As always Pettit was ever so humble in his response.

"To say I'm pleased would be the understatement of the year," Pettit said. "I've achieved other records before, but this is the one I've really worked for and really wanted. I'm proud and humble to be here tonight."

It was a regular-season record only, as Pettit had many more points in play-off competition–194 to be exact. In addition, it was announced in the St. Louis morning newspaper that a local TV affiliate, KTVI, Channel 2, would air a "Bob Pettit Special" based on his life story and his drive for 20,000 points. The irony of the show was that its host was none other than Pettit's longtime teammate and coach, now Channel 2 sportscaster, Easy Ed Macauley.

Interestingly, when Guerin took over as coach in the 34th game of the year, and to its conclusion, the Hawks style was more open and players like Wilkens were getting more scoring chances. The budding NBA star finished the year averaging 16 points and five assists per game. Guerin had 14 and Beaty added 16 a game, a career high, to help the club gain a 45–35 record entering the playoffs.

But that promising regular-season finish was followed by a complete collapse in a brief and ugly playoff appearance. The opponent was the Baltimore Bullets, who finished a dismal 37–43 and a distant third in the standings. The visitors stunned St. Louis at Kiel in Game 1, 108–105 and after the Hawks evened the series smashing Baltimore by 24 points in Game 2, the series shifted to Baltimore. Maryland's favorite team promptly swept the Hawks into the harbor beating them twice to win the series three games to one.

Pettit's fabulous Hall-of-Fame career was over. Injuries had reduced his effectiveness and he realized it was time to retire. As Wilkens said, "We always knew when the ball was thrown up, nobody came to play more than Bob Pettit, and that last season he just couldn't do it consistently. He knew it was time."

Guerin added: "He was truly the greatest competitor. Bob Pettit played that series against Baltimore literally on one leg. The top of his leg and stomach were basically purple from internal bleeding. But he never ever gave up."

Looking back, Gallatin had a discipline and philosophy of coaching that he adhered to and it resulted in a lot of success for the first season and a half, but in his mind, the players strayed from his program, from the start of the 1964–65 campaign.

"Everyone has to understand their role on the ball club and understand that their contribution to the total success is their reward and not how many points they score," he explained. "If their job is to rebound, pass the ball, get the ball to the open man or set screens all day, that's the kind of teamwork you need to win in the NBA and not worry about your personal headlines. You have to constantly stress that team play is more important than individual success.

"I know you're going to say that can't happen in the NBA because when the player is fighting for a contract they talk about individual stats. But I always believed a large part of a player's contract should be based on the team's performance. It sure would help the coach motivate the team as a whole."

Gallatin confirmed the stories that his relationship with Guerin and Bridges was rocky and contributed to his team's inability to get untracked the last year.

"Guerin and I were teammates in New York and I actually recommended to Mr. Kerner that we go get him when he became available before the 1964 season," admits Gallatin. "We needed some experienced help in the backcourt, but it didn't work out well between us because he wanted more playing time and more shots than I did. The same held true for Bill Bridges who also wanted a larger role than I had planned."

Guerin had averaged 29 points per game just a couple of years before in New York as the club's main scorer, but with Pettit and Beaty in St. Louis, the leading scorer's role was taken. Gallatin concluded that Guerin couldn't accept being a contributor and not the main attraction. However in the end, it was Gallatin who paid the price with his job, not Guerin who endeared himself with the owner.

However, Kerner did recommend Gallatin for a job with the Knicks, his old team. It was a kick for Gallatin to coach the team for which he had played with for nine years, if even for only a couple of seasons.

Now it was Guerin's team that would take the floor for the 1965–66 season, the 11th for the Hawks of St. Louis. He was the fourth coach to assume the dual role of player-coach in the Gateway City, though two of those tenures were only days in length. Martin and Pettit combined didn't exceed three weeks as player-coach in their brief tenures.

About to take the floor at Kiel Auditorium was the first Hawks' team ever to begin a season without No. 9 Bob Pettit, Big Blue, the Bombardier from Baton Rouge. Attendance at home games had shrunk to a half filled auditorium although Kerner had boasted early in the year about attendance being up 35 percent over the previous season. It was just after four home games that a story ran in the *Globe-Democrat* proclaiming the increase.

Standing: Bill Bridges, Bob Pettit, Zelmo Beaty, Cliff Hagan. Kneeling: Lenny Wilkens, Richie Guerin.

The four games in question had attendance totals of 10,121 for the home opener vs. Cincinnati, another 8,613 against Philadelphia, some 12,389 at The Arena for Boston and 6,108 for the lowly Detroit Pistons, an average to more than 9,300 per game, which was a huge number for the NBA in those days. Kerner was ecstatic and it was a good promotional ploy to tout the totals in the paper so fans who hadn't attended might think they were missing something.

"We drew the biggest opening-night crowd we ever had at Kiel, and one of the biggest since we came to St. Louis," Kerner boasted. "Yet we were sandwiched between the hysteria of the World Series (won by the St. Louis Cardinals in 1964), the first home game of the football Cardinals and the opening of the St. Louis Braves hockey season (the minor league team played at The Arena). When we moved here in 1955 there were no other local fall or winter sports, yet we're still up a third."

Unfortunately, that growth didn't hold up during the year. Remember, the Hawks were playing in the smallest facility in the NBA. And a winning program was vital to maintain the status quo, which was a tough road to hoe for an owner who couldn't play against the growing number of super wealthy owners.

Chapter Twelve
Jumpin' Joe to Sweet Lou

The 1965–1966 season was a tale of two teams, the first struggling to adjust without the retired Pettit and with Hagan, who was on the downside as a reserve in his final St. Louis season. During the regular season, the club was trying to find its way with a new look, a new fast break style and a new chemistry.

Buying into this new system became essential for customers at Kiel as the roster signaled a new era. Beaty had become a fixture as the hard-working, slick-shooting center surrounded by the rugged Bridges and Villanova rookie Jim Washington at forwards. The Hawks had become a team whose strength was now in the backcourt with veterans Guerin and Wilkens backed by Vaughn and Barnhill.

The regular season was beset with more losses than wins in the first half, and the club needed one of those Kerner-Blake trade jolts to rejuvenate the team. They came up with one of the best deals in club history that restored the credibility and breathed new life into the proud Hawks.

Barnhill and Vaughn joined little-used John Tresvant and were sent to Detroit for the Pistons' former No. 1 draft pick, Jumpin' Joe Caldwell, who had made the NBA All-Rookie and All Defensive teams. Also coming to St. Louis was Rod Thorn, a third-year guard who was averaging in double digits.

"I can't deny it, this was a really good trade the Hawks made giving me up to Detroit for Caldwell," admits Barnhill. "Joe became a tremendous

St. Louis Hawks 1965–66 Team. Front row, L to R: Gene Washington, Mike Farmer, Zelmo Beaty, Gene Tormohlen, Joe Caldwell, Sam Silas. Back row, L to R: Trainer Fred Franz, Richie Guerin, John Barnhill, Len Wilkens, Cliff Hagan, Bill Bridges, Jeff Mullins and Chico Vaughn.

player for them and really ignited their season."

Indeed it was a pivotal trade for the Hawks. It was, in fact, the best deal made since Macauley and Hagan came from Boston almost a decade earlier. Caldwell became a lightning rod for the fans to cheer and the players to rally around. His quickness and leaping ability kept the fans focused every time he was on the floor.

"That trade getting Joe and Rod gave us two key ingredients we were missing to solidify us as a contending team," affirms Guerin. "Joe was a great type of team player. Defensively he was as good, tough and quick as anybody in the NBA, while Rod was an experienced guard to give us tremendous depth with Lenny Wilkens and I. The team immediately got a lot better."

Wilkens agrees: "Joe Caldwell added a spark and was really exciting to watch. This guy could run and jump, but he couldn't dribble two steps without some trepidation. You'd always be worried where the ball was going to go, but he was a great athlete and made good things happen."

Still it was an uphill climb to the playoffs. Los Angeles and Baltimore were the class of the Western Division in the regular season, and St. Louis helped them get there. The Lakers pummeled the Hawks all year, winning twice in St.

Louis and all six games either in L.A. or at neutral sites while losing just twice. The Bullets took the season series from St. Louis, 7–3.

In the Eastern Division, the pendulum had finally swung in another direction and Boston had its streak of nine consecutive regular-season divisional titles snapped by the Philadelphia 76ers, who posted a 55–25 mark. But they didn't exactly run away and hide from the Celts, who finished only one game back at 54–26. Incidentally, the old Philly team that had last won in 1955–56 was the Philadelphia Warriors, now residing in San Francisco.

The Hawks stumbled to a third-place finish at 36–44, which may lulled their playoff opponents to sleep. Guerin didn't understand why the Hawks had a poor regular season, but the strong finish restored his faith.

"We had a very, very good nucleus, even before the trade but especially after it," recalls Guerin. "I couldn't understand why we didn't win more."

Who was what on this "new" version of the Hawks? Beaty was now the team's leading scorer, averaging 20.7 points per game. Wilkens had become a dominant guard in the league, posting 18 points per game. Guerin and Caldwell both pumped in 14 points per game, Hagan (in his final hurrah) averaged a very creditable 13 points, while Bridges tallied 13 and Thorn with 10. Wilkens added seven assists per game, putting him in fifth in the league.

But they call the playoffs "the second season" and the definition certainly fit these ballhawking Birds of St. Louis. They began with the Bullets, who had beat them like a drum all season. However, memories are long and the players who remembered being upset by the Bullets in the same semifinal series one year earlier were ready for revenge.

"I remember the Bullet series in that I played really well after having a horrible regular season series with them," said Wilkens.

While this series didn't mean as much as some other victories in the illustrious St. Louis past, none was more surprising than this three-game sweep of the favored Bullets. Games 1 and 2 in Baltimore were close, but Guerin's boys prevailed, 113–111 and 105–100. The train kept rolling into Kiel Auditorium and the sweep was completed in an easy 121–112 win to advance again to the Western Division finals against Los Angeles.

The fabulous Baylor, the incomparable West and LaRusso, the rugged, unsung hero from Dartmouth, were expected to blow away their conference foes. While the accomplishments and Baylor and West are documented far and wide, LaRusso is noteworthy for his incredible work ethic and determination. Night after night he would guard the opponent's highest scoring forward while being responsible for his own points and rebounds. He wore No. 35 and gave fits to players like Bob Pettit.

The Hawks looked like pushovers early. In Game 1, the only Hollywood ending in town was going on at Grauman's Chinese Theater. At the Los Angeles Forum, the Lakers were ho-humming the Midwesterners, 129–106.

Game 2 was better, but still no cigar. A 125–116 decision gave L.A. a two games to none lead going back to St. Louis where the teams split two games. Going back to L.A. for Game 5, the Lakers were in a clinching mood up 3–1.

But as the line in a good western being filmed down the street at Universal Studios would say, "Not so fast ..." So it was for the gutsy Hawks, who showed signs of those old golden days. Battling all the way, the guys now wearing a powder blue road uniform with the word "Hawks" emblazoned in white outlined in red across their chests, decided to come to the party. The final Game 5 score on "clinching" night in L.A. was St. Louis 112, Lakers 100. Then with some momentum and no Hollywood courtside fans to contend with, the Hawks won a barn burner at Kiel in Game 6, a rousing, high-scoring decision, 131–127, to tie the series at 3–3.

Could the Hawks renew their place in the championship round and bring back the glory of those first five seasons? In the Eastern Division, the Celtics were proving their regular-season second-place finish was just a silly misstep as they buried the 76ers in five games and headed again for the finals. Was this Hawks' team going to rise to the level that only the Pettit-Hagan combination had ever accomplished in this short, but storied history?

The Hawks had them sweating all over those tinsel town outfits, strutting around the floor in Los Angeles. But in the end, they really did need a Pettit to pull off an upset of historic proportions. The battle raged for 48 tough minutes, but the destiny was on the side of the new power in the West. The Lakers pulled out a tough 130–121 triumph to fight off the ferocious efforts of the Hawks to win the series four games to three.

In the NBA Finals, Los Angeles ran into the Boston buzz saw again, but with a stunning added twist. The Lakers had won four straight Western Division championships and played Boston three times in the finals. But the L.A. contingent lost again, dropping the series, 4–3. The shocking twist to the series was the dramatic announcement made after the Lakers Game 1 upset of Boston in the Boston Garden.

Auerbach, the cagey old coach, had pulled some stunts before in his colorful coaching career, but this one was for all-time. After the loss, Red fired up his club by announcing he would retire following the NBA Finals. He also named as his successor the league's first African-American head coach, the Celtics' own Bill Russell. It was truly a bombshell in several respects, but boy, did it work. Boston won three straight and then took a nail biter, 95–93, in Game 7 for another World Championship.

The legendary Wilt Chamberlain won his sixth consecutive and last NBA scoring title, averaging 33 points per game. Like clockwork, the same NBA superstars, L.A.'s Jerry West and Cincinnati's "Big O," Oscar Robertson, would finish second and third in scoring annually.

Chamberlain's run had been remarkable and the numbers eye-popping. In his rookie season, 1959–60, he turned the Philadelphia Warriors from a last-place team into a divisional title contender that knocked on Boston's door. Wilt averaged a record shattering 37.6 points per game and 27 rebounds while scoring more than 50 points in a game seven times!

The 7-1, 275-pounder was a tower of power. He would usually lumber down the court into position. But on March 2, 1962, in Hershey, Pa., Wilt the Stilt played the game of his life in front of just 4,124 fans and no television audience. Chamberlain scored his final basket on a dunk with 46 seconds to play giving him 100 points in a 169–147 win over

Wilt Chamberlain scores record 100 points in single game.

the New York Knicks. He was 36-for-63 from the field and 28-for-32 at the free throw line. Who was the never mentioned leading scorer for the Knicks that night? None other than Guerin, who also was outstanding with 39 points.

Not only has Wilt's 100-point game ever been equaled, but neither has a season like that one ever been repeated—not by Michael Jordan, Kareem Abdul Jabbar or anyone else in NBA history. For the record, Chamberlain broke his own single-game scoring record of 78 points. For the season, Wilt averaged 50.4 points per game, while the second leading scorer averaged 31 point per game. Like him or not, Wilt was a phenomenon that packed arenas and brought a new level of interest to the NBA.

As preparations for the 12th season in St. Louis were being made for the 1966–67 season, little did anyone realize, including the owner himself, that the sands of time were running out on this Mississippi River outpost. On the court, positive things were happening and Guerin seemed to have the club in a positive frame of mind.

The same hassles between owner and players were still hacking away at the stability of the Hawks. Kerner had a new star to wrangle with over salary in Caldwell. Before he arrived in town, Caldwell heard the stories of the "stingy" owner in St. Louis and true to form, Uncle Ben overmatched the newcomer.

A frustrated Caldwell finally came to an agreement on a two-year contract that paid him $27,000 the first season (1966–67) and $30,000 the second year (1967–68) plus an additional $20,000 personal loan to buy a house. Caldwell signed the contract but never received the home loan, leaving the star thinking there was never any intention that Kerner would loan him the money. Caldwell says it was just a ploy to get him to sign the contract.

The Hawks were building a solid nucleus once again, but they were missing that high-scoring forward, which had been a St. Louis trademark when Pettit and Hagan patrolled the frontcourt. Caldwell was a 10–14 points per game man and Bridges was more of a rebounder and defender than scorer. Beaty at center and Wilkens at guard had become the sources of consistent scoring and that wasn't enough to win big in the NBA.

Joe Caldwell

It was time for the Kerner-Blake tandem to team up again and find a player who could be a major contributor quickly. Only this time there was an added challenge. The American Basketball Association (ABA) was forming and actively competing for the best college players.

The Hawks hit the jackpot again when they selected Lou Hudson, a three-time All-Big Ten star from the University of Minnesota, as their No. 1 pick. Hudson's size wasn't overwhelming, but the 6-5, 220-pound forward was a pure shooter with smooth moves around the lane. He averaged 18, 23 and 19 points per game his college years and was known for being able to do more without the ball than some Big Ten coaches claimed to have ever seen. It was Bill Bradley, the NBA Hall-of-Fame forward and later U.S. Senator from New York, who tipped off the Hawks on Hudson's ability by calling him, "the greatest college player he had ever played with or against."

"It wasn't automatic for me to sign with the Hawks when they drafted me and in fact, when Marty Blake and Ben Kerner came up to Minneapolis to see me, on their way home they drove through a snowstorm and slid off the road," said Hudson. "I thought maybe it was a sign.

"I didn't know if I could play in the league. I had been drafted by the Dallas Cowboys in the National Football League as well. The Cowboys were drafting basketball players and I had been down to Dallas twice working out as a wide receiver in front of Coach Tom Landry. He said they really wanted me."

Hudson had not played football in high school or college, which didn't seem to phase the Cowboys. Football was paying a lot more money than basketball, but after experiencing nine contact drills and getting banged up, Hudson decided he didn't want to play a sport where getting hurt was likely.

The ABA team that had selected Lou was Minnesota, right where he was playing college ball. However, a judge was brought in to settle the dispute of having two teams draft Hudson from the two leagues. He ruled Hudson had to sign with St. Louis of the NBA or none at all. Actually there were about 21 similar suits going on in the courts between the leagues, and in this case, the Minnesota team of the ABA chose to stop the suit, save the legal bills and drop out of the Hudson bidding.

"At training camp I knew I was going to make the team, but I did talk to Mr. Kerner and tell him I was concerned about other players not wanting me to shoot the ball much. He answered by saying, 'You're a shooter and they better get used to it,'" laughed Hudson.

"Hudson was a great ballplayer who could really shoot it," said Wilkens. "He became one of Richie Guerin's favorites. They actually hung out together quite a bit."

Wilkens' relationship with Guerin became a little rocky that year after Lenny became the "player rep" for the players' union, a job nobody wanted because it usually was the kiss of death for the player with his team. Wilkens, who was also vice president of the association, had gotten the players to agree to a strike if the owner didn't consent to take over the players' pension fund. At the time, the players had to pay so much towards the pension fund that Wilkens felt the team needed to hold meetings and discuss the situation. Wilkens was vice president of the players association and Guerin didn't like the distraction from the game.

"He was a little upset with me about two issues," said Lenny. "The first were the meetings to discuss what was at stake for the players and the other was about the players' votes for NBA Rookie of the Year. You could not vote for your own player so Richie didn't want players to vote for a particular couple of guys who might beat out Lou Hudson. I kept telling him 'No, no you've got to vote for the best player not against him just to keep him from winning. I think it was Dave Bing in Detroit who was the challenger to Hudson for the trophy."

Whether or not the Hawks' players voted for undeserving rookie candidates, Hudson lost a close vote to Bing, who averaged 20 points per game for the Pistons. Guerin used "Sweet Lou" sparingly the first 24 games of the season. Over the last third of the schedule and playing everyday, Hudson rattled in 24.7 points per game for a season average of 18.4 points per game, eclipsing Pettit's Hawk rookie record. The sensational rookie had scored 41 points in one game against Cincinnati and 38 in another contest with Philadelphia.

With a competitive, basically young team on the floor led by the veteran guards Wilkens and player-coach Guerin, the Hawks were an exciting bunch to watch. However, only about half of the crowd that packed Kiel in the Pettit-Hagan days were now in attendance.

Through the first 47 games, St. Louis muddled along with a 20–27 record, but the Hawks began turning things around on January 22 at Kiel against Guerin's old team, the Knicks. A big effort pulled off a tense 104–101 victory that night and victories in 10 of the next 15 games boosted their record to 30–32 on the season.

The remainder of the regular season was marked by one five-game losing streak in early February, but the club regained its balance and at the end went into the playoffs having won seven of their last nine for a 39–42 record and in second place, five-games behind San Francisco. Los Angeles finished third and the new expansion team, the Chicago Bulls, in fourth position.

The Baltimore Bullets, who just the season before had buried the Hawks in the first round of the playoffs, had moved to the Eastern Division to accommodate Chicago. As a result, the NBA had two five-team divisions with an adjusted playoff scenario that saw the first place team playing the third place team in a first-round series. Thus, San Francisco squared off against their West Coast rival Lakers, who they demolished in three straight games.

The Hawks' playoff magic seemed to return in the first round. They cleared out Chicago in three straight games, 114–100, 113–107 and 119–106. However, they would not be the favorites against the towering and physical Warriors in the league championship series. San Fran had a terrific club with the 6-11 Nate Thurmond jamming the middle and the league's most exciting new scoring machine, Rick Barry, who was the league scoring champion at 35 points per game.

A pattern was set early in the best-of-seven finals. The Warriors won by two points in the first game and then exploded for 143 points to win by seven in Game 2. To the Hawks' credit, they battled back and won a pair of hard-fought contests in St. Louis to force the series back to the West Coast with the series even at 2–2. Unfortunately the pattern persisted in a San Francisco rout in Game 5.

"They were a really good team led by Thurmond at center and the Hall-of-Famer Rick Barry shooting the eyes out of the basket," said Guerin. "They also had two real gamers in forward Tom Meschery (10 points per game) and our former player from the year before Jeff Mullins, who really blossomed at guard for them."

"I found the series very disappointing in that I really thought we could beat them after having played them so well during the season," said a discouraged Wilkens. "We were healthy and excited about the playoffs, but just didn't finish the job."

San Francisco finished the job by going back to St. Louis and ending things on the road in Game 6, 112–107. It was a bitter and frustrating loss because the Hawks had led by 18 points at the end of the first period, 39–21, and seemed on the verge of a blowout.

But by the end of third quarter, the Warriors had surged to an 85–80 lead setting the stage for a frantic fourth period. It began to look like the series would go back to the Bay for a Game 7 when St. Louis took a 102–99 lead halfway through the fourth quarter and the Warriors were deep foul trouble.

The Warriors 7-foot Wilt Chamberlain rebounds over Hawks Cliff Hagan in Kiel game.

Then a key backcourt foul by Caldwell gave Frisco new life and ultimately a tie at 102 as guard Al Attles knocked down two free throws.

With time running out and the score tied at 105, Hudson, who tossed in 15 points for the game, missed on a drive to the bucket and then fouled Mullins, who made two free throws. Seconds later Guerin's driving shot was blocked by Thurmond. A Bridges foul followed leading to two more Warriors' points.

Besides Hudson's 15 points, Beaty played his best game of the playoffs on both ends, scoring 28 points, while Wilkens added 21 points and Caldwell 17. But it wasn't enough to derail the Warriors, who were led by Barry's 41 points. Mullins chipped in with 26 and Meschery 14.

It was after St. Louis' rousing victory in Game 4 that Barry had blasted the fans, so before Game 5 in San Francisco the normally passive Bay Area folks lost a little of their sophistication and hurled a few dozen eggs in the direction of the Hawks' players that led to the retaliation by St. Louisans.

Before Game 6 in St. Louis, Barry also categorized St. Louis fans as "strictly for the birds" in a newspaper article. Hawks' fans responded to those remarks by splattering Barry and some of his Warriors teammates with raw eggs as the players came onto the court for the beginning of the game. The opportunity to beat the Warriors and boo Barry brought out a big crowd of more than 8,000 to Kiel Auditorium—a reminder of crowds past in St. Louis.

In his "Benchwarmer" column in the *St. Louis Globe-Democrat*, the venerable Burnes chastised the crowd for the egg-throwing episode, but applauded the spirited effort by the "shorthanded" Hawks, who had lost some players to nagging injuries during the series:

"(The fans) Their wrath, fanned by the intensity of the competition and the ridiculous statements (by the Warriors' Barry) brought on a boorish demonstration of hoodlumism throughout the game.

"Rick Barry, who will be the league's next super star, was the target of the fans' indignation. Whether they were justified or not in their reaction to Barry's open challenge is besides the point. All they did Wednesday night was prove Barry was right.

"St. Louis fans were out of line in their pelting of players with eggs, apples, candy bars, cigarette lighters, cigars, rubber balls and ripe tomatoes. They hit their intended target only once. Barry was hit on the foot by an apple."

Burnes ended his column by summarizing, "The fans can be proud of the Hawks. Tragically, they can be more proud of the Hawks than the Hawks can be of their fans in the last game of the season."

The Hawks lost the series four games to two, but had played it with just nine players and with other complications and distractions. Kerner had taken many home games away from St. Louis and played them all over the country as an experiment during the season. He may have cost his club "home court advantage" in the playoffs by neutralizing those regular-season games. By midseason there was the first talk of a possible sale of the team.

That season, the NBA clearly belonged to Chamberlain and Philadelphia. The stranglehold on the Eastern Division title finally had the cord cut as the Boston Celtics run of 10 straight NBA Finals appearances, including eight straight championships, was snapped. Philadelphia put an exclamation on their first NBA title by setting a league record in the regular season with 68 wins against 13 losses. At one point they had posted an incredible 46–4 mark!

The 76ers cruised to the East title, whipping Boston by eight games in the standings. After the Celts took care of New York and Philly thumped Cincinnati in first round playoff series, the 76ers weren't in awe of the defending champs. They dispatched Boston in just five games, including a 24-point shellacking in the final Game 5, 140–116.

Chamberlain listened to the critics who said he was a ball hog who just shot all night and didn't do the "team" things needed to win. Wilt changed his style and became a rebounder and passer first. His points per game averaged dipped from the record-setting 50 back in 1961–62 to a modest 24 points per game finishing third in the league.

Chamberlain's name popped up in two new categories in league statistics. He was third in assists, averaging more than seven per game and was first in rebounds, averaging 24 boards per game. Russell was second with an average of 21 rebounds. Wilt set an NBA record on February 24, 1967, when Philly blew out Baltimore, 149–118. Chamberlain shot a perfect 18–18 from the field, a record that still stands.

Philadelphia, the new power in the West, met the Barry-led San Francisco Warriors. This match-up had Philly fans rolling up their sleeves wanting to get even with the team that had left their city before the 1962–63 season leaving them out of the league for a year. Revenge is sweet as the team of Chamberlain, a fabulous shooting guard who averaged 22 points a game Hal Greer, plus the team's leading scorers, forwards Billy Cunningham and Chet "the Jet" Walker led their club to a six-game win over San Francisco for the championship.

The 1967–68 season would be highlighted by a couple of more new franchises and the sad ending of another. New into the fold were the Seattle Supersonics and San Diego, both entering the Western Division with the Hawks sending their old rival, the Detroit Pistons, to the Eastern Division. The NBA was now a 12-team league and would play an 82-game schedule for the first time in history.

Pro basketball was gaining such popularity that a rival league popped in all the big metropolitan areas the NBA had ignored to date. The ABA began in cities like Denver, Dallas, Houston, Oakland and San Antonio. Credibility

George Mikan

came quickly from NBA stars. Former superstar George Mikan was selected as the league's first commissioner and the league's leading scorer, Rick Barry from San Francisco, sent up the shock waves taking his 35 points per game from the Warriors to the new team across the bay in Oakland. The ABA was a colorful group of teams and players right down to the rainbow basketball they used on the court.

Chapter Thirteen

One of the Best, for Last

ocally, the St. Louis Cardinals were in the midst of a great run that began with the 1964 World Championship. The Birds of '67 were nicknamed "El Birdos" because of their colorful Latin first base slugger, Orlando Cepeda. Besides "Cha-Cha" at first, they were led by Hall-of-Fame pitcher Bob Gibson, base-stealing sensation Lou Brock, second baseman Julian Javier, center fielder Curt Flood and major league single-season home run king, Roger Maris. They won the National League pennant in a runaway by 10 1/2 games and then won a hard fought seven-game World Series battle over the Boston Red Sox.

The Cardinals' fan base was elevating to new heights thanks to the Redbirds' exciting ball club. With popular Hall-of-Famer Red Schoendienst at the helm, the Cardinals went 101–60 and drew an all-time record 2,090, 145, smashing their single-season attendance record.

Then when Busch Stadium switched from baselines to goal lines, the football Cardinals grabbed the interest of sports fans after coming off of their second-best season since their move from Chicago in 1960. The Big Red under head coach Charley Winner had gone 8–5–1 and were threatening to win the division before losing their last three games.

For those seven Busch Stadium home appearances, the Big Red averaged 45,274 spectators per game, a healthy number that spread the sports entertainment dollars even further. But it wasn't football that started hammering nails in the Hawks' coffin in St. Louis.

In 1965, when the National Hockey League planned a six-team expansion for the 1967–68 season, it was Baltimore, not St. Louis that was suppose to get the sixth and final franchise. However, at the last second the William Wirtz family, the owners of the Chicago Blackhawks, realized they had a white elephant building sitting in St. Louis called "The Arena."

A St. Louis family by the name of Salomon showed interest in purchasing a hockey team and playing in The Arena. Wirtz enticed Sidney Salomon, Jr., to get into the NHL ownership group by packaging the team and the building. Wirtz made a killing off the building, which he overpriced at $4 million, after he had once offered The Arena for sale to another group for just $250,000. In addition, the Salomon's paid a league franchise fee of $2 million. The NHL redirected its expansion interest to St. Louis because The Arena satisfied the minimum of 12,000-seat requirement, the Chicago owner was obviously supporting the Salomon's bid, and the buyers had the right credentials financially and politically.

Salomon, a highly successful insurance agent and well-known political heavyweight in the Democratic party, drastically overspent for the building to get the hockey franchise for his 20-year-old son, Sid Salomon, III. Unlike the Hawks, whose owner moved to St. Louis with nothing in his pocket to purchase players or building upgrades to get a running start, the Salomon's bought veteran star players and paid to renovate the rundown Arena. They established a private dinner club inside, added seats, a fresh coat of paint and air conditioning, then cleaned it to the extent that it would pass a Marine Corps barracks check.

What made the St. Louis Blues Hockey Club an even bigger bet to succeed was the sports background of Sid, Jr. He had served on the board of directors of both the St. Louis Browns and the St. Louis Cardinals. He'd also owned a minor league team in Syracuse that he moved to Miami to play in the International League. He had plenty of experience operating a sports franchise.

St. Louisans had a taste of hockey with the Chicago minor league franchise, the Braves, so there was a small base of hockey fans in town when the major leaguers arrived. The acquisition of would-be Hall of Famers such as goalies Glenn Hall and Jacques Plante, defenseman Doug Harvey and forward Dickie Moore, followed later by Barclay Plager, Noel Picard and Red Berenson achieved the goal of gaining local headlines and establishing the franchise quickly.

Hockey became what the Hawks had been in their hey-day, "the thing to do" on a Saturday night in St. Louis. People came well dressed in coats, ties and dresses as if they were attending the opera. There was a glitz and a glamour to the new game inside the now-sparkling Arena and it became a huge competitor to the Hawks, who were still playing at the dingy looking Kiel Auditorium. Remember, Kerner had asked the city many times to help upgrade the look and comfort of Kiel, but his request only fell on deaf ears.

The puck dropped at The Arena on October 11, 1967, as 11,339 paid to watch the St. Louis Blues play a rousing 2–2 tie with another expansion team, the Minnesota North Stars. St. Louis sports fans had a new toy, and as is always the case with children, the old toys go back in the closet when the new ones arrive. The Blues had veteran NHL stars that were only winning occasionally early on, but regardless, the atmosphere in The Arena, now seating 14,000, was electric. The organist, Norm Kramer, became a catalyst for fan reaction throughout the games, and he became famous for his heart-stirring rendition of "When The Saints Go Marching In" as the Blues skated from the locker room to the ice before every period.

The Blues even had a jump in the schedule on their downtown counter-parts. The Hawks season didn't open until three days later, October 14, on the road at the home of a new NBA team, the San Diego Rockets. It was a first night squeaker, with the Hawks winning the first of three consecutive road games, 99–98. They reported for their home season opener on October 19 where they knocked off the Lakers, 100–95, for a snappy 4–0 start.

The Hawks roster included Beaty and Tormohlen at center, Bridges, Hudson, Silas, Jim Davis, Tom Workman and Jay Miller at forward, and Wilkens, Caldwell, Don Ohl, Dick Snyder and George Lehmann in the backcourt. Guerin was strictly a head coach now. As many had done in the past, Hudson had military duty, which it cost him all but 46 games of the season. "Paul Silas and I were both in the military, but he was in the National Guard," said Hudson. "We both came back to the Hawks in January."

Make no mistake, the Hawks were off to their best start in their 13 seasons in St. Louis. They were 7–0 before being stopped by Boston in the Garden, but undeterred, Guerin's squad reeled off nine victories in a row blasting out to a 16–1 record by mid-November. A few years back that kind of record would have sold out Kiel every night, but alarm bells were going off in the owner's office as an average of only 5,000 fans were spinning the turnstiles.

Did the players recognize that the fans had fallen off and did they see signs that the team could be sold? The answer to both questions was "yes," they noticed and they heard the whispers.

"Yeah, I heard the rumors about selling the team," said Wilkens. "I went and asked Mr. Kerner if he was selling the team because my wife and I were about to buy a new house in town and we needed an honest answer.

"Of course, he vehemently denied all the rumors and said 'No, no, no. I'm not selling you guys,' so we bought the house."

So what was really happening to the Hawks as their spectacular regular-

Bob Pettit shooting over Tom Heinsohn in Boston.

season rolled on? The wins were piling up at record levels. In January there were two streaks of five and six wins apiece and a 13–4 record between December 29 and January 27. Were people making a choice between hockey and basketball because unlike today, the same people and corporations didn't buy season tickets to both sports?

"It was like people weren't interested all of a sudden," recalls Kerner's wife Jean. "The fans weren't coming in big numbers, and Ben was getting concerned that maybe it was time for him to get out. He was 55 years old, still living with his mother, and he wanted to be sure he could get out of the game with his money.

"He'd worked hard all his life for little to nothing for a lot of it. He was one of those people who worked seven days a week and didn't want a vacation, but now he wanted to smell the roses a little bit."

The 1967–68 season was a banner one. In February, the Hawks leveled out winning 13 and losing 10, but in March, another five-game win streak got them going strong towards the playoffs. And on the final day, March 16, a 124–106 win over the expansion Seattle Supersonics, gave St. Louis the shiny regular-season final record of 56–26. They headed into the playoffs the favorite to get to their fifth visit to the NBA Finals.

This magnificent season, witnessed by far fewer fans than in the past, had some marvelous performances. Unlike the great teams of Pettit and Hagan, this one had a balanced offensive attack that didn't rely on just one or two players. Wilkens led the way with 22 points per game, followed by Beaty with 21, Bridges 17, Caldwell 16, Ohl with 14, Silas with 13 and Hudson with 12 during limited duty. They were also one of the top rebounding teams in the league with Bridges finishing with 1,102 for the year or 13.5 rebounds per game, Silas and Beaty each averaged 11.7 boards, and even little Wilkens grabbed five rebounds per game.

The final standings showed the Hawks winning the Western Division by four games over the Lakers and a 13-game bulge over third-place San Francisco. In the East, Philadelphia continued to dominate, winning 62 games and beating out Boston by eight full games.

What doesn't make sense and turned out to be fatal to the Hawks was the first-round pairing in the playoffs. Instead of the first-place team playing the fourth-place team and the second and third place clubs meeting, the NBA in their wisdom had the first-place Hawks meet the third-place Warriors, while the Lakers were offered the fourth-place fodder, the Chicago Bulls.

During the season, the Hawks had completely dominated San Francisco by a margin of seven wins to one loss. Fans and writers alike were looking ahead to the L.A. series and a meeting with Baylor and West for the right to go to the finals. Could an NBA championship be the tonic to restore the full houses to the Hawks' nest and stop the nasty rumors?

Then the unthinkable happened. The semifinal round began on March 22 just like a year earlier in the conference finals, San Francisco won Game 1 in St. Louis, 111–106. Regaining their balance, the Hawks eked out a Game 2 win, 111–103, and headed for San Francisco where they had success all season.

Back at home, though, the Warriors crushed the Hawks by 15 in Game 3, sparked by old Hawks' nemesis Nate Thurmond, the controller of the boards, who averaged 22 rebounds per game that season, and another St. Louis adversary, Rudy LaRusso, moved from L.A. to S.F. Another player who kind of came out of nowhere to be a key performer for the Warriors was Fred Hetzel, a 6-8 forward out of Davidson College, who averaged 19 points per game that season.

The Hawks had one more shot to get back in the series in Game 4, and almost pulled it off. But it didn't happen. San Fran pulled out a 108–107 triumph, taking a commanding 3–1 series advantage.

One positive note was the Hawks won what would be their last game in St. Louis in the fifth game. Playing like they had all year against their West Coast visitors, they trounced the Warriors, 129–103, under the gleaming lights that would soon go dark in the Kiel Convention Center. Trying desperately to return to St. Louis for a Game 7, the Hawks fought the fight but couldn't overcome the strength of the Warriors, who qualified for the conference finals with their 111–106 verdict. However, the Lakers shut the Warriors out in four straight games for the Western Conference title, while the Celtics were upsetting Philadelphia in the Eastern Conference finals. Boston then grabbed their 10th championship by beating L.A. in six games for the NBA title.

Before going on to what followed next, mention must be made of Guerin's successful 3 1/2 seasons as the head coach in St. Louis. He won 159 games, lost 131, made the playoffs all four seasons, and won those 56 games in the 1967–68 regular season, the best ever for a St. Louis team. Guerin outlasted any other coach and tells the story of how he conquered the "Kerner Curse" with coaches.

"I'll give you one story that's a typical Ben Kerner story," said Guerin. "It was my first full year as the coach after I took over for Harry Gallatin in December 1965. Now it's my team. The next year we go to training camp, we have exhibition games and now we're playing the second or third game of the regular season at Baltimore, which had a very good team with Gus Johnson, Kevin Loughery, Wesley Unseld and Earl "the Pearl" Monroe. They beat us by 30 points and I was really ticked off at our team after the game.

"I told the players (Hawks), 'We'll call your families and tell them when we get to the airport in St. Louis that we're going right to the gym and practice. I'm a playing coach so I've got to go up and bust my butt right with you to get this thing straightened out. We are never going to lose like that again.'

"At practice the next day, Marty Blake comes down and tells me Ben wants to see me in his office after practice. Well, it didn't bother me then because I knew I could still play if he was going to fire me.

"I go into his office and the first thing Ben says is, 'Jesus, Richie, what the hell was going on last night in Baltimore? Weren't they hustling for you?' I stop Kerner right there.

"'Ben, stop right now,' I said. Here's the game. If you think I'm going to come in here after we win a game by 30 and tell you why we won, or that I'm going to come in here after we get whacked by 30 points, you're crazy. Get another coach. I'll go back to being a player. But I am not going to live my life like this. Make up your mind right now, either fire me or get off my case, and don't talk to me again about a game. If I can't do the job, I'll be the first one to walk into this office and tell you to get another coach.'

"Never ever again was I summoned to Ben's office and I think I gained a little respect from him for standing up to my beliefs. I had a wonderful relationship with Ben after that for sure and was the coach for eight seasons."

"We didn't win any championships, but we did contend and had some really good people playing for the Hawks," said the coach. "Billy Bridges, to me, was one of the hardest working players I'd ever been around and he didn't care if he scored, he was totally unselfish. He took a lot of pride in his defense and rebounding, but I always made sure we had some plays that would call Bill's number out and get him involved on the offense to keep him in the flow.

"Then there was Zelmo Beaty who we utilized as a high-post center because he had that terrific jump shot from 15-feet, unusual for a big man. He did very well taking Wilt Chamberlain, Bill Russell and Nate Thurmond away from the basket on defense to guard him, and he did a pretty good job too of guarding them.

"Zelmo was tough and at times he was labeled a little dirty, which some of his opponents said but it wasn't a big deal."

Though Guerin might have competed with Wilkens as a player when he arrived, he had nothing but compliments for his play as his coach.

"Len Wilkens was one of the greatest all-around players in all of basketball," said an admiring Guerin. "He was a really good penetrating guard, a very good defensive player, handled the ball extremely well, had a nice mid-range shot and was a team leader. He had everyone's attention and respect.

"Finally Lou Hudson was probably one of the finest shooters in the game of basketball at the time, one of the great, great, great jump shooters," emphasized Guerin. "His biggest weakness as a player was that he wasn't a good ball handler. We used to work on drills tying one of his

Shooting phenom Lou Hudson

hands behind his back, making him dribble the ball up and down the court, which gave him more confidence.

"We relied heavily on Lou and when it came to the last shot of the game, we always designed it for him. I had all the confidence in the world in him."

One of the many disappointments of losing the Hawks was that St. Louis fans never got to see "Sweet Lou" develop into one of the premier shooters in the NBA. He played 11 more years in the league averaging 20.2 points per game with 4.4 rebounds and 2.7 assists over his career. Only Pettit and Hudson had their numbers retired by the Atlanta Hawks.

"I was a shooter, I could usually make the open shot," Hudson said. "I had the highest scoring game of my career in St. Louis. One night I was 25–30 from the field and made seven free throws for 57 points. That tied the all-time team record of 57 set by Bob Pettit." (Pettit 57 vs. Detroit, Feb. 18, 1961)

As good as Hudson was, there was a team he didn't care to play. Guerin experimented with Hudson at both forward and guard, so when they played the Boston Celtics, a tough defender, forward Bailey Howell, would play Lou. When he played guard, the great defensive star K.C. Jones "would hold me all night," laughed Lou.

"Sometimes Satch Sanders would guard me and he would try to beat me up physically."

193

Lou Hudson (#23) passes the ball to teammate Zelmo Beaty (#31) around New York Knicks (and former U.S. Senator) Bill Bradley (#24).

Hudson talked about playing with Beaty and Bridges on the front line. Beaty wasn't as large as the league's centers, but he would get the ball in the pivot, fake up, then drive around his defender or take his jump shot.

"Zelmo was really strong, he would play hard and was a great competitor," said Hudson. "I liked playing with him. He always had your back when you got beat. He would talk to me as a young player about the tradition of St. Louis. He and Bridges were big on the Hawks tradition.

"I really did like St. Louis. The fans were very vocal in our favor. They really did care. People always stopped me on the street, in the stores or at the airport."

Incidentally, the Hawks couldn't be sold without Hudson being under contract, particularly after Wilkens held out for more money after the season. Lenny had become a big star having just finished second in the MVP voting, and he was vastly underpaid at $30,000. He wanted $60,000 and the team wanted to pay him just $40,000. Chamberlain, the NBA's MVP, was taking down a cool $250,000 annually.

Wilkens said, "pay me or trade me," and Kerner refused to budge. Ultimately, Wilkens would be traded to Seattle where he continued his stardom at a great loss to the Hawks. Lenny wanted to stay and play for the Hawks, whom he considered a championship contender. But not at the price of being underpaid.

"It was the dumbest thing we ever did not signing Wilkens," said Blake. "It was a stupid move. He was our leader and a great player."

These were the Hawks who had gained a reputation as a "blue collar squad" that worked hard together to get to the point of having the best regular-season record in the NBA. There was great potential for good seasons ahead but St. Louis fans didn't seem to care to support their former NBA champions anymore?

It wouldn't be long before the stories and rumors got cranked up again—this time with some teeth in them. The stories had began circulating back in January 1967, that the club was for sale.

Chapter Fourteen
The Sign Says "For Sale"

he warning signs that Kerner was prepared to sell the club for the right deal began a year and a half before an announcement was made so that St. Louis businessmen and fans couldn't say they were ambushed by any move out of time. There was plenty of time and opportunity for St. Louisans to package a deal to own the Hawks and keep them in St. Louis. Nobody, however, stepped up.

The process began in January 1967 when, just before the NBA All-Star Game in San Francisco, Kerner announced to the public that the team was for sale. There was a press conference at the Sheraton-Jefferson Hotel at which team spokesman, attorney Michael Aubuchon, a director for the club, made the initial statement. No price was mentioned and he quickly stated the hope was to find a St. Louis buyer. Still, the announcement stunned St. Louis sports fans.

Kerner, just 50 years old at the time, cited failing health and an inability to be at the office regularly as reasons for the sale. He was struggling with a painful arthritic condition, and Aubuchon was quick to dispel any speculation that the Hawks had any money problems.

"The club is in good shape financially and has made a profit every season since coming to St. Louis in 1955," claimed the attorney. "Last year (1965–66) the Hawks made a profit of $243,975 and will make the same amount this season (1966–67). This would include one of the best television contracts locally in the NBA."

In fact, there had never been a losing year financially for the St. Louis Hawks. Pro basketball had made a lot of money for Kerner and made money for the city of St. Louis. If dollars and cents weren't the primary reason for selling the team then what was the trigger?

The real answer unfortunately can't be answered by the late owner who passed away November 22, 2000, four days after his 87th birthday. But the answer could lie in a number of issues. Season tickets were down to a point of concern with the new hockey team taking sports dollars, but even though Kerner was still making money, it bugged him to look at empty seats.

A second issue no one liked to talk about then or now is racism. Clearly, racism played a role in all walks of life in St. Louis back then, but how much is debatable. Bob Burnes of the *Globe-Democrat* was one of Kerner's best friends, and he, too, had heard from many in the public that racism might have been the cause and stated so in his column.

Kerner responded to complaints about too many Negro players on the team by saying, "We try to please people. If we didn't we'd be crazy. As to the complaint about players, every club in the NBA has Negro players. They dominate the sport, Bill Russell, Wilt Chamberlain, Oscar Robertson, Elgin Baylor and many more, and yet their teams are selling out every night. So it can't be a big deal."

Jack Levitt, team statistician, timekeeper and Ben's friend, was much more blunt about it, but he didn't blame society's shortsightedness for the team's ultimate departure.

"Sure, St. Louis was a racist town in the '50s and '60s," he said. "Black players couldn't eat a meal in downtown restaurants no matter who they were The most repeated story was the one about the trio of Boston stars, Bob Cousy, Coach Red Auerbach and Bill Russell, who couldn't get served in the restaurant across from the Sheraton-Jefferson Hotel because of Bill's color. What a sorry chapter in our history."

One Hawk member who wished to remain anonymous said he spent some off seasons selling season tickets to businesses. He said he was told to his face that racism was the reasons why they wouldn't buy season tickets.

"If you think I'm going to spend my cash to support those such-and-suches, you're out of your mind," the player remembered in astonishment. "I was completely floored by the attitude. It floored me, it really, really did."

A source close to the team said the owner would get all kinds of hate mail about the number of African-Americans on the Hawks with statements like, "Why don't you just change your nickname to the Globetrotters." Another said, "We're not coming anymore to watch all those black players."

The same source said Ben didn't want to believe that St. Louis fans could be so far out of step. He talked about how millions of fans went to Busch Stadium to watch the great African-American stars of the Cardinals. He asked himself whether basketball fans were more sensitive because they were closer to the court. Were people really that bigoted? Was that why it didn't matter in pro football because the fans were far away in the stands and the players were covered up with their uniforms and helmets?

It's said that when Wilkens came to town the first time and Ben wanted to take him out to dinner he first called some of the fine restaurants and asked the proprietors if they had a problem with him bringing his African-American No. 1 draft choice. They said they personally didn't have a problem, but their customers might feel uneasy. Ben then took Lenny to the Sheraton-Jefferson dining room where there was no problem.

Those stories aside, former players and many fans don't think race issues were the overriding factor in the team's demise in St. Louis. Again Burnes was the closest thing to a Hawks' guru with his relationship with Kerner. He offered these theories about what was causing the owner's dissatisfaction with St. Louis in his column.

"For a year or more, owner Kerner has stated flatly on many occasions that he could not go on indefinitely playing in Kiel Auditorium. Last fall (1966) he amplified that by saying that if he could not have a new building in St. Louis he would have to make other arrangements.

"That Kerner's argument was sound cannot be denied. Kiel Auditorium by standards of athletic buildings around the country is antiquated. It was not

Opening tip, Championship Series at Kiel Auditorium

designed for sports in the first place and the dressing rooms are a horror. The area is bad and the parking is no better.

"The seating is bad. What improvements do exist in the facility at Kiel—the floor, the clock, some of the seats were provided by Kerner although in the final summation the city did pay for them."

Burnes saw the facility failures as the top reasons for the owner's irritation, but one other item probably got into Kerner's craw that caused him more anguish. When pro football came to town and then pro hockey, they both drove hard bargains with the city. As a result the squeaky wheel got the grease, and both franchises prospered from various concessions, financial and otherwise, given by city officials. Frankly, no concessions were given to save the Hawks.

Finally, there was the "success factor" that may have backfired on Kerner's legions. The Hawks had quick success. The second season in St. Louis they played for the world championship. The third year they won it with a glamorous roster of players like Pettit, Hagan, Macauley, Martin and McMahon. The fans were spoiled for five fantastic seasons early. When those heroes departed, the newcomers were neither as good nor as glamorous.

When Kerner first announced he was looking for a buyer in 1967, the buzz was about who would step up and make offers to purchase the franchise. It was assumed the team was safe in St. Louis and a local buyer would emerge. But even if an out-of-town buyer was the best offer, it was taken for granted the league would demand the team stay in St. Louis. Besides, a new owner would be silly to leave this established NBA town that just needed a touch up.

Burnes didn't think Kerner would let the club leave town. He presumed new owners would be found here. He urged the city to get with it and help fill the needs that Kerner that had been asking for to improve the environment for the NBA. He wrote:

"The announcement that the ball club is for sale ends an era. The Hawks started an era of unmatched sports prosperity in St. Louis when they came here. Perhaps another one, even better one will be born.

"That could happen if things are done by the city for the new owners of the club—things that were not done for the Hawks but which, ironically, were done for some other sports enterprises (football Cardinals, Blues) that followed them here. In the final analysis, this was probably the primary determining factor in Ben Kerner's decision to sell."

For awhile, it looked like the sale talk was just that, "all talk," and a way to wake up the city fathers about what could happen if some of the demands weren't met. Just one month after announcing the team was for sale (January 4), Kerner notified his attorney Aubuchon that he was terminating all sale discussions and would just continue the battle to keep his team.

On February 2, 1967, Kerner said, "We turned down several bids of better than $3 million from groups who wanted to move the franchise away from St. Louis. No St. Louis group approached the figure. From the start I have made it plain that I wanted the ball club to stay here if at all possible. I think our action in calling off the negotiations proves that point. The Hawks will remain here."

Kerner had received verbal support from NBA president Walter Kennedy, who urged him to continue to operate the team. Some owners in the league were very vocal about their displeasure of any attempt to move the franchise from St. Louis.

Franklin Mieull, president of the San Francisco Warriors, had a strong message for Kerner and potential buyers:

"I'll have a lot of questions to ask and I'll want weighty answers before I'll vote to approve any sale. I'd also want some real reasons why we (the NBA) should leave St. Louis, which is a good sports town."

The cause of the commotion amongst the owners was the first offer thrown out to Ben by a group calling themselves the New Orleans Pro Basketball Associates, headed by S.M. Downey, Jr. Their group floated out a $3.8 million figure for the team just a few days after Kerner announced his intentions to sell the team. J.R. Kimble, a 24-year-old vice-president of the New Orleans group, made the initial offer but bowed out of the New Orleans syndicate once Kerner put a 10-day grace period on the contract so that any St. Louis group could match it and pledge to keep the team in St. Louis.

It was called a conditional sale offer and it did arouse the ire of several league owners. Fred Zollner of the Detroit Pistons was very upset over the news of a possible deal to sell the Hawks.

"I heard there was a joker in the deal and if there is I'm going to find it out and vote against the sale. No one is going to sway my vote even if Ben is a good friend of mine."

Ned Irish, president of the New York Knicks, said he couldn't give his opinion yet since he didn't know all the facts, but then he added, "It takes three-quarters of the club owners to approve such a deal."

Most interesting was NBA president Walter Kennedy's comment that if the Hawks were moved his feeling, shared by many other owners, was that the city of St. Louis would be totally successful in bidding for a new team since it was an established NBA city.

Aubuchon added an insurance clause for the city by announcing that the conditional deal with the New Orleans group contained verbiage that prohibited the team from leaving St. Louis—period. He reiterated that anyone from out of town who wanted to buy the team must agree to keep it in St. Louis or "no deal with Ben." That's what he said publicly.

Incidentally, there were a few St. Louis inquiries into the purchase, the most prominent one by Ed Arthur, president of Arthur Company and his associate, Harry Kessler. They felt the price offered by the New Orleans group was surprisingly high and would allow a minimal 10 percent return on investment at best with risk. The only other St. Louis potential buyer mentioned was Harold Koplar, the owner of KPLR-TV and the Chase Park Plaza Hotel, but his interest passed quickly.

Kimble, by the way, was the son of a Louisiana state senator who had been left with a reported $40 million inheritance. Blake listened to the deal with suspicion as Kimble made the offer. Kimble then turned to Blake and offered him big money and an airplane to take on his scouting trips. Sound too good to be true? It was.

"As it turned out," said Blake, "The guy lived in a shack and was a complete nut."

The local press simply reported that the New Orleans group lacked proper financing. One other group that was considered came in from Cleveland, Ohio. A stock broker, Larry Schmelzer, and his three brothers had the controlling interest in the Columbus, Ohio, hockey team of the International League. They said they were serious about buying the Hawks and Larry vowed to move to St. Louis to run the team himself.

However, the Schmelzer family thought the now $3.5 million price Ben had on the team, dropped from the $3.8 million asked of the New Orleans group, was still too high. In 1964, they had bid for the Boston Celtics franchise, which sold for $3.2 million and didn't believe the Hawks could be worth more than the greatest franchise in the NBA.

When Schmelzer was asked why he wouldn't shuttle the franchise to his hometown Cleveland, he said, "We don't feel we can battle Art Modell (owner of the football Cleveland Browns). He's got a 55,000 person mailing list and an established organization. We hear he's been promised an NBA franchise."

A few days later the Schmelzer interests faded away as did an inquiry from a Los Angeles syndicate composed of L.A. movie film people. Aubuchon said up to "50 interested groups" made passes at the Hawks franchise.

As the 1966–67 season moved on, Kerner seemed resigned to keeping the team and diverting some of the daily operational duties to Aubuchon and others so he could concentrate on improving his health. The Hawk players were happy talks had ended as many of them were now permanent residents of St. Louis and didn't want to be uprooted.

It all sounded good, but those who knew Kerner knew this was just a lull in the action. He'd made up his mind and was committed to selling to somebody soon.

"Remember Ben was living with his mother and he wanted to get out of the game while he could get out with money," said the wife of the late owner. "As he would say to me, 'I want to get out, smell the roses and take it easy for awhile.' He'd worked hard and risked everything he had all the time. He was happy working seven days a week and never taking a vacation."

Wilkens, who was there as a player when all this posturing and proposing was occurring, reflects on what he thought was going on with Kerner.

"When what turned out to be the last season started, Kerner didn't advertise, didn't promote the team in town like he'd done in the past," said Wilkens. "I think he was losing interest. It was tough to run a franchise because the salaries were changing. When you're a one-man ownership group and this was your whole income with no other outside business to support rough spots, that had to be scary.

"He was right. We really needed a new building to play in and get the people excited about. He wasn't going to make it in the future on 9,400 seats in this league. I think Ben Kerner did the best he could for as long as he could without a big radio deal, a big national television deal or much, if any, support from his own city fathers. He sold it when he had a chance to make a decent profit."

What is unfathomable in a city considered to be a major sports town, is that 15 months could go by after Kerner put up his "for sale sign" without anyone in St. Louis ever stepping forward to put a solid group together to save this precious commodity. The Hawks were a treasure in St. Louis. Shamefully, the city went to sleep and ignored the signs, letting the team slip away.

Ben Kerner discusses sale of Hawks with Atlanta buyer Tom Cousins.

And slip away they did with a very quiet, one-week negotiation in late April of the 1967–68 season. After many false alarms and empty talks with potential buyers, Ben got a call from Tom Cousins, a 36-year-old real estate developer, and an associate, former Georgia Governor Carl E. Sanders, who wanted to discuss purchasing the Hawks. Ben's immediate thought was that Atlanta doesn't have a facility in which to play pro basketball. Even though that was the case, Cousins and Sanders wanted to meet with Kerner.

Not knowing what Cousins' plan was for Atlanta, Kerner entertained the pair thinking it was just another big waste of time. Guerin remembers the initial visit and Ben's ho-hum attitude.

"Cousins and his partner came to our little offices in Brentwood above the bowling alley where we'd moved to from downtown because Ben had bought the building," said Guerin. "Ben told me he wasn't even going to bother to take them somewhere nice to eat like he usually did with visitors because it was just a waste of time and not going anywhere. He just took them downstairs in the bowling alley for chili and a hot dog and then they went home."

Two weeks later Cousins called back and told Kerner he had secured a deal to play games at Georgia Tech University while The Omni, a new shopping mall and arena complex, was being built in Atlanta. Cousins was the builder of the complex, so he knew he could play there and needed a pro sports tenant. Guerin said Cousins was instantly charming, sincere and one of the nicest men he'd ever met.

This proposal was different from the other offers and Kerner dropped his demand that the team stay in St. Louis basically because no business group in the city cared enough to put a real offer on the table. He figured he was kidding himself and the city really didn't care whether they left or not.

Timing was everything as Cousins didn't quibble and Kerner became reasonable with the price. The purchase price was reported at $3.5 million, a middle of the road figure for a franchise back then. In the end, after their bold

Ed Macauley, Greg Marecek, Buddy Blattner and Bob Pettit celebrate Ed Macauley Tribute Night in May 2004 at the Missouri Athletic Club in downtown St. Louis.

statements about saving St. Louis as a franchise city, the owners in the NBA voted overwhelmingly for the sale to support the wishes of their friend, Ben Kerner. They also wanted to see him leave with a lucrative deal after coming into basketball 20 years earlier.

In retrospect, how sad it was for this storied and proud St. Louis professional basketball franchise that had propped up the sinking stature of a city as a "sports town." The Hawks had turned cold, dark, dreary St. Louis winters into hot nights of fast-paced entertainment at a championship level.

Would Bill Bidwill have really brought his National Football League team to St. Louis if some pro franchise hadn't reversed the negative fortunes of a failed baseball team, the Browns, and a failed hockey team, the Flyers? The Hawks proved St. Louis fans were more than just Cardinals' fans and would adopt heroes other than baseball players.

Meanwhile, the players proved to be a classy group. At the height of popularity, Hawks players like Pettit, Hagan, Share, Macauley and Martin couldn't walk a downtown street without stopping every few yards to sign autographs and have pictures taken with the people.

"When you walked down the street in St. Louis at 6-5, 6-9 and 6-11 you drew a lot of attention from the folks," Share fondly recalled. "We were like movie stars walking around, going to the grocery store or into restaurants in St. Louis. If it was New York we wouldn't have even been noticed. We were proud to be the Hawks."

Looking back at the sale, Wilkens said, "I have a lot of fond memories of St. Louis. We won a lot and that was great. Then there were the three All-Star games (1958, 1962 and 1965 at The Arena) and they were memorable playing in front of the hometown fans.

"There were the places we went to eat all the time like Tony's Restaurant, and living in the Plaza Square apartments where my wife, Marilyn, and I had our first child. They were right across the street from Kiel. We loved the Cardinals, who were champions themselves. We had a lot of friends on the baseball team. The city was great to us."

Jack Levitt still bemoans the fact that the city and fans gave up on the Hawks at the end. After all, in 13 seasons in St. Louis the Hawks won six division titles, went to the NBA Finals four times, captured a World Championship and were in the playoffs a remarkable 12 times in 13 seasons. Absolutely no St. Louis sports franchise can claim that kind of success over any 13-year period.

On Friday, May 3, 1968, a glum-looking Kerner made the announcement that his team had been sold to the Atlanta interests of Cousins and Sanders, effective immediately and subject to the rubber stamp approval of the NBA Board of Governors. It took just one week of negotiations to hammer out the deal.

"We had to do it, there was no way we could continue in St. Louis," explained the owner who should have been happy with his $3.5 million windfall. "We had tried hard to find a St. Louis group to buy us out but none came forward. They just don't want our product here anymore."

The NBA, meanwhile, never followed up on their promise to bring a new expansion franchise to what the president had called a "loyal franchise city of the NBA." To this day professional basketball has not come back to St. Louis except for a few sporadic practice games that are always reasonably attended.

The Hawks left for Atlanta without a Pettit or Hagan, who had retired, and without Hall-of-Fame guard Len Wilkens, who refused to sign and go to Atlanta. The city of Atlanta was actually in shock at the transfer. It was considered a sure-fire losing proposition to bring basketball into the football crazed South.

Now 38 years later, after no championships, only a few good seasons, several more owners and few fans, the Hawks history can only look back to their days in St. Louis to find greatness. All but one Hall-of-Famer, the late Pete Maravich, was bred in St. Louis—Pettit, Hagan, Macauley, Martin, Lovellette, Wilkens, Hannum and Gallatin—all had connections to the River City.

The St. Louis Hawks belonged to the people. There are endless stories of individuals who have warm, fuzzy memories of interaction with Hawks' players or at Hawks' events. But at the head of the class were stories involving Kerner because, above all, he was the Hawks. Blattner tells this one that typified Kerner as the people's choice of those magical days and times in St. Louis sports history.

This man called Bob wanted to tell his story. He began by saying his dad had Hawks' season tickets when he was growing up. On one occasion, the Hawks were in the NBA Championship Series against the Celtics, he recalled. "We were headed downtown to the game, but as we looked around for our usual seats we couldn't find them. What happened was the national media had taken over the seats that we owned all season by the floor.

"My dad was really mad, and he went storming down to the floor right before the game was to start because we didn't have any seats. He went up to the owner Ben Kerner seated at Murderer's Row at center court and said, 'Mr. Kerner, you don't know who I am, but I'm one of your season ticket holders back to day one of the team, and look what you've done. Your people have taken my prime seats away for something.'

"Kerner listened intently for a minute with the basketball about to be tossed into the air and the game to begin when he said, 'Wait right here, I'll be back.' Sure enough a minute later he came back and said with a grin, 'You're sitting here with me.' He sat us down in the first row, asked the people, including his mother, to move over a seat and we sat down. Imagine, watching the sixth game of the NBA Finals against the Boston Celtics at center court with Ben Kerner and his mother. It was unforgettable and a lifetime thrill."

Woven deep in the fabric of St. Louis sports history and now never to be forgotten, they were the St. Louis Hawks, and once the champions of the world.

Appendix A

BUDDY BLATTNER'S ON-AIR VOCABULARY
(as told by Buddy Blattner)

"They're Walkin' the Wrong Way!"

The St. Louis Hawks were playing the New York Knicks one night in 1955 at Madison Square Garden, and sometime during the latter stages of the game a foul was called. I waited for the referee's signal, and saw that the foul was called against the Hawks. I then extemporaneously proclaimed on the radio airwaves, "They're walkin' the wrong way." I have no idea what prompted me to use this never-declared-before expression, but it was merely a reaction to describe what was really happening to the Hawks.

Tens of thousands of words are delivered during the play-by-play broadcasts of a lengthy NBA basketball season. It, therefore, becomes beyond the realm of imagination how one particularly short phrase can spark such a responsive chord as to become indelibly etched in the listener's memory file. This happening actually allowed the phrase to take on a life of its own and preserved it for decades following the Hawks' broadcasts. In addition, it established a lasting link between the Hawks' listeners and me, the announcer.

I'm still greeted on occasion by that very acknowledgment when out in a crowd, "Hey, Bud, they're walkin' the wrong way!" It invariably gives me a warm feeling to know people remember a special time in history now some five decades ago.

During the course of my 800-plus Hawks' game broadcasts, which encompassed more than 2,000 hours of play-by-play description, there were numerous phrases and nicknames I used to make it easier to envision the action and the characters playing the game for my listeners. But nothing has come close to enjoying the shelf life of those five little words—"They're walkin' the wrong way."

There are no specific guidelines or a prescribed formula to be followed in the creation of a nickname. It's a distant stretch from an exact science and is merely a product spawned from one's physical appearance, lifestyle, style of play, nationality, unusual trait . . . well, you get the picture. Just never let a nickname be degrading or insulting, particularly when you have thousands of radio listeners out there.

Given the responsibility of presenting the play-by-play action during the course of an NBA season, I needed to avoid redundancy, thus boredom, for the fans when describing the action and in recognizing the players on the floor. If you say the same phrases or play on words over and over, the broadcast will be tarnished and impact the quality of the game for the listener. If I properly educated the listener to the extent that they could connect the dots from my nicknames to the players, then I succeeded.

Here are a few of those nicknames I applied to describe those colorful stars of the St. Louis Hawks on every radio broadcast:

BOB PETTIT—"Big Blue," "The Bombardier from Baton Rouge"
Bob's bold approach at making a winter fashion statement was to wear the longest, widest, most monstrous blue coat known to mankind. When walking away from you he resembled the front wall of a blue handball court. The tag "Big Blue" was used sparingly because it prompted an explanation since it was appreciated and understood only by a limited number of insiders. On occasion I used the second nickname, "The Bombardier from Baton Rouge" as his shots were always on target and Bob played at Louisiana State University.

CLIFF HAGAN—"Lil' Abner"
This name was inspired by the popular comic strip character. "Lil' Abner" was the personification of all that is good, a strong silent type, handsome and the All-American hero look. That was what Cliff Hagan was all about.

ED MACAULEY—"Easy Ed"
This one was not my creation, but came with the man up front. He was dubbed "Easy Ed" during his great playing days at St. Louis University. He always fit the billing as throughout his lengthy Hall-of-Fame NBA career with Boston and St. Louis he made his special shooting talents look awfully easy.

DUGIE MARTIN—the "Tornado from Texas"
Dugie was a great performer at the University of Texas. Even though he was the smallest man on the team, he played BIG! When he brought the ball down the court, it was with speed and fury, like a TORNADO. He was a funnel cloud in action.

JACK MCMAHON—"Jack Mac," "Irish"
Just look at this ruddy, red-faced man built in a sturdy round shape and then come up with any better nicknames!

AL FERRARI—"Bronco"
This name evolved as Al dribbled and bounded around the court, always a hard-charging, competitive drive, just like a bucking bronco. He was also known as "Mugsy."

JACK COLEMAN—the "Old Rancher"
Jack had a horse farm in Kentucky, possessed the rugged look of the Marlboro Man, and was one of the senior members of the Hawks' cast. He also had the appearance of someone who would be very comfortable in the saddle during a roundup.

MED PARK—the "Bulldozer from Missouri"
Med was built along the lines of an earthmover and performed in the grand fashion reserved for a piece of heavy machinery. He had an outstanding career at Mizzou.

ALEX HANNUM—"Sergeant York"
He was big, strong and played the role of a physically bruising style on the court. He would enter a game with the assignment of taking charge of the forward area, pick off members of the opposition and take no prisoners on defense. Gary Cooper couldn't have done it better!

CLYDE LOVELLETTE—"Boom Boom," "Boomer"
Clyde was deputy sheriff in Indiana during the offseason and fashioned himself as being the fast draw good guy who always shot all the bad guys. In the real world, he established himself on the basketball court as a bonafide fast draw with the set shot and "Boom, Boom," he outgunned the opponent often.

WOODY SAULDSBERRY—"Sling Shot"
He never seemed to come set before launching one of his long, one-handed line drive shots that could barely clear the rim. He was always in motion.

OTHERS WHO BROADCAST HAWKS' BASKETBALL ON RADIO AND TELEVISION

Jack Buck, Harry Caray, Skip Caray, Jerry Gross, Don Cunningham, Gene Kirby, Jim Butler, Al Ferrari, Cliff Hagan and Bill Sharman.

Appendix B

THEY CALLED THEM "MURDERER'S ROW"

At every Hawks' game, owner Ben Kerner sat courtside with his mother, Mrs. Helen Kerner, seated next to him. But they were hardly alone. On both sides of Ben and mom sat a group of highly vocal, fiercely loyal businessmen, whose raucous behavior caused broadcaster Buddy Blattner to dub them "Murderer's Row."

"I was cleaning the Title Guarantee office building downtown and I saw the Hawks' offices were there, so I went in and introduced myself to Marty Blake and Ben Kerner," remembers the instigator of the group, the president and owner of Modern Maintenance, a local building maintenance firm, Mitch Murch. "I told them I was the guy who was cleaning the building. We had a nice visit and I told them I thought I could get a bunch of guys together to buy some season tickets.

"We ended up to be six or seven couples every night and we had seats between the basket and the Hawks' bench. Next to our seats was an aisle, which led from the court up to the visiting players and the officials' dressing rooms. That really gave us a chance to converse with them in our own way," he smiled. "I rarely missed a game."

All members of the group were in their 20s—a bunch of good friends, fraternity brothers and neighbors. It just so happened that they were assigned to those courtside seats that put them right in the action. The guys weren't lacking in exuberance, which led to Buddy Blattner's awareness of them and his decision to tab them with the nickname.

"We were all exuberant and in the stage of our lives where we weren't just beginning in our businesses," said Murch. "We were starting to make some money and could afford to buy good season tickets by sharing them with people."

The names of the Murderer's Row group included: Mitch and Elaine Murch, Ollie and Toni Trittler, Russ and Nancy Meister, Jim and Mary Lee

Svehla, Van and Sonya Parriott, and Frank and Alice Hamilton. Another frequent member of the courtside squad was the esteemed longtime owner of Grey Eagle Distributing, the Anheuser-Busch distributor for St. Louis County, Jerry Clinton. Others such as Bob and Susan Debasio sat there at different times. They all held to the theme of letting the officials and the opposing team know they were held accountable for everything that happened in the game.

"Kerner used us to help him with a couple of promotions, one which had us raising money to buy center Charlie Share an automobile," said Murch. "Share didn't get the headlines for his hard work rebounding, passing, setting up picks for the shooters and playing great defense, so we were happy to help Kerner in this effort.

"Kerner gave us tickets to sell and he set aside the money raised to fund the kitty to buy Share a car. We succeeded and Kerner held a "Charlie Share Night" and presented him with a brand new Cadillac. Unfortunately, the 6-11 Share couldn't get into the car, so Cadillac took out the seat and mounted it on the floor. That night 10,000 fans showed up to honor Charlie. We did such a good job, Ben had us raise money to get cars for Cliff Hagan and Jack McMahon as well."

Kerner loved the group sitting near him on the court. They said all the things to opposing players and officials to get under their skin that Kerner would have liked to have said himself but couldn't as the team owner. No question their biting remarks would get into the heads of the players and just make it that much tougher to play the Hawks at Kiel.

Appendix C

THE HAWKS LINE SCORES

Hawk's Box Score

HAWKS (123)

	FG.	FT.	F.	Pts.
Coleman	4	2-5	6	10
Hagan	7	10-14	6	24
Share	0	5-7	4	5
Macauley	2	5-8	6	9
Hannum	0	0-0	1	0
Pettit	14	11-13	4	39
McMahon	3	0-0	6	6
Martin	6	11-12	6	23
Park	3	1-2	1	7
Totals	39	48-61	37	123

BOSTON (125)

	FG.	FT.	F.	Pts.
Heinsohn	17	3-10	6	37
Loscutoff	2	3-3	5	7
Ramsey	4	2-5	3	10
Risen	6	4-7	6	16
Nichols	4	0-0	3	8
Russell	7	5-10	5	19
Sharman	3	3-3	3	9
Cousy	2	8-10	4	12
Phillip	1	1-2	3	5
Totals	47	31-52	37	123

1 & 2   4 OT. OT.

Boston ....26 25 32 20 10 12—125
Hawks ....28 25 24 26 10 10—123

1957–58 Championship–6th Game Score

ST. LOUIS (110)

	G.	F.	PF.	P.
Pettit	19	12	1	50
Hagan	5	5	6	15
Macauley	0	2	5	2
Davis	2	1	2	5
Share	3	2	6	8
Coleman	3	2	3	8
Martin	0	4	4	4
Park	1	3	1	5
McMahon	4	1	5	9
Wilfong	1	2	1	4
Total	38	34	34	110

BOSTON (109)

	G.	F.	PF.	P.
Heinsohn	5	13	5	23
Tsiropoulos	4	6	1	14
Ramsey	3	2	6	8
Risen	4	4	3	12
Nichols	0	0	0	0
Russell	2	4	4	8
Cousy	4	7	3	13
Sharman	10	6	4	26
Jones	1	1	0	3
Phillip	0	0	4	0
Total	33	43	30	109

St. Louis ....22 35 21 32—110
Boston ....18 34 25 32—109
Free throws missed—Pettit 3, Hagan, Davis, Martin 2, McMahon, Wilfong, Heinsohn 4, Risen, Russell, Cousy.

1957–58 Championship–Final Game Score

GAME 9: January 21, 1958

GAME 10: January 22, 1960

GAME 11: January 17, 1961

GAME 12: January 16, 1962

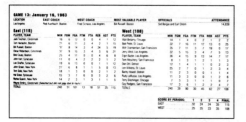

GAME 13: January 16, 1963

LOCATION	EAST COACH	WEST COACH	MOST VALUABLE PLAYER	OFFICIALS	ATTENDANCE
Los Angeles	Red Auerbach, Boston	Fred Schaus, Los Angeles	Bill Russell, Boston	Sid Borgia and Earl Strom	14,838

East (115)

PLAYER, TEAM	MIN	FGM	FGA	FTM	FTA	REB	AST	PTS
Jack Twyman, Cincinnati	16	6	12	0	0	4	1	12
Tom Heinsohn, Boston	21	6	11	3	4	2	1	15
Bill Russell, Boston	37	8	14	3	4	24	5	19
Oscar Robertson, Cincinnati	37	9	15	3	4	3	6	21
Bob Cousy, Boston	25	4	11	0	0	4	6	8
John Kerr, Syracuse	11	0	4	2	2	2	1	2
Lee Shaffer, Syracuse	19	6	13	0	0	1	1	12
John Green, New York	27	6	8	1	1	5	0	13
Tom Gola, New York	18	1	3	0	0	2	1	2
Hal Greer, Syracuse	15	3	7	0	0	3	2	6
Richie Guerin, New York	14	2	3	1	3	1	1	5
Wayne Embry, Cincinnati (*Selected but did not play due to injury.*)								
TOTALS	240	51	101	13	18	51	25	115

West (108)

PLAYER, TEAM	MIN	FGM	FGA	FTM	FTA	REB	AST	PTS
Walt Bellamy, Chicago	14	1	4	0	2	1	2	2
Bob Pettit, St. Louis	32	7	16	11	12	13	0	25
Wilt Chamberlain, San Francisco	35	7	11	3	7	19	0	17
Jerry West, Los Angeles	32	5	15	3	4	7	5	13
Elgin Baylor, Los Angeles	36	4	15	9	13	14	7	17
Tom Meschery, San Francisco	8	1	3	1	2	1	1	3
Don Ohl, Detroit	12	1	4	1	1	0	2	3
Len Wilkens, St. Louis	25	2	7	0	1	2	3	4
Bailey Howell, Detroit	11	2	3	0	0	1	1	4
Rudy LaRusso, Los Angeles	11	3	3	0	0	1	2	6
Terry Dischinger, Chicago	7	3	3	1	1	1	0	7
Guy Rodgers, San Francisco	17	3	6	1	2	2	4	7
TOTALS	240	39	90	30	45	62	27	108

SCORE BY PERIODS:	1	2	3	4	FINAL
EAST	32	24	24	35	115
WEST	25	25	23	35	108

GAME 14: January 14, 1964

LOCATION	EAST COACH	WEST COACH	MOST VALUABLE PLAYER	OFFICIALS	ATTENDANCE
Boston	Red Auerbach, Boston	Fred Schaus, Los Angeles	Oscar Robertson, Cincinnati	Sid Borgia and Mendy Rudolph	12,464

East (111)

PLAYER, TEAM	MIN	FGM	FGA	FTM	FTA	REB	AST	PTS
Jerry Lucas, Cincinnati	36	3	6	5	6	8	0	11
Tom Heinsohn, Boston	21	5	12	0	0	3	0	10
Bill Russell, Boston	42	6	13	1	2	21	2	13
Oscar Robertson, Cincinnati	42	10	23	6	10	14	8	26
Hal Greer, Philadelphia	20	5	10	3	4	3	4	13
Tom Gola, New York	7	0	0	1	2	0	1	1
Chet Walker, Philadelphia	12	2	5	0	0	0	0	4
Len Chappell, New York	12	1	5	2	2	1	2	4
Wayne Embry, Cincinnati	21	6	14	1	1	7	1	13
Sam Jones, Boston	27	8	20	0	0	4	3	16
TOTALS	240	46	108	19	27	61	21	111

West (107)

PLAYER, TEAM	MIN	FGM	FGA	FTM	FTA	REB	AST	PTS
Bob Pettit, St. Louis	36	6	15	7	9	17	2	19
Elgin Baylor, Los Angeles	29	5	15	5	11	8	5	15
Walt Bellamy, Baltimore	23	4	11	3	6	7	0	11
Guy Rodgers, San Francisco	22	3	6	0	0	[illegible]	2	6
Jerry West, Los Angeles	42	8	20	1	1	4	6	17
Wilt Chamberlain, San Francisco	37	4	14	11	14	20	1	19
Terry Dischinger, Baltimore	13	2	4	3	3	2	1	7
Bailey Howell, Detroit	6	1	3	0	0	2	0	2
Don Ohl, Detroit	18	3	9	2	2	2	0	8
Len Wilkens, St. Louis	14	1	5	1	1	0	0	3
TOTALS	240	37	102	33	46	64	16	107

SCORE BY PERIODS:	1	2	3	4	FINAL
WEST	22	27	28	30	107
EAST	25	34	27	25	111

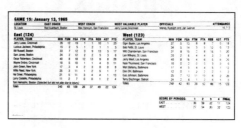

GAME 15: January 13, 1965

LOCATION	EAST COACH	WEST COACH	MOST VALUABLE PLAYER	OFFICIALS	ATTENDANCE
St. Louis	Red Auerbach, Boston	Alex Hannum, San Francisco	Jerry Lucas, Cincinnati	Mendy Rudolph and Joe Gushue	16,713

East (124)

PLAYER, TEAM	MIN	FGM	FGA	FTM	FTA	REB	AST	PTS
Jerry Lucas, Cincinnati	35	12	19	1	1	10	1	25
Lucious Jackson, Philadelphia	15	2	5	1	2	1	1	5
Bill Russell, Boston	33	7	12	3	9	13	5	17
Sam Jones, Boston	24	2	12	2	2	5	3	6
Oscar Robertson, Cincinnati	40	8	18	12	13	6	8	28
Wayne Embry, Cincinnati	19	5	10	1	1	4	0	11
John Green, New York	17	3	4	2	3	0	0	8
Willis Reed, New York	25	3	11	1	2	5	1	7
Hal Greer, Philadelphia	21	5	11	3	4	4	1	13
Larry Costello, Philadelphia	11	2	7	0	0	1	2	4
Tom Heinsohn, Boston (*Selected but did not play due to injury.*)								
Totals	240	49	109	26	37	49	22	124

West (123)

PLAYER, TEAM	MIN	FGM	FGA	FTM	FTA	REB	AST	PTS
Elgin Baylor, Los Angeles	27	5	13	8	8	7	0	18
Bob Pettit, St. Louis	34	5	14	3	5	12	0	13
Wilt Chamberlain, San Francisco	31	9	15	2	8	16	1	20
Len Wilkens, St. Louis	20	2	6	4	4	3	[illegible]	8
Jerry West, Los Angeles	40	8	16	4	6	5	6	20
Nate Thurmond, San Francisco	10	0	2	0	0	3	0	0
Walt Bellamy, Baltimore	17	4	5	4	4	5	1	12
Don Ohl, Baltimore	12	0	1	2	2	2	1	2
Gus Johnson, Baltimore	25	7	13	11	12	8	2	25
Terry Dischinger, Detroit	24	2	6	1	2	5	1	5
Totals	240	42	93	39	52	66	15	123

SCORE BY PERIODS:	1	2	3	4	FINAL
EAST	36	39	32	17	124
WEST	27	34	30	32	123

PLAYER STATISTICS

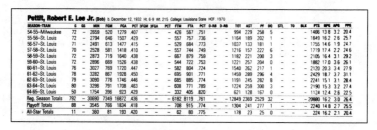

Pettit, Robert E. Lee Jr. (Bob) b. December 12, 1932 Ht. 6-9 Wt. 215 College: Louisiana State HOF: 1970

SEASON–TEAM	G	GS	MIN	FGM	FGA	PCT	3FGM	3FGA	PCT	FTM	FTA	PCT	O-RB	D-RB	TOT	AST	PF	DQ	STL	TO	BLK	PTS	RPG	APG	PPG
54-55–Milwaukee	72	–	2659	520	1279	.407	–	–	–	426	567	.751	–	–	994	229	258	5	–	–	–	1466	13.8	3.2	20.4
55-56–St. Louis	72	–	2794	646	1507	.429	–	–	–	557	757	.736	–	–	1164	189	202	1	–	–	–	1849	16.2	2.6	25.7
56-57–St. Louis	71	–	2491	613	1477	.415	–	–	–	529	684	.773	–	–	1037	133	181	1	–	–	–	1755	14.6	1.9	24.7
57-58–St. Louis	70	–	2528	581	1418	.410	–	–	–	557	744	.749	–	–	1216	157	222	6	–	–	–	1719	17.4	2.2	24.6
58-59–St. Louis	72	–	2873	719	1640	.438	–	–	–	667	879	.759	–	–	1182	221	200	3	–	–	–	2105	16.4	3.1	29.2
59-60–St. Louis	72	–	2896	669	1526	.438	–	–	–	544	722	.753	–	–	1221	257	204	0	–	–	–	1882	17.0	3.6	26.1
60-61–St. Louis	76	–	3027	769	1720	.447	–	–	–	582	804	.724	–	–	1540	262	217	1	–	–	–	2120	20.3	3.4	27.9
61-62–St. Louis	78	–	3282	867	1928	.450	–	–	–	695	901	.771	–	–	1459	289	296	4	–	–	–	2429	18.7	3.7	31.1
62-63–St. Louis	79	–	3090	778	1746	.446	–	–	–	685	885	.774	–	–	1191	245	282	8	–	–	–	2241	15.1	3.1	28.4
63-64–St. Louis	80	–	3296	791	1708	.463	–	–	–	608	771	.789	–	–	1224	259	300	3	–	–	–	2190	15.3	3.2	27.4
64-65–St. Louis	50	–	1754	396	923	.429	–	–	–	332	405	.820	–	–	621	128	167	0	–	–	–	1124	12.4	2.6	22.5
Reg. Season Totals	792	–	30690	7349	16872	.436	–	–	–	6182	8119	.761	–	–	12849	2369	2529	32	–	–	–	20880	16.2	3.0	26.4
Playoff Totals	88	–	3545	766	1834	.418	–	–	–	708	915	.774	–	–	1304	241	277	1	–	–	–	2240	14.8	2.7	25.5
All-Star Totals	11	–	360	81	193	.420	–	–	–	62	80	.775	–	–	178	23	25	0	–	–	–	224	16.2	2.1	20.4

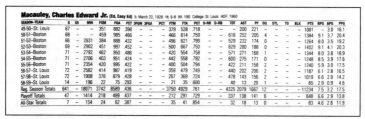

Macauley, Charles Edward Jr. (Ed, Easy Ed) b. March 22, 1928 Ht. 6-8 Wt. 190 College: St. Louis HOF: 1960

SEASON–TEAM	G	GS	MIN	FGM	FGA	PCT	3FGM	3FGA	PCT	FTM	FTA	PCT	O-RB	D-RB	TOT	AST	PF	DQ	STL	TO	BLK	PTS	RPG	APG	PPG
49-50–St. Louis	67	–	–	351	882	.398	–	–	–	379	528	.718	–	–	–	200	221	–	–	–	–	1081	–	3.0	16.1
50-51–Boston	68	–	–	459	985	.466	–	–	–	466	614	.759	–	–	616	252	205	4	–	–	–	1384	9.1	3.7	20.4
51-52–Boston	66	–	2631	384	888	.432	–	–	–	496	621	.799	–	–	529	232	174	0	–	–	–	1264	8.0	3.5	19.2
52-53–Boston	69	–	2902	451	997	.452	–	–	–	500	667	.750	–	–	629	280	188	0	–	–	–	1402	9.1	4.1	20.3
53-54–Boston	71	–	2792	462	950	.486	–	–	–	420	554	.758	–	–	571	271	168	1	–	–	–	1344	8.0	3.8	18.9
54-55–Boston	71	–	2706	403	951	.424	–	–	–	442	558	.792	–	–	600	275	171	0	–	–	–	1248	8.5	3.9	17.6
55-56–Boston	71	–	2354	420	995	.422	–	–	–	400	504	.794	–	–	422	211	158	2	–	–	–	1240	5.9	3.0	17.5
56-57–St. Louis	72	–	2582	414	987	.419	–	–	–	359	479	.749	–	–	440	202	206	2	–	–	–	1187	6.1	2.8	16.5
57-58–St. Louis	72	–	1908	376	879	.428	–	–	–	267	369	.724	–	–	478	143	156	2	–	–	–	1019	6.6	2.0	14.2
58-59–St. Louis	14	–	196	22	75	.293	–	–	–	21	35	.600	–	–	40	13	20	1	–	–	–	65	2.9	0.9	4.6
Reg. Season Totals	641	–	18071	3742	8589	.436	–	–	–	3750	4929	.761	–	–	4325	2079	1667	12	–	–	–	11234	7.5	3.2	17.5
Playoff Totals	47	–	1414	218	499	.437	–	–	–	212	291	.729	–	–	337	138	141	6	–	–	–	648	6.6	2.9	13.8
All-Star Totals	7	–	154	24	62	.387	–	–	–	35	41	.854	–	–	32	18	13	0	–	–	–	83	4.6	2.6	11.9

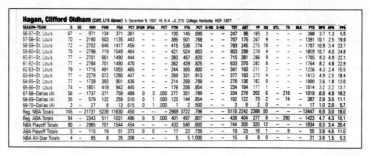

Hagan, Clifford Oldham (Cliff, Li'l Abner) b. December 9, 1931 Ht. 6-4 Wt. 215 College: Kentucky HOF: 1977

SEASON–TEAM	G	GS	MIN	FGM	FGA	PCT	3FGM	3FGA	PCT	FTM	FTA	PCT	O-RB	D-RB	TOT	AST	PF	DQ	STL	TO	BLK	PTS	RPG	APG	PPG
56-57–St. Louis	67	–	971	134	371	.361	–	–	–	100	145	.690	–	–	247	86	165	3	–	–	–	368	3.7	1.3	5.5
57-58–St. Louis	70	–	2190	503	1135	.443	–	–	–	385	501	.768	–	–	707	175	267	9	–	–	–	1391	10.1	2.5	19.9
58-59–St. Louis	72	–	2702	646	1417	.456	–	–	–	415	536	.774	–	–	783	245	275	10	–	–	–	1707	10.9	3.4	23.7
59-60–St. Louis	75	–	2798	719	1549	.464	–	–	–	421	524	.803	–	–	803	299	270	4	–	–	–	1859	10.7	4.0	24.8
60-61–St. Louis	77	–	2701	661	1490	.444	–	–	–	383	467	.820	–	–	715	381	286	9	–	–	–	1705	9.3	4.9	22.1
61-62–St. Louis	77	–	2784	701	1490	.470	–	–	–	362	439	.825	–	–	633	370	282	8	–	–	–	1764	8.2	4.8	22.9
62-63–St. Louis	79	–	1716	491	1055	.465	–	–	–	244	305	.800	–	–	341	193	211	2	–	–	–	1226	4.3	2.4	15.5
63-64–St. Louis	77	–	2279	572	1280	.447	–	–	–	269	331	.813	–	–	377	193	273	4	–	–	–	1413	4.9	2.5	18.4
64-65–St. Louis	77	–	1739	393	901	.436	–	–	–	214	268	.799	–	–	276	136	182	0	–	–	–	1000	3.6	1.8	13.0
65-66–St. Louis	74	–	1851	419	942	.445	–	–	–	176	206	.854	–	–	234	164	177	1	–	–	–	1014	3.2	2.2	13.7
67-68–Dallas (A)	56	–	1737	371	759	.489	0	3	.000	277	351	.789	–	–	334	276	202	6	–	216	–	1019	6.0	4.9	18.2
68-69–Dallas (A)	35	–	579	132	259	.510	0	1	.000	123	144	.854	–	–	102	122	73	2	–	74	–	387	2.9	3.5	11.1
69-70–Dallas (A)	3	–	27	8	13	.615	0	1	.000	1	2	.500	–	–	3	6	2	0	–	–	–	17	1.0	2.0	5.7
Reg. NBA Totals	745	–	21731	5239	11630	.450	–	–	–	2969	3722	.798	–	–	5116	2242	2388	50	–	–	–	13447	6.9	3.0	18.0
Reg. ABA Totals	94	–	2343	511	1031	.496	0	5	.000	401	497	.807	–	–	439	404	277	8	–	290	–	1423	4.7	4.3	15.1
NBA Playoff Totals	90	–	2965	701	1544	.454	–	–	–	432	540	.800	–	–	744	305	320	12	–	–	–	1834	8.3	3.4	20.4
ABA Playoff Totals	5	–	115	19	51	.373	0	0	–	17	23	.739	–	–	19	23	16	1	–	9	–	55	3.8	4.6	11.0
NBA All-Star Totals	4	–	65	8	26	.308	–	–	–	5	5	1.000	–	–	15	6	8	0	–	–	–	21	3.8	1.5	5.3

THE HAWKS FACTS AND FIGURES

Played As: Tri-Cities Blackhawks* 1946/47–1950/51
Milwaukee Hawks 1951/52–1954–55
St. Louis Hawks 1955/56–1967/68
Atlanta Hawks 1968/69–Present
*-Played in NBL 1946/47–1948/49

Nickname: The team's named shortened from Blackhawks to Hawks upon moving to Milwaukee from the Tri-Cities region, where the Blackhawk war took place in 1831.

Logo: A Hawk wearing a basketball uniform with the name "Hawks." The bird is holding a basketball at its left side waiting to make a pass.

Colors: Red, White, Blue

Coaches: (10)		Season W	L	Finish	Playoffs W	L
1955–56	Red Holzman	33	39	3rd	4	4
1956–57	Red Holzman	34	38	1st	8	4
	Slater Martin					
	Alex Hannum					
1957–58	Alex Hannum	41	31	1st	8	3
1958–59	Andy Phillip	49	23	1st	2	4
	Ed Macauley					
1959–60	Ed Macauley	46	29	1st	7	7
1960–61	Paul Seymour	51	28	1st	5	7
1961–62	Paul Seymour	19	51	4th	—	—
	Andrew Levane					
	Bob Pettit					
1962–63	Harry Gallatin	48	32	2nd	7	5
1963–64	Harry Gallatin	48	34	2nd	7	5
1964–65	Harry Gallatin	45	35	2nd	1	3
	Richie Guerin					
1965–66	Richie Guerin	36	44	3rd	6	4
1966–67	Richie Guerin	39	42	2nd	5	4
1967–68	Richie Guerin	56	26	1st	2	4

Arenas: (3) Kiel Auditorium 1955/56–1967/68; The Arena 1955/56–1967/68; Washington University Fieldhouse 1955/56–1967/68

NBA Championships: (1) 1958

NBA Finals: (4) 1957, 1958, 1960, 1961

Conference Finals: (10) 1956, 1957, 1958, 1959, 1960, 1961, 1963, 1964, 1966, 1967

Division Champions: (6) 1957, 1958, 1959, 1960, 1961, 1968

Playoff Appearances: (12) 1956, 1957, 1958, 1959, 1960, 1961, 1963, 1964, 1965, 1966, 1967, 1968

Hall of Famers: (8) Cliff Hagan, G, 1956–1966
Alex Hannum, Coach, 1956–1958
Red Holzman, Coach, 1955–1957
Clyde Lovellette, C, 1958–1962
Ed Macauley, F, 1957–1959
Slater Martin, G, 1956–1960
Bob Pettit, F, 1955–1965
Lenny Wilkens, G, 1960–1968

All-Star Games Hosted: (3) 1958, 1962, 1965

All-Star Game MVP: (4) 1956 Bob Pettit F
1958 Bob Pettit F
1959 Bob Pettit F
1962 Bob Pettit F

AWARDS

Coach of the Year: (2) 1963 Harry Gallatin
1968 Richie Guerin

NBA MVP: (2) 1956 Bob Pettit
1959 Bob Pettit

Best Season: 1967/68 (56–26)

Worst Season: 1961/62 (29–51)

Bibliography

Hubbard, Jan. *The Official Encyclopedia of the NBA*. Doubleday, a division of Random House, Inc. 2000.

Denberg, Jeffrey; Lazenby, Rolland; Stinson, Tom. *From Sweet Lou to 'Nique*. Longstreet Press, 1992.

Packer, Billy; Lazenby, Rolland. *The Golden Game*. Jefferson Street Press, 1991.

Bjarkman, Peter C. *Boston Celtic Encyclopedia*. Sports Publishing, Inc., 1999.

St. Louis Globe-Democrat newspaper at the St. Louis Mercantile Library at UMSL, excerpts from game stories and columns written by Executive Sports Editor Robert L. Burnes.

St. Louis Hawks' official press guides between 1955 and 1967 as provided by the National Basketball Association Research Department.

Credits

The author wishes to thank the following people for granting interviews for the book: Ed Macauley, Bob Pettit, Cliff Hagan, Charlie Share, Slater Martin, Al Ferrari, Jean Kerner, Len Wilkens, Clyde Lovellette, Richie Guerin, Lou Hudson, Harry Gallatin, John Barnhill, Bob Cousy, Bill Sharman, Frank Ramsey, Tom Heinsohn, Max Shapiro, Jack Levitt, Marty Blake and Buddy Blattner.

A personal thanks for their accommodation, diligence and support to: Zelda Spoelstra, Senior Director of NBA Alumni, Andrew Stephens, NBRPA I.T. Coordinator, Peter Steber, Manager NBA Market Research and Communications, Brian McIntrye, Senior V.P. of NBA Basketball Communications, and the Atlanta Hawks.

A special thanks to the legendary cartoonist of the *St. Louis Post-Dispatch* Amadee Wohlschlaeger. His contribution of several cartoon drawings about the St. Louis Hawks were much appreciated. Amadee drew the famous Weatherbird in the daily *Post* for more than 60 years, and many of his sports cartoons spanning the decades are available for purchase from MathisJones Communications in Eureka, Mo.

Interior photo credits go to: The Naismith Memorial Basketball Hall of Fame, NBA Photos, Mack Giblin, Jerry Buckley, Buzz Taylor for the panoramic view of Kiel Auditorium, Paul Bathis for the photo of Wilt Chamberlain, and the Hawks' players themselves who provided personal photos.

Every effort has been made to determine ownership of copyrighted photos. If we have failed to give adequate credit, we will be pleased to make corrections in any future printings.

Special Acknowledgments

This book was a labor of love for the author, a kid of the '50s in St. Louis who each winter, listened on his crystal radio to the play-by-play call of St. Louis Hawks' basketball. With 17 years as a local St. Louis sportswriter prior to being a broadcaster and station owner, I felt compelled to write the story that has never been written about the history of this great sports franchise.

I am the storyteller, but it took the help of many to record and transcribe interviews, edit copy, then design, layout, publish and promote the book.

My thanks to a dedicated friend and talented professional, Chris Hoss Nupert, a radio engineer and broadcaster at 590 The Fan KFNS Radio in St. Louis, who arranged various technical aspects of player interviews. The interview text was transcribed to perfection by Ellen Brewer of Tulsa, Okla., and Karen Klemmer of KFNS Radio, whose expertise in managing details of the book's preparation was so helpful.

A special thanks to my longtime friend and the book's editor, Myron Holtzman, the former sportswriter and sports editor of St. Louis' former daily morning newspaper, the *St. Louis Globe-Democrat*. Myron's involvement as editor assured the quality of the text and guaranteed the rules of grammar and punctuation would be followed!

I want to congratulate a young man who wrote several important pages of this book. His name is Eric J. Wittenauer from St. Louis University where he is enrolled in the John Cook School of Business as a member of the MBA Class of 2006. I chose Eric from a number of applicants from various local colleges to whom I put out the word that I wanted a college student to research and write a piece describing what was going on in St. Louis in the mid-1950s when the Hawks arrived. He has done a wonderful job giving readers an accurate picture of the city. Eric discusses the St. Louis region's politics, economics, building projects, social issues and other dynamics that made up the setting for the Hawks of 1955. Eric gets an A-plus for his excellent contribution.

Marketing of the book was kicked off well in advance of printing by a donation of promotional flyers by my good friends at one of St. Louis' top printing corporations, Kohler and Sons, Inc. It was coordinated by Kent Kohler, executive vice-president, and I'm sure supported by his brother and company president, Kevin Kohler, and their now-retired father, Charles Kohler, who gave me an office when I started my first business.

Those who read along, offering suggestions and advice as we went were former Hawks' players Easy Ed Macauley and Al Ferrari, plus banker and brother-in-law David Reed. A very special nod of thanks goes to NBA Hall-of-Famer Macauley, whose friendship I cherish and without whom some interviews wouldn't have occurred. Ed was invaluable with his insight interjected into the interviews.

To my wife and No. 1 supporter, Helen Marecek, for 34 years of sports endeavors. Thank you for the encouragement to keep going night after night sitting at the computer for more than nine months in addition to the first four months of nothing but research and interviews. She kept sending me into the office until it got done. I do the sports and she keeps everything else in our lives in order. She's the best.

Finally, to the duo of William Mathis and Ellie Jones of MathisJones Communications, LLC in Eureka, Mo., who designed the book and gave it the quality look that has attracted the readers. From them I have learned much about how a book should be put together. Enjoy the images that they made to look of recent vintage when in reality, they're all 40 to 50 years old.

To any others who've touched the makings of this book my humble thanks and I hope it was worth the sacrifices.

Greg Marecek

Index